YOUR SPOUSE
IS NOT
YOUR ENEMY!

YOUR SPOUSE IS NOT YOUR ENEMY!

God's Ten Principles for Marriage

Larry and Beverly J. Bentley
www.NotYourEnemy.info

WESTBOW®
PRESS
A DIVISION OF THOMAS NELSON
& ZONDERVAN

Library of Congress Cataloguing-in-Publication Data: Bentley, Beverly J., 1936–

WestBow Press books may be ordered through booksellers or by contacting:
WestBow Press
A Division of Thomas Nelson & Zondervan
1663 Liberty Drive
Bloomington, IN 47403
www.westbowpress.com
1 (866) 928-1240

Front cover photography: © Zoonar RF in Zoonar Collection.
Back cover photography: © Bluefont in iStock Collection.
Cover design and interior editing and design: Bob Lingo.

Scripture quotations marked *NIV* are taken from *The Holy Bible, New International Version®*, NIV®. Copyright © 1973, 1978, 1984, 2011 by Biblica, Inc.®. All rights reserved worldwide.

Scripture quotations marked *NASB* are taken from *The New American Standard Bible.* Copyright © 1960, 1962, 1963, 1968, 1971, 1972, 1973, 1975, 1977, 1995 by The Lockman Foundation.

Scripture quotations marked *Amp* are taken from *The Amplified Bible.* Copyright © 1954, 1958, 1962, 1964, 1965, 1987 by The Lockman Foundation.

Scripture quotations marked *NKJV* are taken from *The Holy Bible, New King James Version.* Copyright © 1982 by Thomas Nelson, Inc.

Scripture quotations marked *KJV* are taken from the *King James Version* of the Bible. Public domain.

Scripture quotations marked *ESV* are taken from *The Holy Bible, English Standard Version.* Copyright © 2001 by Crossway Bibles, a division of Good News Publishers.

ISBN: 978-1-4908-2564-9 (sc)
ISBN: 978-1-4908-2566-3 (hc)
ISBN: 978-1-4908-2565-6 (e)

Library of Congress Control Number: 2014902563
Printed in the United States of America.
WestBow Press rev. date: 8/21/2014

This book is dedicated

—To visionary couples contented in their marriage who...

- Want to know more on how to nurture their marriage

- Are motivated to capture God's plan for their marriage

- Choose to grow stronger in their covenant marital vows

- Aspire to model a heritage of matrimonial victory to their children

- Simply desire to express more gifts of the Holy Spirit

- Desire to spread a moral marriage concept to their neighbors, in the work place, with friends, and in family relationships

—To struggling marriages that are unaware that...

- They entered into a covenant with God when they got married

- Marriage was designed by God and not by mankind

- Marriage takes three: a husband, a wife, and God

- God has a plan for authority and responsibility in marriage

- "Selfishness" is the root of all quarrels

- The enemy is not your spouse

- All problems heal in the realm of repentance and forgiveness

To Bob Lingo
A loyal and precious friend, without whom
I never would have finished this book.
Even though you said you haven't a way with words,
you are the world's best editor.
Thank you for your valued fellowship
and mutual love of our Lord Jesus Christ.

Foreword

Divorce is alive and well! In this twenty-first century, divorce is killing marriages. For those of you who are in your first marriage, you have less than a 50-50 chance of survival with the mate you promised to love in sickness and in health. If you are a "born-again" Christian, believe it or not you have a lower marriage survival rate than the "world" rate. My precious brother and sister, you have a 40-45 percent chance that you will stay together "til death do us part." Those of you who are planning to marry for the second tine or are in your second marriage have about a 30-percent survival rate, and if you are on your third marriage have a 20-percent survival rate!

Love is *not* necessarily lovelier "the second time around." Why, I hear you asking, is there such a low survival rate in subsequent marriages? In simplest terms, the majority of divorces resulting from second, third, or even fourth altar visits are due to the startling fact that most couples have gone from "personal" love into a "blended family" in about eighteen short altar minutes. There have been little or no meaningful, thoughtful, sacrificially demanding plans made ahead of time for the blended families. Consequently, when the ceremonial part is done, they are in spiritual warfare almost constantly. Usually both marital spouses are working. When trouble appears, they usually forget the proper order of discipline and the teaching of God's word, and slip into the quarreling they experience in their first marriage. Frequently, the blended family's important decisions are reached with hasty conclusions rather than thoughtful consideration.

In most blended-family situations, the majority of adults entering into remarriage are unable to first successfully blend into a "one-flesh" relationship, before they tackle the challenging work of handling children in the marriage.

Let us not forget the remarriage of people over fifty. Even though they may love each other dearly, they may have to deal with each other's grown children and grandchildren—and these may not be as accepting as you would like them to be. Their jealousy often causes hurt feelings.

In a *"godly one-flesh marriage"* the husband is commanded: (1) to hold himself accountable to God for the covenant marriage that God, Himself, witnessed at the wedding altar; (2) to hold his wife in highest esteem, second only to God; and (3) to accept family responsibility in delegating authority, taking charge of discipline, and teaching God's morals in the home. As we ponder the other side of the marriage equation, we find the character traits of the twenty-first century woman have been altered by the world's definitions. The woman of today is striving to "be equal with man" in all things, whether it be climbing a power pole, entering the boxing ring, or just simply desiring any and all male-dominant positions. The godly wife is willing to learn the sweet obedience of "submission" to her husband, as God commands her. She elevates her husband to head position in the family who is making decisions. Then the husband can take on the role of being a "protective umbrella" for his wife and family, as God intended in marriage.

This book was not intended for just "troubled marriages" that are badly in need of healing, but it was also designated for "solid marriages" that could use some "freshness" in their relationship. It was created for children, friends, neighbors, fellow workers, and married couples, everywhere, who will receive the many blessings from this book as they apply "God's Ten Principles of Marriage" to their own marriages. We have labored at this "love for marriage" ministry to defuse the confusion for the average person who has tried to assess the marital discontentment by using only the formats of this troubled world they're surrounded by, rather than to operate in the words of God's marriage manual—the Bible.

Marriage is more important to God than any one of us could envision. The Bible starts with marriage in the very first chapter of Genesis and ends with a marriage in the last chapter of the Bible, Revelation. Between the two, the Bible is full of narrations on how we should conduct ourselves within a covenant marriage setting throughout the life of our marriage. We offer two biblical examples of covenant marriage: (1) the New Testament speaks of Christ and His bride, the Church, as a "new covenant marriage," and (2) in the Old Testament, Scriptures illustrate the marital "covenant" relationship between God and Israel, the wife of God:

Ezekiel 16:4-8 (NKJV) speaks of God's love for Israel:

> ... *on the day you were born* ... (16:4)

> ... *you were thrown out into the open field* ... (16:5)

> ... *I passed by you and saw you struggling* ... *I said, Live* ... (16:6)

> ... *And you grew, matured, and became very beautiful. Your breasts were formed; your hair grew, but you were naked and bare.* (16:7b)

> *When I passed by you again... your time was the time of love; so I spread my wing over you and covered your nakedness. Yes, I swore an oath to you and entered into a covenant with you, and you became mine,"* says the Lord God. (16:8)

God continues in Jeremiah 3:1 and 6, 31:31 (NKJV)

> ... *for I am married unto you* ... (Jeremiah 3:1)

> ... *Israel* ... *has committed adultery* ... (Jeremiah 3:6)

> ... *thought I was a husband to them* ... (Jeremiah 31:32)

It's a mystery to ponder.

For I am jealous for you with a godly jealousy. For I have betrothed you to one husband, that I may present you as a chaste virgin to Christ. (2 Corinthians 11:2 NKJV)

Paul is addressing "the Church" which is all believers, whether Jew or Gentile, as the "bride of Christ." We will come to see that much of the New Testament's language speaks in the form of a "spiritual marriage relationship."

God, in His wisdom, created marriage and all the elements of marriage. He was the first to call marriage a "covenant" as He fashioned His first two human beings into a "one-flesh" union. As a wedding present He gave them sex and intimacy, calling it "an act of worship." And, then, He elevated them into a partnership position in His creation by giving them the command to take dominion over all of the earth and, in His anticipation to participate in all of it, He blesses it and called it a "triune" marriage. He created it, He protects it, He sustains it, and He nourishes it; this is the basis of all His relationships toward mankind. He loves us.

Our goal is to share with you the knowledge we were given by our Almighty God who taught us what He wanted us to know as we enter the holy state of matrimony. It is Beverly's third time at marriage and the second time for Larry. If we were to "walk together" in a godly marriage, we had no choice but to be obedient to God's words on marriage.

Contents

Contents

Chapter 1
Covenant Marriage?

A covenant creates a binding relationship between two persons where the "promises" and "terms" are expected to be fulfilled.

In a covenant, *promises* are itemized personal commitments of each partner to the other partner, whereas the *terms* are conditions under which the agreement is sealed. The content of the covenant agreement obligates the partners to the relationship, and ensures its continuation.

God is the Father of all covenants. He sees our marriage as a *covenant*! Therefore we must examine God's covenants and determine what God honors in a covenant.

Godly Principle 1:
Marriage is a covenant between a man, a woman, and God.

The Wedding

"Dearly beloved we are gathered here together, in the presence of God to unite this couple in holy matrimony." Sound familiar? Many weddings start with these words. Did yours? Or did you, perhaps, write your own words? If you wrote your own words as many couples do, it probably had the same elements as those spoken words from a pastor or priest or even a justice of the peace. You may have added some words of your own; like a poem that expressed your deepest feelings of an eloquently spoken love that would never cease.

However, did you know that even with all the added extras such as your poem, the guest singer and the "Wedding March" music that accompanies that long walk down the isle; the average wedding ceremony contains about 235 words and lasts, in time, about eighteen minutes.

But let us get back to the wedding ceremony. Just as you are getting back your breath from the long walk down the aisle, and reciting the words, the ceremony is over! You really didn't get the chance to savor the words that probably would not be said again. You, as the groom, wanted to tell her how beautiful she looked coming down the aisle, and what's more, you had not knowingly contemplated that you would spend the rest of your life with her. Your life was coming together, and you were accomplishing one more of those "once in a lifetime" human experiences. You, as the Bride, wanted to keep this moment forever in your mind's eye as you saw him waiting to receive you as his wife. You held the flowers tightly, knowing that from now on your life would never be the same. As you approached the man of your dreams, your senses take in the flowers, the lighting, and the sound of the music you picked out to be played. You are so happy! Ah, the romance and excitement of it all! Even if you were married in front of a Justice of the Peace, the essence of the honorable place you stood gave forth the silence of a holy allegiance that burns with an intense passion to accept, protect and honor. Women cry, and men feel powerful and exceptional.

You were so absorbed in the progression of events that you simply did not stop to realize that you had entered into a holy state of matrimony. Hours before the ceremony, you made a mutual and solemn written agreement by signing the marriage certificate, and, now, you have verbally announced in front of God and all your family and friends, that you intent to enter into a *life-long position of unity with another person of the opposite sex.*

Knowingly or unknowingly, the power of the words you spoke transformed your "singleness" into a birth that united two people in making a "one-flesh" marriage. You spoke an oath! You entered into a *covenant*! It's done. It's forever! And God agreed to it all!

Oh, yes, God was there, and of course you knew that, but when the minister said, "You may kiss the bride," and the music starts bounding, and the audience starts laughing and clapping; you two are announced as "Mr. and Mrs." The celebration begins and you're off and running. The cameras flash! You wave to others as you proceed down the aisle to enter the car. The rice is falling everywhere. Even the ride to the wedding reception doesn't seem very far away. You find yourself rushing from one phase of the wedding to the next phase. As you enter the reception hall, someone announces your arrival…and the feast begins. The dancing, the cake cutting, the rush to the airport to leave for the honeymoon—the further the celebration gets into the evening hours, the more distant the words of the ceremony become, and the words begin to fade away.

The Anniversary

By your first anniversary, things are very different. A lot of changes have occurred, and there is barely a remembrance of the pre-marital classes you and your spouse took just a little over a year ago in preparation for the wedding. You are busy adapting, as most newly married couples, to the generalized activities of married life. First, right after, or during the honeymoon, there were important questions that demand immediate action, such as: what side of the bed do you sleep on? Which sink in the master bedroom is your? Who makes the coffee in the morning? Who's the keeper of the alarm clock? And, which side of the garage do I park on?

As the days passed, little irritations that you didn't know you had about your spouse's behavior begin to invade your awareness. He snores! Ah, ha, she doesn't roll the toothpaste tube! Oh, no, he leaves his shaving hairs in the sink! For Pete's sake, the toilet paper is on backwards! That's the start of the day, and then you remember: it's your first anniversary! Oh, how times flies!

Do some of you do what Larry and I did on our first, second, and even our third anniversary? We had a quiet cozy dinner for two with candlelight. I brought out the top of the original wedding cake that was kept in the freezer. It was sectioned off for future dessert portions to be eaten on each anniversary year. We would snuggle on the living room couch to watch the video of our marriage ceremony, and ended up in the hot tub together. It was fun, and I'm not putting that down. There's nothing wrong with that! That's what making a memory is about. However, I don't remember inviting God to the "memory-making celebration," and nor do I remember seeing Him in the video. We were just two people falling in love with a marriage ceremony, reliving "our day" and forgetting what really had transpired that day…"the making of a covenant."

Larry, too, had forgotten that God was there at our marriage. Our marriage ceremony was ancient history to him. As he watched the tape, he was taken back by the seriousness of the event. In fact, he did not realize the marriage ceremony was so complicated. The vows and promises he had made were still important to him, but a *covenant*? Just what does God mean by a *covenant*?

The First Groom

Let us start from the beginning of time, where we meet the first groom.

> Then God said, *"Let us make man in Our image, according to Our likeness; let them have dominion over the fish of the sea, over the birds of the air, and over the cattle, over all the earth and over every creeping thing that creeps upon the earth. So God created man in His own image, in the image of God He created him; male and female created He them."* (Genesis 1:26-27 NKJV)

First things first, let us deal with Bible translations. Genesis 1:26 states that when God created man, He created this creature in His own image, after His own likeness! Does "in His own image" translate into the possibility that the first man—or for that fact, and any man thereafter—can become some sort of a god? Or, maybe, even attain a position in the Godhead? The resounding answer is a big "No!" We can get a clearer meaning when we look up the Hebrew meaning of the words "image" and "likeness." The Hebrew word for *image* is *"pecel"* (Strong's, *image*) which translates to "carved image." The Hebrew word for *likeness* is *"t'meunah"* (Strong's, *likeness*) which translates to "something portioned," "a shape," "embodiment," or "manifestation."

Let me give you an example. Envision an artist using brush strokes on his canvas to copy an image of, let's say, a bowl of flowers sitting on the table near his northerly-faced window. The artist wants to capture the vision of the various hues of color in the bouquet, in particular, the bright yellow rose that has a touch of peach making the flowers look so flourishing. The artist's aspiration is to provide that spark of splendor that lights up a spring day—a

3

moment of peace and calmness for the onlooker. He wants to make it so real and lifelike that in the "likeness" of that yellow rose; the joy of the on-looker goes beyond the use of his eyes for enjoyment; he experiences with ease an inner spiritual sense of "almost being able to smell the flowers."

As the artist closes the canvas with his last stroke for effect, the wind flows through the window ever so softly to caress the rose of reality, the one in the flower bowl. His eyes flow to the canvas, the rose of "likeness" does not respond to the delight of the wind's flutter. The one on the canvas only reacts within its limited capacity of "likeness" as created by its master. It is beautiful to look at. You can move it from wall to wall, but again, its limited functioning is captured within its maker's limits. So, we too, are limited to function within our maker's limits. We always carry the image of God better when we are being used as a channel by our Heavenly Father for Him to flow through us in the blessings of other people. But we are limited when we try to act within our own image.

Genesis 1:27 can be confusing when he is describing the groom. Note that the Bible says, "He created him," and then in the same sentence the Bible says, "male and female He created them." God formed Adam to be the first human being, the first man, father of all mankind. God delighted Himself in His new creation. He put this new creation in a garden and called the garden "Eden," which in Hebrew means "delight." God exalted this man above all the other creatures He had created. This mannish creation He had created was going to rule over all other life that lived on the earth. There was no mistaking; there was to be an "Order of Authority" in this new world. There would be an undeniable division between man and the rest of all nature; for God did something to man that He did not do to any other creations.

God preserved this division by breathing into Adam's nostrils, creating a "Spiritual" component to man. This put all of nature on notice: this was a superior creation! It was an act of God that the entire kingdom of nature had never before seen. Man, the jewel of God's creation, would ultimately be the final foundation upon which would reveal the most appealing attributes of God: love, mercy, grace, and suffering. Within Adam's God-created being, he possessed all of God's attributes. Let's look at the attribute of gender. In order to do this we must go back to the first five words spoken in the Bible.

In the beginning God created ... (Genesis 1:1 NIV)

In Hebrew, it is written as "Berishit Bara Elohim." When we break down the Hebrew meanings we come up with:

- *Berishit:* any Hebrew word ending in "it" denotes female attribute
- *Bara:* to create ... to call into existence something that never was
- *Elohim: El* means *God* in Hebrew. Any Hebrew word ending in *-im* means plural male

In these first three Hebrew words, we can get an idea about God Himself. We get a sense that there is a female gender attribute in God. We also know that *Elohim* is a name for God that means plural male. So, in God's name for Himself, *El*, there must be more than one person within the *Elohim*. We can therefore state that the one true God, *Elohim* in Hebrew, is described as *plural male*. Although the term "trinity" was first used in the second century and means "three-in-one," it is not written in the Bible, but seems to address the "plural male" description. The one true God of the Hebrews becomes, through translation, the Christian's "one triune God" defined as three persons in one God—the Father, the Son, and the Holy Spirit—and each is co-equal, co-powerful, and co-eternal together in a unity that results in oneness. This *Elohim* who created the heavens and the earth now seems to have attributes of "male" and "female."

Let me give you a task to expand your thinking about God. Take a sheet of paper and with your pen write the words: "God is" and under the heading write: "Father, "Son," and Holy Spirit." That is where most of us stop when we are asked to describe God. But we know that these are *persons* in God that express the essence of God, *not attributes*. Here are some hints on attributes:

Attribute	Scriptural Truth	Reference
Life	Breathed into his nostrils the breath of life	Genesis 2:7
Love	Love comes from God	John 4:7
Spirit	God is Spirit	John 4:24
Light	I am the light of the world	John 8:12
Joy	My joy may be in you	John 15:11
Grace	My grace is sufficient	2 Cor. 12:9
Peace	The God of Peace	1 Thess. 5:23
Judge	God, the judge of all	Hebrews 12:23
Kindness	The kindness of the Lord	1 Peter 2:3
I AM	I am the Alpha and the Omega, the first and the last, the beginning and the end	Revelation 22:13

Then add the Hebrew translations "male" and "female" (Genesis 1:1).

Lastly, when you think you have run out of attributes, add "And many more."

The Bible says that God declares Himself as "the Bread," "the Water of life," etc. It is in the "And many *more*" that we try to comprehend God's ability to understand the female uniqueness, as well as the usage of the male gender in which He communicates His laws, His self-existence, and His personal being. God is neither female nor male, but within the vastness of what God is; there is a male and a female attribute. There is no way we can comprehend the vastness of what God really is; our only clues are in the words of God as He describes Himself.

At first glance we may be tempted to ask the question, "Hey, wait a minute, is God male and female?" And, if so, is it wrong to call God a "she'? The answer is "yes." The Hebrew word for God, J°hovah (Strong's, *Jehovah*), translates to "self-existent" indicating that God is "non-gender." It is in the language that hints at the attributes of male and female within the one triune God. The value of the language witnesses to the fact that God understands all feeling, desires, hurts, and pains in the person we are, whether male or female. God comprehends the makeup of the male, as well as that of the female, and therefore, all of mankind can go to God with confidence trusting in His ability to understand us in our own gender. Remember, now, we are talking about attributes, qualities and characteristics of God, not any physical images.

Some people refer to God as a "she," indicating you can approach God by calling him a female. This is unacceptable, as evidenced in His Holy Bible; nowhere is it written in Holy Scripture that God refers to himself as a female.

It is written all over the Old Testament and New Testament how we are to address Him, when we refer to his gender. In the first chapter of the first book of the Bible, Genesis, there are at least five times God declares Himself to be a "He": (1) *God called the light day, and the darkness He called night* (1:4); (2) *God called the dry land earth, and the gathering of the waters He called seas* (1:10); (3) *He made the stars also* (1:16); and (4) *God created man in His own image, in the image of God He created him* (1:27). In example 5—Larry's favorite—God says, "*And God saw every thing that He had made, and, behold, it was very good*" (1:31 KJV).

In the New Testament, God chose to come to His people in the form of His Son Jesus, a male. The Holy Spirit of whom Jesus spoke about was referred to as male. Even the heavenly order has "the Father," who is depicted as the Godhead figure, and is male. God has selected the model of a male as the standard in which He would communicate to all mankind.

God specifically took on the traits of a male, using names He Himself designated for the purpose of self-identification so that all mankind can interact with the almighty, holy, spiritual God. This standard of communication to mankind is called "anthropomorphism." It is a system using terms in human language we can more easily "identify with" as He tells us about Himself in a manner that accommodates our understanding.

As we previously discussed, God is so much more that we can even imagine, that some times we fail to understand the vastness of what God is, or the fact that God the Spirit has a language all His own. In the New Testament there were so many times Jesus' own disciples didn't understand Him. Jesus, who was all-God-all-man, the Spirit clothed in flesh, tried to communicate to man

6

the things God wanted mankind to know. Jesus always talked in God language, but many listened without the ability to understand. He spoke in many parables knowing that the spirit of a man who had become a believer would be able to interpret its meanings. And, yet, even then, Jesus had to tell the disciples the meanings of many of the parables. So it is today.

Adam was created in the image of God. It isn't until Genesis 3:17 that we find the first man was given the name "Adam." There are many meanings attributed to the name *Adam*. Perhaps my favorite is the Hebrew translation for *ground* and is spelled *Adameah*. Translated, the word *Adameah* means *Adam* (ground) + *e* (divine) + *ah* (in joyfulness). Do you see it? This suggests that a divine being, in conjunction with the ground, made a man called Adam in sheer delight!

We have used the words *create* and *made* in relationship to Adam's beginning: the first groom of mankind. For clarification, "create" means to make something out of nothing, whereas "made" or "make" means to use a substance to form something. Adam was *made* out of the ground that God had created when He created the world. Adam was like all the rest of creation until God breathed the *Spirit of Life* into his body. Now, Adam was a new creation, unlike any other creature in the world. He became a living human being that had a Spirit plus he was a created in God's image! His Spirit could communicate with God's Spirit. He could understand and talk with God, something no other creation could do. All the rest of creation was subject to service and obedience to God. But God had given Adam a "will" and only in the possession of a "will" could a relationship be formed and flourish.

Adam possessed many of the attributes of God. In fact, when God made Adam He created him fully mature: physically and spiritually with a soul that was tuned into obeying God. With His breath, God blew into man the soul of a perfect companion. Adam was able, in his own will of choices to respond to God spiritually, enjoying total fellowship with God. In fact, Adam was so holy that he was "worthy" to walk with God. He daily had an intimate communication with God. He walked the walk, and talked the talk with God. Adam uniquely reflected the image of God that he had been created in: God's love, God's glory, and even God's righteousness. The first man and future husband of Eve was sinless and holy, with a heart of love that possessed wisdom and the will to do right, as well as the attributes of both "male" and "female"—more about this in chapter 2.

The First Bride

Then the Lord God said, "It is not good for the man to be alone; I will make him a helper suitable for him. So the Lord God caused a deep sleep to fall upon the man, and he slept; then He took one of his ribs, and closed up the flesh at that place. And the Lord God fashion into a woman the rib

which He had taken from the man, and brought her to the man."
(Genesis 2:18, 21-22 NASB)

The scriptures tell us it was *not good* for man to be "alone," so God fashioned a "woman" for Adam. Now, don't get this wrong. Nowhere in the Scriptures does it say that Adam was "lonely." There is a difference between being *alone* and being *lonely*. Even when "alone," a man can find complete satisfaction in walking and talking with God. He can find love in his communication with God. At the same time, God knew it was not good for man to be alone because in his "aloneness" God's total plan for all His creation could not be accomplished.

Apply this concept of God's life to your life: He decided that you needed something in your life, something that you were not aware of and in His caring nature for you; He brings that something into your life without you even asking or praying for it. For some, God brings a faithful spouse the "second time around" even though you feel very comfortable being single. For some, the marriage brings a heritage of loving people that present opportunities for sharing an empty space from childhood that you've never been able to express.

For others, God gives you an unquenchable desire to have that certain dog, not knowing that the very same dog will save the life of your future child in a car/street situation or swimming pool accident.

> *"For I know the plans I have for you," declares the Lord, "plans for welfare and not for calamity to give you a future and a hope.*
> (Jeremiah 29:11 NASB)

We read that God took a rib from man to form woman. The Hebrew word for translated as "rib" means *volume*. God simply took a volume of material from Adam's own body to make the helpmeet Adam needed: a woman. God did not create Eve. Woman was fashioned from the finished product that made up Adam. She was made from and of his flesh!

> *And the man said, "This is now bone of my bones, and flesh of my flesh; she shall be called "woman," for she was taken out of man."*
> (Genesis 2:23 NIV)

Adam was "right on"! Woman was made of his very bone and from his very own flesh.

> *" ... and the two shall become one flesh."* (Matthew 19:5 NASB)

This is the reality of what happened when God formed a woman. The first human who was created in the image of God, was now being used to form another human being. Woman was not made from a different material than that of Adam: she was made *from Adam*. Every essence of her being *came* from Adam. Every "life-giving" cell in her body was once in Adam.

Then how do we explain the difference between the sexes? Am I saying that the sex of male and the sex of female were both in Adam? Yes, that is exactly what I am saying. Adam, who was created in God's image, was given, along with other godly attributes, the attribute of "femininity." When God took this particular "volume" out of Adam to form Eve: God, along with taking bone and flesh, also took the femininity quality out of man and gave it to the helpmeet. That is evident in the last half of the Scripture, "male and female He created them." (Genesis 1:27b NIV)

God had separated that which was *one*, into *two* individual parts that were the same in every other way accept sexually. When God instituted sex and marriage, which was almost immediately after the formation of woman: He simply brought back together that which was once "one," hence, the term "one flesh." Did God intend to make female distinct from male? Yes, He did! (In chapter 5, we will discuss the emotional and physical attributes, which differ greatly, between males and females.) Are some persons born with physical attributes of both male and female? As a retired nurse, I would have to say, "Yes, this does happen." But I must say that this is not the only physical abnormality we see in childbirth, nor is it even close to being a common abnormality. Before I go any further, I must direct you who suffer from this abnormality, to an Almighty Lord God that knows your hurts and pains: go to Him for physical and mental healing, for He loves you! He knows what has happened to you. And it is not in His will for you to suffer all alone the devastation that sin has inflected upon mankind. (We will discuss God's will in our lives in chapter 9.)

As for those of you who "feel" you are a sex other than the physical sexual characteristics you were born with, run to God for protection and healing. You are in spiritual warfare (more about this in chapter 10). God did not intend His separation of male and female to have any ungodly outcomes. The entrance of sin into man's existence altered all forms of man's godly inherited attributes.

Mankind lost its holiness, its righteousness, its ability to communicate with a spiritual God when its innocence was shattered. God did not intend for sin to blemish the behavior of His most prized possession in creation. Now, a holy God has to impose physical death for the lack of obedience and honor to Him! That is what sin is, and does: it brings distortion and chaos in all of our earthly lives.

It does us no good to compare our conduct with the behavior of animals, or any part of nature, for they, also, were perfect before sin came into the world. Just as all of mankind's "godly attributes" were altered by sin, so was nature's way of life. As we view creation, we see that God instituted marriage before the bride and groom had committed sin. God fully knew what He was doing in regard to human sexually. He wrote laws for His people concerning their sexuality: they are imbedded within the code of moral laws.

Woman was formed for the sake of man, to be a loving companion and helper for him. God inspired the Apostle Paul to remind us of the order of mankind:

> *... a man ... is the image and glory of God: but the woman is the glory of man. For man does not originate from woman, but woman from man; for indeed man was not created for woman's sake, but woman for the man's sake.* (1 Corinthians 11:7-9 NASB)

When we read the scriptures carefully, it reveals that God fashioned Eve after (1) He made Adam, (2) He planted a garden for him, (3) He put a river in that garden, and (4) He instructed him on the upkeep and rules of the garden! As such, woman was to share Adam's responsibility and cooperate with him in fulfilling God's purpose for his life and the life of their family. In this first marriage, there were no "self-image" problems. Adam got his glory from God, while Eve got her glory from Adam.

Let's pause for a just moment, and think how things would have been different if we had applied the no "self-image" concept of Adam and Even to our marriages. Husbands who get their glory from God are humble, trustworthy, steadfast, faithful, and protective and honor their wives … because that is what God requires from a husband.

> *You husbands likewise, live with your wives in an understanding way as with a weaker vessel, since she is a woman; and grant her honor as a fellow heir of the grace of life, so that your prayers may not be hindered.* (1 Peter 3:7 NASB)

God requires the husbands to be a "priest and prophet" to the entire family, spending hours in prayer: applying training principles to the children and to his loving wife.

> *Husbands, love your wives, just as Christ also loved the church and gave Himself up for her that He might sanctify her, having cleansed her by the washing of water with the word, that He might present to Himself the church in all her glory, having no spot or wrinkle or any such thing; but that she should be holy and blameless. So husbands ought also to love their own wives as their own bodies. He who loves his own wife loves himself.* (Ephesians 5:25-28 NASB)

All self-centeredness is gone. He waits upon the Lord God for guidance and assurance as he sets his daily life to follow the teachings of Jesus Christ. Smart man! His reward: a peaceful home and a loving wife.

What about you, wife? If you got your "self-image" from your husband, what would you be like? Wives who get their glory from their husband are respectful, humble, submissive, and cleaving to their husband as they honor him in allowing him to be the head of the home.

In the same way, you wives be submissive to your own husband....
(1 Peter 3:1 NASB)

Not to just any man: but to your husband alone. There is a distinction that God has made. A godly woman submits only to her huband! Your reward is great: freedom from worry, anxiety and resentment. You have a protector who, with the help of God, can handle all the world can throw at you. You can experience contentment in a loving and sexually moral husband. Your "nesting" desires become complete as your husband participates in the activities and discipline of the entire family. You feel fulfilled and you will understand the blessings that God intended when He created marriage and family.

The Marriage Outcome

We are barely into the second chapter of the Bible when we learn that God has set boundaries for the first human marriage. This requirement would bless future generations.

Therefore shall a man leave his father and mother and shall cleave unto his wife: and they shall be one flesh. And they were both naked, the man and his wife, and were not ashamed. (Genesis 2:24-25 NIV)

This is the first time the word "wife" is used in the Bible. Both in the Hebrew and in the Greek language it means "woman." The provisions of "leaving and cleaving" were set forth by God to establish unity in the marriage between man and woman. Adam and Eve had no earthly mother or father. Their marriage was to be the main relationship in their lives where intimacy was shared just between the two of them.

Man and woman were charged with being fruitful: To rule and subdue the earth and all its contents. They were created to form family relationships. This indicates that God considers a godly family by the raising of children in God's words. God expected Adam and Eve to consecrate all things in the earth to him and to manage it in a God-glorifying way.

But there is a place where someone has testified: "What is man that you are mindful of him, the son of man that you care for him? You have made him a little lower than the angels; you have crowned him with glory and honor, and set him over the works of your hands. You have put all things in subjection under his feet. (Hebrews 2: 6-8 NKJV)

It was God's divine purpose to place the future of His earth under mankind's dominion. God had established a union of one man and one woman for life, and, He, Himself intended to be a covenant partner in a marriage that would have dominion over all He created.

Covenant or Contract?

The subject of this chapter is "covenant." In the beginning of this chapter, we used the word "covenant" as a verbal description of marriage. We all have a "covenant marriage" when we say words like: "for better or worse," "for richer or for poorer," "in sickness and in health," and "til death do us part." These are ceremonial "covenant" words purposely describing an action we promise to maintain in a marriage. In speaking these words we seal a binding and solemn agreement; a promise to perform the action the rest of our lives.

Many Christians often refer to their marriage as a contract until they become aware of the meanings of "covenant" verses "contract." They differ in three major ways. First, a covenant has no termination date; the very nature of its "terms" (until *death* do us part) declares no ending, whereas, a contract calls for a specific amount of time. Second, a covenant calls for the full participation of the person, whereas, a contract involves only a part: usually a skill or a talent that is possessed by that specific person. Thirdly, a contract may involve from two persons to a dozen persons depending on the nature of the contract. However, a marriage covenant consists of only 3 persons: husband, wife and God. For example: one may contract to have a house built, and when it is completed (including various subcontractors), the relationship is over. But when one enters into marriage, they make a covenant for life not only with their spouse, but also God and in the presence of God who was called to witnesses the ceremony.

Covenants are made through mutual agreement. Every covenant contains promises and terms specific to the covenant. The *promises* are itemized personal commitments from each partner, whereas, the *terms* are conditions in which the agreement is sealed. The beauty of the content of the covenant agreement is that it obligates the partners to the relationship and to ensure its continuation.

Two Kinds of Covenants

There are two kinds of covenants:

1. God-to-man, based on love

    In all God's covenants with man, He requires obedience. This is expected because God allows man to express his will by being in "mutual agreement." God's words are His covenant.

2. Man-to-man, based on fear

Covenants contain the exchanging promises with personal items, making it a compulsory and solemn agreement. It involves a binding sense of commitment to the relationship. In today's world there are godly men who still keep their word, but sin has caused many a man to request collateral: something to back-up another man's word.

The God-to-Man Covenant: Based on Love

In order for us to understand what a covenant means to God, we must study the covenants He made with mankind. In the contexts of a covenant of *God to man*, a covenant is an agreement between God and mankind in which God initiates the *promises* and *terms* of the covenant, and brings it to completion. Covenants are very important to God, for everything He does toward mankind is based on a covenant, and it is always a blessing. In all of God's covenants, He is training us to understand the depth of the relationship we share with the Almighty Creator of the universe.

God's First Covenant with Mankind

God made His first covenant with Mankind in the Garden of Eden.

> *And the Lord God took the man, and put him in the Garden of Eden to work it and take care of it. And the Lord God commanded the man, "You are free to eat from any tree in the garden; but you must not eat from the tree of the knowledge of good and evil, for when you eat of it you will surely die."* (Genesis 2:15-17 NIV)

God's first covenant with mankind was in the Garden of Eden: hence it is called "The Edenic Covenant." God's covenants are His promises, His oaths, and even His counsel whereupon exist, wholly, the bestowal of all blessings. The contents of the covenant were: (1) the *promises* made by God for "eternal life" or for "death"; and (2) the *terms* were, "when you eat of it." God was making a covenant that said Adam could have eternal life—until he disobeyed and ate from that specific tree. At first glance, the scripture context appears to simply be an agreement about "not to eat the fruit of a certain tree," and it was. But in fact, there were deeper meanings: (1) to be "obedience" to the word of God in the exercise of Adam's own will; and (2) the faithfulness of God to His own word.

In this Garden of Eden conversation God is telling him, (in my own words; "Hey, Adam, don't eat the fruit of this tree or else you will die. We have created you just as you are to live forever; providing that you obey My words. I can only give it to you if you remain pure, innocent, and holy. If you do eat the fruit, you will lose these qualities and you will suffer death.") Even though Adam had not yet seen human death, the threat of death had a reality to him because his faith was based on what God said, and Adam in his "holy" state always believed God. Adam's spirit, given to him by the breath of God, was bound to God through belief and obedience, knowing God's word to be "absolute truth." Hence, we can "see" that there was *mutual agreement* between God and Adam, for he had a will and he could have said "No."

Well, we know the outcome of this Edenic Covenant. Adam didn't keep his part of the covenant: not to eat of the tree. But God kept His part of the covenant: to provide eternal life. By adding another covenant (promise) to His relationship, Adam would still have eternal life. God established His authenticity to His first covenant with Adam by announced there would be a coming Messiah that would save man and restore him as an "eternal" being.

When God was handing out His "Judgments" to the three offenders He said to the snake:

God said to the serpent, "And I will put enmity between thee and the woman, and between thy seed and her seed; it shall bruise thy head, and thou shall bruise his heel." (Genesis 3:15 KJV)

And what was the "thy seed" and "her seed" relationship all about that would cause the existence of rivalry for all mankind? (We will study this is length in chapter 10.) This we do know, God had a plan to bring all of mankind back to His presence; a plan that would "bruise" (the Cross) "her seed" (the Messiah) for mankind" disobedience (sins); His name is Jesus The Christ. God is proclaiming in Genesis 3:15 that sin has now entered His creation and that there would always be a spiritual conflict between the offspring of the woman and the evil practiced by the coming generations who would serve Satan just as the serpent did. The bruising of the woman's seed is sealed in the crucifixion, yet, in His resurrection, He would rise to deliver man from Satan, death and hell! From Adam to Noah: God's plan of salvation for all mankind was time-honored in His covenants with Abraham, Isaac and Jacob, which found its fulfillment in the birth, death and resurrection of Christ.

The word of God contains eight different revelations where God reinforces the imminence of His first Covenant in the Garden of Eden. Each covenant was built upon the previous covenant in which mankind had difficulty understanding or being obedient, until the eighth covenant; "eight" meaning "a new beginning." It is called the "New Covenant" in which God, Himself, would make the final sacrifice for mankind through His only begotten Son, Jesus the Christ. (The word "Christ" means "Messiah.") Only the shedding of His Son's blood could remove the presence of sin from His cherished creation: mankind. With the removal of sin, God, who is holy and cannot look upon sin, could once again, walk and talk with His beloved creation.

Covenant as a Verb

The Old Testament Hebrew word for *covenant* is "beriyth," derived from a root word that means "to cut." Hence, a covenant is a "cutting"—it is an action word. Most of us have heard the saying, "to cut a deal"? The Hebrew word broadens the English meaning by further indicating that the "cutting" is in reference to the cutting or dividing of animals into two parts with the covenant parties passing between the pieces, declaring their intent to keep their word.

The men who have violated my covenant and have not fulfilled the terms of the covenant they made before me, I will treat like the calf they cut in two and then walked between its pieces. (Jeremiah 34:18 NIV)

This is a very serious statement by God. Here we see that God holds men to their covenants. Both parties walking between the two halves signifies that by mutual agreement either deserves to be cut into pieces if he breaks the covenant. God is solemn about His covenants. Not only does He keep His covenants (His Word), but He *also* declares that every man (and woman) should keep his own covenants, as well.

There is actually a *sequence* of God's promises in order to keep His very first covenant: the promise of eternal life for mankind. In God's love for man, He continued to reveal and develop His original promise seven more times, in seven successive covenants.

Insight: *God's Covenants with Mankind*

Covenant Name	Covenant Meaning and Purpose
1. Eden/Edenic	In the Garden of Eden, man was called to be an "eternal" being
After the fall into sin	
2. Adam/Adamic	The coming Messiah that would save man and restore him as an "eternal" being
After the flood	
3. Noah/Noahic	God loved man, saved a remnant and would never again destroy the earth with water
4. Abraham/Abrahamic	God now selected a specific group of people from which the Messiah will come
5. Moses/Mosaic	The Law—the Ten Commandants—to show man's need for the coming Messiah
6. Wilderness	• To the new generation after the forty years of wandering • Reinstated by Moses (Deut. 29:1-29, 30:1-10)
7. David/Davidic	Established the final foundation through David's seed
8. New Covenant	• Fulfills all previous covenants • Through Jesus Christ, man will live an "eternal life"

Covenant 1: Eternal Life

In reviewing the eight covenants, we see God establishing His original covenant, in Genesis 2:16-17 (Edenic Covenant) with Adam for eternal life.

The *promise* was eternal life if they did not eat of the fruit of the tree, or death if they ate the fruit of the tree. They would have eternal life as long as they kept away from the eating of the fruit of the tree. The covenant *terms* were death. "*When* you eat of it" was a mutual agreement. Adam committed the first sin by disobeying God's warning not to eat of the tree. God kept His word and death was inherited by all mankind.

Covenant 2: A Coming Messiah

While God was assigning judgment to the failure of His finest creation: mankind, and to the serpent in the garden, God once again, established with His word: a covenant. In the covenant, the Adamic Covenant, God had to cover the purpose of His "original covenant." God is going to bring around His promise of "eternal life" for mankind. So He *promises* a Messiah that will save man and restore him as an eternal being.

The war was on! Satan had entered the serpent to destroy and mislead God's treasure: mankind. God accepted the challenge to purify His people; Himself. God no longer demanded a mutual agreement from man, for there is nothing mankind can do to achieve the "Holy" state that Adam once had. It is at this point in scripture that God demanded "Faith" from man, along with "obedience." The keeping of the covenant promise is now all up to God, for He will not forsake His word! There are no terms; God's word will be enough! God's very character is expressed in His covenants, and He remembers them.

He remembers His covenant forever, the word He commanded, for a thousand generations... (Psalms 105:8 NIV)

Covenant 3: A New Beginning for Mankind

Evil continued to prevail in God's created Earth.

The Lord saw that the wickedness of man was great in the earth and that every intention of the thoughts of his heart was only evil continually. And the Lord was sorry that He had made man on the earth, and it grieved him in His heart. (Genesis 6:5-6 ESV)

Yes, God was sorry He made mankind and He decided to destroy all of them. In all the multiplying of mankind, there was only one man who found favor with God. In fact, scripture says that he "walked with God." (Genesis 6:9) It was Noah. And God decided to save Noah, his wife, and his three sons and daughter-in-laws from the destruction that was about to cover the entire earth— the Flood! After the flood (Genesis 9:11), God gave His word to Noah that "never again shall there be a flood to destroy the earth." In fact, God placed a rainbow in the sky after each rainfall as constant proof to mankind that He would keep the heavenly waters from ever flooding the earth again. The rainbow is proof of His words.

Covenant 4: A New Nation of People and Messiah's Genealogy

God initiated His covenant to Abram, whose name means "exalted Father."

Now the Lord had said to Abram, "Get out of your country, from your family and from your father's house to a land that I will show you. I will make you a great nation. I will bless you and make your name great: and you shall be a blessing. I will bless those who bless you, and I curse him

who curses you; and in you all the families of the earth shall be blessed."
(Genesis 12:1-3 NKJV)

God would only ask of Abram what He asked of all mankind since Adam: faith and obedience!

In Abram's time, the world was just as evil as it had ever been, sin continued to flourish. The flood only served to reduce the number of people on the earth, not the presence of evil and temptation. Abram was from the line of Shem, Noah's son. God had elected Abram as the man to bring forth a nation; a specific group of people from whom the Messiah would come. God intended to have mankind know Him and to serve Him with devoted faith. The generations that would come from Abram's loins would become a nation that would keep the words and ways of God. He would call this nation to be a separate people, His holy people, away from the ungodly ways of a sinful world. The original covenant for eternal life was the first covenant for moving in the direction of completion. God would rise up prophets to foretell the coming of the Messiah in a genealogy time-line, and the people would recognize the promised Messiah as the host of eternal life! It would be a long time in coming to its fruition as man counts time, but God would keep His Eden Covenants.

In Genesis 15:5 as God shows Abram the land He is giving to him and the offspring that will result from God's Covenant, God tells him, "Look up at the heavens and count the stars – if indeed you can count them." Then He said to him, "So shall your offspring be." Even though Abram trusted God and relied on God for everything, he still asked, in verse 8 "Lord God, how shall I know that I will inherit it?"

God, knowing Abram's heart of righteousness, answered him by the ceremonial sacrifice. God would keep His word and He would show Abram in no uncertain terms that He always keeps His covenants. In the following verses we see the sacrifice being made ready:

> *So the Lord said to him, "Bring me a heifer, a goat and a ram, each three years old, along with a dove and a young pigeon." Abram brought all these to Him, cut them in two and arranged the halves opposite each other; the birds, however, he did not cut in half. Then birds of prey came down on the carcasses, but Abram drove them away. As the sun was setting, Abram fell into a deep sleep, and a thick and dreadful darkness came over him.*
> (Genesis 15:9-12 NIV)

Here we also see that there is an element of ceremony in most of God's covenants. We use the word "ceremony" in the sense of a "ritual," "performance," or a "formal procedure." It was while Abram gathered the sacrifices for the ceremony that God prophesied the Egyptian slavery and oppression of 430 years for some of his descendents. (See Genesis 15:13-14.)

After Abram prepared the sacrifice, we see God's presence:

When the sun had gone down and it was dark, behold, a smoking fire pot and a flaming torch passed between these pieces. (Genesis 15:17 ESV)

Here, we see God active in the covenant He made with Abram. The description of the "smoking firepot with a blazing torch" which appeared and passed between the pieces is *God's presence*. Note that although a covenant usually establishes responsibilities (promises and terms) for both parties, in this instance only God passed between the pieces of the animals. God alone established the promises, terms, and obligations of the covenant. God is confirming to Abram that He will keep His word to Him. Abram had only to accept them in obedient faith. Abram did and God changed his name to Abraham, which means "father of a multitude."

Covenant 5: "The Law" to Reveal Sin and the Need for the Messiah

God had selected a specific group of people, through Abraham, whom He now called "the children of Israel" and sent them to Egypt for growth and humility training for over 400 years. Through Moses, He brought them out of the land of bondage and slavery of the Egyptian masters, to lead them to "the Promised Land" of milk and honey. God would feed them, preserve them and perform miracles. He was establishing their trust and so was He increasing their faith. But as their journey continued on the original eleven-day trip to "the Promised Land," doubt and grumbling began set in the people's heart. God redirected Moses and the two million people that left Egypt to another route—through the wilderness of the Red Sea toward Mount Sinai, which took an additional forty years of travel. Here, at Mount Sinai, the people would understand God's purpose and plan for their lives. God called Moses to the mountain:

Thus you shall say to the house of Jacob, and tell the children of Israel: "You have seen what I did to the Egyptians, and how I bore you on eagles" wings and brought you to Myself. Now, therefore, if you will indeed obey My voice and keep My covenant, then you shall be a special treasure to Me above all people: for the earth is Mine. And you shall be to Me a kingdom of priests and a holy nation. (Exodus 19:3-6 NKJV)

It was here, at Mount Sinai, that God gave Moses His Ten Commandments for His people to follow. Besides the Ten Commandments, there were laws and commandments for worship (ceremonial laws) and for morality among the people (civil law).

And Moses came and told the people all the words of the Lord, and all the judgments: and all the people answered with one voice, and said, all the words which the Lord hath said will we do. And Moses wrote all the words of the Lord, and rose up early in the morning, and built an altar under the hill, and twelve pillars, according to the twelve tribes of Israel. And He sent young men of the children of Israel, which offered burnt offerings, and sacrificed peace offerings of oxen unto the Lord. And Moses took half of the blood, and put it in basins; and half of the blood he sprinkled on the altar. And he took the book of the covenant, and read in the audience of the people: and they said, "All that the Lord hath said will we do, and be obedient." (Exodus 24:3-7 KJV)

The sacrifice, the spilling of animal blood, was not entered into until the congregation said they would obey the laws. Once man has accepted the conditions of the "book of the covenant" and the terms with a vow, man cannot go back on them. Here, we see again, as between Adam and God: a mutual agreement between the children of Israel and God.

If a man vows a vow unto the Lord or swears an oath to bind his soul with a bond, he shall not break his word; he shall do according to all that proceedeth out of his mouth. (Numbers 30:2 KJV)

This verse makes it very clear that God requires His people to keep their promises to Him and others.

Covenant 6: A New Generation of Faith

The first generation of the children of Israel to leave Egypt never did give up their murmurings, nor develop the kind of faith needed to "rest" in the covenant. Due to their murmurings and lack of faith, a second generation now replaced all the adults of the first generation that had died.

The Promised Land came into view, and entrance into the Promised Land would be by Joshua and Caleb, along with persons who were under the age of twenty years old. A little over two million people entered the Promised Land.

The Giving of the Ten Commandments

It was never God's purpose in giving the Ten Commandments to demand full obedience to His law, because He knew the Israelites couldn't do it.

For He Himself knows our frame; He is mindful that we are but dust. (Psalms 103:14 NASB)

The Ten Commandments were given as a guide, as a "signpost" to show them (and us) that no one could ever attain, nor deserve eternal salvation in the sinful state we inherited from Adam. They had to see their sin (inability to obey the Ten Commandments) and the need for a redeemer—the promised *Messiah* who would be the only one to fulfill obedience to the law.

God then had Moses reinstate all the laws and the covenants to the second generation in the wilderness that He given to the descendants of Abraham, Jacob, and Isaac. God intended to keep His covenant, and added another commandant for this generation: the law and commandments are to be read before all the people of Israel every seven years. It would be a celebration, a time to remember and reflect, a time to give thanks, a time to celebrate the covenant, and a time to establish an anniversary!

Covenant 7: The Nation of God's People Births the Messiah

God is setting up a final foundation from which the Messiah shall come. It will be through Israel's second king, King David.

> *God instructs Nathan, the prophet to tell David, "When your days are fulfilled and you rest with your fathers, I will set up your "seed" after you who will come from your body, and I will establish His kingdom."*
> (2 Samuel 7:12 NIV)

God is about to come to earth, to save His people from the sin of Adam. The triune God, the only true God of this world, will sacrifice His own son to meet His standard of holiness so that He, once more, may walk and talk with and amongst His people.

Covenant 8: A New Covenant that Fulfills All Previous Covenants

The "New Covenant," the last covenant by God is the one in which we see the fulfillment of all the rest of the covenants. It is Jesus, the last blood sacrifice.

> *In the same way, after the supper He took the cup, saying, "This cup is the new covenant in my blood, which is poured out for you."*
> (Luke 22:20 KJV)

Death came through Adam, but eternal life comes through Jesus.

> *Therefore, just as through one man sin entered the world, and death through sin, and thus death spread to all men, because all sinned...*
> (Romans 5:12 NKJV)

> *Therefore, as through one man's offense, judgment came to all men, resulting in condemnation ...* (Romans 5:18 NKJV)

> *But God demonstrates His own love toward us, in that while we were still sinners, Christ died for us. Much more then, having now been justified by His blood, we shall be saved from wrath through Him* [the Messiah] ... *We also rejoice in God through our Lord Jesus Christ, through whom we have now received the reconciliation* [with Father God]. (Romans 5:8-11 NKJV; brackets added for clarification.)

Read chapter 15 of 1 Corinthians regarding mankind's future for those who have faith and obedience in the risen Messiah. Savor the words of hope—your enemies are destroyed, and the exchange of your lustful flesh is for a glorious heavenly body.

Summary: God's Covenant with Man

What are the terms and promises of God's last covenant with mankind? The same as in the Old Testament; God makes all the promises and terms, and we agree mutually by faith in Jesus Christ to obey God's word (that is all God asked of Adam). The Old Testament sacrifices are no longer required, Jesus was the last sacrifice—the last *blood sacrifice*. There is just one thing we must do "on our own," and that is to *decide* that we want to be "born again." In John 3:3, Jesus declared, "I tell you the truth, no one can see the kingdom of God (eternal life) unless he is born again."

Sacrifices are now substituted by saying "the Sinner's Prayer"! This prayer brings us to an admission of our sins and acknowledging that Jesus took them on the Cross for us in order to be reconciled with our holy God. This now puts us in a relationship with the Almighty God that mankind had lost in the Garden of Eden. When we are born again we walk through the pieces, accepting His death. We take on Jesus' robe (his identity and righteousness) and He takes on our sin. We become one with Him, sharing all His possessions in the anointing of the Holy Spirit. We die to self and live for Jesus, our covenant partner.

We put to death all other relationships, as a priority, and in self-denial, we take up His Cross. His words become as sweet as honey to our lips. His protection grants us freedom from fear of want and encourages us to serve others. Every covenant promise spoken in the Bible is now ours.

God's purpose for mankind has always been to bring us to Him and establish a covenant relationship where God says "they are mine and I will be their God." Aren't we a lot like that? We go into a marriage relationship that says, "you will be mine, and I will be your wife/husband." As married couples we feel this way because of the nature of our creation, we need to complete the "wholeness of one flesh."

> God said to Israel, *"I will betroth you to me forever. I will betroth you to me in righteousness and in justice, in steadfast love and in mercy."* (Hosea 2:19 ESV)

God considers Israel to be his wife. Jesus Christ considers "the Church" to be his bride!

The Sinner's Prayer

If you have never said the Sinner's Prayer to be born again, receive the following as your prayer. Say it out loud and don't be ashamed, it gives *you* the promise of *eternal life*.

> *Dear Heavenly Father, how wonderful is your faithfulness in your covenant to me. I confess that I have sinned against You, Your word and heaven. I repent of all my sins and seek your forgiveness. Thank you for fulfilling your promises in your Son, Jesus Christ the Messiah, who died on the Cross and rose from the dead so that I might have eternal life. Today, I ask Jesus to come into my heart, to open my ears and eyes, and become my Lord and Savior. I turn away from my own way of life, and seek your plans for my life. I love you, and thank you for bringing me into the family of God, and appointing me a resident in your kingdom. In Jesus' holy name I pray. Amen!*

If you have just said the Sinner's Prayer, please, sister and brother in Christ, find a church to worship in and be baptized; or if you have a church, then be baptized. Baptism is an outward, public sign of your commitment to change your life and grow toward the image of Jesus Christ.

The Man-to-Man Covenant: Based on Fear

Let us examine more elements of a covenant by studying a biblical example of a *man-to-man* covenant by David and Jonathan:

And Jonathan made a covenant with David because he loved him as himself. Jonathan took off the robe he was wearing and gave it to David, along with his tunic, and even his sword, his bow and his belt.
(1 Samuel 18:3-4 NIV)

This covenant contains the exchanging of promises with personal items. It involves a binding sense of commitment to the relationship. David knew that King Saul, Jonathan's father, was trying to kill him. David needed to know the movements of Jonathan's father in order to hide from him. The symbolism in the *robe* is that of taking on the identity of the covenant partner. As one would put on a robe, one is *putting on the other person* and becoming "one" with that person. The belt, weapons and armor symbolize tools of protection for the wearer, whereas a person without them is subject to death in bouts with an enemy. When Jonathan gave them up to his covenant partner, it implies that Jonathan would give his life for David if it were needed.

You might ask, does God expect us to keep an oath or covenant we've made even if it is not in His will? The answer is *yes!* We find the answer in the next example of a *man-to-man* covenant in the book of Joshua. During the book of Exodus, Joshua was constantly in training to take over for Moses when the Israelites would enter the Promised Land. He was privy to many conversations between God and Moses. Here is a very important message that God gave Moses in the presence of Joshua.

Take care, lest you make a covenant with the inhabitants of the land to which you go, lest it become a snare in your midst. (Exodus 34:12 ESV)

God told the Israelites that they were not to make treaties with the tribes in the "promised land." God knew that if they "mixed" with them there would be the problem of Idolatry. As Joshua, God's appointed military leader and judge, entered the promised land; God gave him a list of all the heathen tribes and nations that he was lead in conquest. Joshua had instructions to kill all the tribes; every man, woman and child, cattle and livestock—destroy everything.

As Joshua was moving into the area, God gave him military victory. The news spread and the idolatrous Kings began to fear Joshua and His God. One tribe, the Gibeonites, resorted to a ruse; they dressed as if they were from a distant country, asking to make a treaty of peace with Joshua and the Israelites. The leaders of the assembly looked at their sandals and wineskins; they appeared to be weathered and old. And on this evaluation, without consulting God, Joshua and the people agreed to a treaty to let them live. Three days later, when Joshua and his army came upon the towns of the Gibeonites, they realized that they were neighbors living close to them.

And the sons of Israel did not strike them, because the leaders of the congregation had sworn to them by the Lord, the God of Israel. And the whole congregation grumbled against the leaders. But all the leaders said to the whole congregation, "We have sworn to them by the Lord, the God of Israel, and now we cannot touch them. (Joshua 9:18-19 NASB)

The Israelites were bound by their oath, even though they went against God's command not to spare anyone.

The Elements of God's Covenant as Seen in the Wedding Covenant

From what we have learned about covenants, let's look at the elements of a covenant and the elements of a wedding ceremony. As you view the diagram "Elements of a Covenant," below, the similarities are striking.

It is in this comparison we can "see" how God feels about our covenant marriage. God gives His covenant partners (us) all that is dear to Himself: His creation. He expects no less from us in our marriage: the sharing of all our earthly goods, the pooling of all our resources.

God ratifies His promises to all mankind by the bloodshed of His own son, Jesus Christ. Just as God walked between the sacrificial pieces to show Abraham He meant what He promised to him, so the husband passes through the sacrificial blood of his virgin wife (that is their mutual sacrifice: to remain virgins until the covenant marriage is sealed by promises and terms) to consummate his promises during the covenant wedding vows. The sealing of the covenant is the giving of something—Jonathan gave his robe and sword, and God gave His Son!

In modern day marriages, we give rings as a seal of the covenant. The giving of rings, for centuries, has stood for "a blood covenant." Earliest mankind felt that the heart's blood ran from the heart, down the left arm to the fourth finger; this was the route of a true, heartfelt vow. In the earlier century marriages, each partner in the ceremony would cut their own inside left hand fourth finger and, then, grasp their left hands together, mixing their blood. This was translated to into a "blood covenant" that could not be broken. Today, we simply apply rings to the left hand fourth finger to signify the same covenant. Changing of names; feast; the celebration after the covenant becomes a reception; and, of course, for annual celebrations, we have our anniversaries.

Insight: *Elements of a Covenant*

God's Covenant	Wedding and Marriage
Promises made (Genesis 12:1-3) • Abram's land • Abram's descendents • Abram's seed • Everlasting promises	**Vows exchanged** • "I bequeath all my possessions" • "For better or for worse" • "In sickness or in health" • "Til death do us part"
Ratified by bloodshed (Genesis 15:17) God Himself walked between the pieces of animal sacrifices	**Life and death commitment** Husband passes through the pieces (the legs) on the wedding night (breaking the hymen; blood is shed, the veil broken)
Seal or token (1 Samuel 18:3-4) David and Jonathan: "robe, sword, belt"	**Exchanging of rings** • Stands for "blood covenant" • Blood covenants cannot be broken • Heart to left hand, to 4th finger (cut fingers and grasp hands)
Changing of names (Genesis 17:4) Abram to "Abraham"	**Bride takes groom's last name**
Sanctuary Where the divine presence of God resides	**Ceremony at church** "The house of God"
Feast Celebration after the covenant	**Reception** Eat a memorial meal
Annual celebration (Deuteronomy 31:9-13) "Feast of the Tabernacle"	**Anniversaries**

Closing Prayer

Dear Heavenly Father, we confess that we have not always understood the full meaning of the marriage covenant. We have not been the husband and wife you planned for us. We repent and ask your forgiveness. I ask your Holy Spirit to come into our hearts with the plans Our God has for us. I turn away from my own way of life and seek your guidance for the path you will walk with us. Thank you for your covenant promise of Jesus Christ. We love you and thank you for bring us into the family of God. In Jesus' name we pray. Amen and Amen.

Chapter 1: Covenant Marriage?
Summary and Applications for Marriage

- Marriage has three elements: (1) the wedding; (2) the marriage itself; and (3) the family. The wedding is the *celebration* of the covenant. The marriage is the *living* of the covenant, and the family is the *teaching* of the covenant.

- God witnesses our marriage and becomes a covenant partner. The Wedding vows are indissoluble and irrevocable after accepting the terms and promises. God expects us to honor our covenants marriage vows because they are said in mutual agreement.

- We have a "triune" marriage. Jesus is the *power source* that brings about the joy and happiness of our marriage. God is the ultimate *authority* in our marriage! The power of the Holy Spirit *cements* our marriage.

- We are "one flesh"; our two souls become one, and we live for the covenant partner. Our lives are held in common, where all wealth, debt and possessions are combined into unity of oneness.

- We take on our covenant partner's identity. Marriage is death to independent living. Any selfish interests must take a back seat to the growth of the marriage. All other earthly relationships have secondary importance.

- When you enter into the marriage designed by God, you also are entering into a personal ministry that will witness to others. In your love for each other that reflects Christ's love, in a very special way you enhance all that you do in the name of Christ and in the way you serve the Lord.

- Second Corinthians 6:14 said you should not be yoked with a non-believer.

Visit our website for this book, at **www.NotYourEnemy.info**, where you will be welcome to ask questions or make comments. Enjoy!

A covenant made in the presence of God is a binding vow that ends only in death. God, the original covenant maker, has been called to be a witness to our oaths and therefore takes our covenant seriously. He walks between the pieces, becoming the center of our marriage. Read Deuteronomy 23:23. Together, review the vows you said at your wedding in the presence of God.

1. What were some of the promises you made?

    Husband: _____

    _____

    Wife: _____

    _____

2. What were the *terms* of your marriage covenant as to length of time?

    Husband: _____ Wife: _____

3. Did you invite God's presence as a witness to hear your ceremonial vows?

    Husband: ☐ Yes ☐ No. Why? _____

    Wife: ☐ Yes ☐ No. Why? _____

4. Write in your own words what a "marriage covenant" means to you.

    Husband: _____

    Wife: _____

5. Going back to your wedding day, husband, do you remember how you felt when you saw her in her wedding dress, and looked into her eyes and said you loved her? Write it here:

    _____

    _____

6. Wife, write down your feelings, when your husband put the ring on your finger. Were there feelings of tenderness? Did you have a sense of belonging? To share this with your husband, write them down here:

    _____

    _____

7. 2 Corinthians 6:14 says that you should not be yoked with a non-believer. When you got married were you "unequally yoked"?

   ☐ Yes ☐ No

   a. ☐ If you were unequally yoked and you said the "Sinner's Prayer," you no longer have to be concerned about the past. Today, you live in a "triune covenant" marriage between you, your spouse, and God.

   b. ☐ If you were unequally yoked and chose not to say the "Sinner's Prayer," we would recommend a local church to help you understand the prayer.

   c. ☐ If you are equally yoked now, hallelujah! Run into God's arms, and with all the ups and downs of your marriage, He will bring you joy in all things.

8. After reading the chapter on *Covenant Marriage*, do you feel that God *holds you to your marriage vows*?

   Husband: ☐ Yes ☐ No. Why? _____

   _____

   Wife: ☐ Yes ☐ No. Why? _____

   _____

9. Do you believe and trust God to take an active role in the daily routine of your marriage life, and why?

   Husband: ☐ Yes ☐ No. Whether *yes* or *no*, please give reasons why:

   _____

   Wife: ☐ Yes ☐ No. Whether *yes* or *no*, please give reasons why:

   _____

Chapter 2
One Flesh

Godly Principle 2:
God sees us as "one flesh" in a covenant marriage.

God's number-one issue in marriage and Satan's number one target:

- To get the husband to submit to the "understanding" of his wife, especially when she displays aspects he doesn't understand.
- To get the wife to respectfully submit to her husband's authority, especially when he can be wrong.

God completes our "one flesh" by designating earthly roles of authority and responsibility. We will look closely at these roles for both husband and wife.

The Situation

Before considering the definition of what one "one flesh" means, let us examine and evaluate a common situation we all have been in, where a conversation presents itself in rather unguarded innocence, yet obligatory compromise with someone other than your spouse.

Suppose someone, whether a neighbor or a friend or a fellow worker, or even a church member, engages you in conversation and tells you about a certain situation, asking you not to repeat this situation to anyone, maybe saying something like, "it's just between you and me." Some people unwittingly start off conversations with that very phrase. It sounds like a command that demands action on your part! In fact, the speaking of those very words creates an environment that seems to take on the existence of one of those "self-fulfilling" conversations that suggests a secrecy all of its own. You've "been there." You meet your Bible-class friend or neighbor in the local grocery store, and as you stop for a chat, you ask how the job is coming along—or the youngsters, or the illness in the family, etc. They lean over and say, "Well, just between you and me .... " And before you've even said a word, you get the feeling that they are about to make you "privy" to some sort of personal information. The private information is not intense, but in your hesitancy to speak your opinion openly to this person, your silence becomes a gesture of agreement to a "hush-hush" confidence that lends itself to the beginning of a "secret pal" society.

On the way home you remember the conversation, and disregard it as unimportant. It's the kind of information that you wouldn't have passed along anyway. Hours later, at the dinner table with your family, the conversation moves to sharing daily experiences. You just happen to mention that you met "so-and-so" at the market today. Showing interest in your day, your spouse asks innocently, "How are things with them?" Well, there you sit—the holder of an off-the-cuff conversation that you are not sure you should share with anyone because you are not sure they would like for you to repeat what they told you. And, now, the discomfort comes. Thinking that friendship involves loyalty, you sort through your thoughts, looking for something to share about the conversation that doesn't violates the seemingly "secret pal pact" you made with your friend.

The feelings that you are struggling with is not the withholding of some juicy piece of gossip that you know is wrong in the eyes of both you and your spouse, it is the loss of the freedom to be in "complete union" with your spouse. It is the loss of intimacy that you and your spouse share in the liberty of your "one-flesh" relationship. The fact that you are the "owner" of private information that you cannot or should not repeat, now, puts you in a "bondage-like" silence of a secret that forever keeps you from sharing it with your "soul-mate." It is one of those situations that, although small, can start a disconnection between you and your spouse.

It is one of those situations that can start to form a bit of isolation in your marriage. The act of prohibiting yourself from sharing even the slightest part of yourself can lead to a division in intimacy between you and your spouse.

What could you have done differently in that conversation with you friend? Should you go back and tell them how you feel, or should you just chalk it off to a bad experience? Was it a big deal? What do you do if you disregard the same comment next time, and pass it on to someone else, and your friend get hurt feelings? Does one need to set conversational precedence? Yes!

We feel it is very important to void any cliques or language that lends its self to questionable outcomes. Anyone using slang sayings such as "just between you and me" is sending an invitation of intimacy. It personalizes the conversation, excludes all others and establishes a familiarity that can be re-engaged.

So you have choices: (1) you can confront the issue, or (2) you can ignore the issue. Confronting the issue can have some "present discomfort" where as, ignoring the issue brings on future pain, over and over again. Ignoring any issue that touches our feelings in a negative way, can, and usually does return. It is called "unresolved conflict." Each time you experience "that same feeling," the pain comes back again and again with more intensity than the first time you experience it. Future conversations may lead toward deeper personal subjects such as moral attitudes, private disappointments, or just plain "flirting."

A true friend, when confronted with the issue, will offer a willing apology, understanding the position their unguarded conversation put you in. That is a worthy friendship.

30

Answer to the Situation

First of all, you need to protect your marriage from any situation that involves matters of secrecy between you and anyone else other than your spouse. To prevent any future episode of this nature, you need to make clear to all people, even your children and family members, that you do not keep any information or "secrets" from your spouse, and that you usually share your daily conversations with your spouse. They may laugh at you and reassure you that they meant no harm to your marriage, stating, "Oh, you're being foolish, how could you think that there would be any other meaning than just playful nonsense?" This gets them "off the hook" and makes you look like an old fashioned, "get-a-life" traditionalist.

Don't take their comments seriously. Their main agenda is making themselves look good at the cost of your feelings. Don't even take their remarks on a personal level, as you have just established a high moral ground, a marital standard that provides a safety net for your marriage. You have just eliminated any fear or doubt that may arise in any other situations where you "hear stuff."

You see, when anyone asks for something to be between you and him/her alone, it violates the unity of the marriage. It places a "wedge" between the "oneness" of your marriage, oneness that can only be played out by the two of you. In revealing to a person that you share your daily life-style activities and conversations with your mate, it is giving them notice that any conversation will be repeated.

The beauty of this announcement is this: it not only decreases future topics that may injure their relationship with you, but it also eliminates conversational information that may invade the harmony of the "one-flesh" relationship you have with your spouse. It's a win-win situation for you!

"One Flesh": What Does God Mean?

For this cause shall a man leave father and mother, and shall cleave to his wife: and they twain shall be one flesh. Wherefore they are no more twain, but one flesh. What therefore God hath joined together, let no man put asunder. (Matthew 19:5-6 KJV)

Jesus is repeating what His Father said.

Therefore a man shall leave his father and his mother and hold fast to his wife, and they shall become one flesh. (Genesis 2:24 ESV)

God sees us, in our marriage, as "one flesh." This is so important that God had Paul repeat the same words.

Therefore a man shall leave his father and mother and shall hold fast to his wife, and the two shall become one flesh. (Ephesians 5:31 ESV)

Three times we have read scriptures that attests to the reality that we, husband and wife, are "one flesh" in God's sight. God's perfect plan for marriage is fundamentally about *two people* who mysteriously become and remain *one flesh* for the rest of their lives. God did it. He made it and called marriage. It is not some social event that man declared for the purpose of moral controls in the community. God made marriage and all the beauty that surrounds it. In fact, it is here within the relationship of marriage that He formed the "one-flesh" covenant.

To put it another way, God's design for marriage is that it is to be a covenant of spiritual unity to which the souls and hearts of both partners are joined *before* Him and *with* Him into a "three-fold cord."

> *Two are better than one, because they have a good return for their work. If one falls down, his friend can help him up. But pity the man who falls and has no one to help him up! Also, if two lie down together, they will keep warm. But how can one keep warm alone? Though one may be overpowered, two can defend themselves. A cord of three strands is not quickly broken.* (Ecclesiastes 4:9-12 NIV)

Solomon is telling us that marriage has a deeper meaning than just meeting our own needs. The entire passage speaks to life's advantages when there are "two people" caring for each other.

The "unity of two people" caring for each other will render protection and safety from many of the world's troubles. God not only joins the married couple to each other making them "one flesh," but also joins the "one flesh" to Himself, making a "triune marriage" that is protected by His presence in the marriage, becoming like "a cord of three strands," which is much stronger than a single or double cord. The cord of marriage *must* contain *all three* elements: the husband, the wife, and God Himself. God gives reference to the marriage being united with God and therefore the protection is even greater. Even in a marriage between a godly woman and a godly man, there continues to be stresses in life here on this earth. But when we include God into every fiber (strand) of our married life, there is more peace and calmness because we learn from God that godly priorities result in blessings.

Jesus, when approached by the Pharisees about divorce, pointed out that the God-given "one-flesh" marriage was "unity." The Pharisees were asking if it was "lawful" for a man to divorce his wife; but in essence, and more to the point, they were looking for an answer that would legalize divorce for any reason! Jesus reminded them of the Old Testament where God created Adam, and formed Eve, joining of the twos of them in a covenant marriage. God sees the "one-flesh" marriage and the "triune" marriage as a relationship of permanence: "Until death do us part." Only until the death of one of the "flesh" partners does the marriage end. The "three-strand cord" that is not easily broken was meant to be broken only through death.

Yet, even in the course of the death of one of the spouses, God in His never ending love continues to support and care for the other spouse that is left behind. The living partner can re-marry and still be in the will of God. Because of death, there is no law forbidding the remaining spouse to re-marry again in a new covenant with God.

You see, the main problem with divorce is not in the act of having sex with someone other than your ex-mate, although we can relate this to the "adultery" Jesus speaks about; the "adulterous act" is in *not keeping with the covenant—* the promises and terms of the *first marriage* vows. Keeping a covenant is straightforward with God; He heard His name called at your wedding ceremony, "Dearly beloved, we are gathered here in the sight of God, family and friends." He lends His presence to the ceremony by pledging His part of the covenant to the marriage. God says, (my sense of what he would say) "Great! My children are getting married. I want to be part of their *one flesh*, to guide them and to protect them. They are going to go through a lot of changes, and I will help them cope." Sounds silly, but all marriages are God-covenant issue. Divorce and re-marriage while the first spouse is still alive is the act of making another covenant with God when the first covenant has not been honored. However, when death brings about an end to the covenant, then the marriage promises and terms have been kept.

As we said, we have no reason, wisdom or knowledge to not accept the fact that God does see our marriage as "one flesh." The mystery around the "one flesh" involving two people in marriage leads us to, at least, ask the following questions for a better understanding; that is, "What are the individual and oneness components of the "one flesh?" "Why did God see a need to bond a male and female in such a manner?"

"One Flesh": When and How?

Let us return to Genesis for a summary rundown of mankind. Let us go back to man's creation.

> *Then Lord God formed the man of dust from the ground and breathed into his nostrils the breath of life and the man became a living creature.* (Genesis 2:7 ESV)

God specifically imparted *life and breath into* the first man, creating a uniqueness of "divine life and human life" (a spirit and a soul).

> *So God created man in His own image, in the image of God He created him: male and female He created them.* (Genesis 1:27 ESV)

Here we see that Adam was created in the image of God, having the likeness of God. When God had completed Adam's creation, he was complete and whole, perfectly containing within one person all the attributes we now know as male and female. In chapter 1, we learned in Genesis 2:21 that God removed from

Adam a "rib," or a "chamber." In some Bible translations, it says, "Took part of the man's side." In Hebrew, the word "rib" translates into the words "volume" or "container." With this "volume" God formed Adam's helper from the perfection of Adam, his own body and substances. All the various characteristics such as discernment, sensitivity, dependency, love, and nurturing that were given to Eve came from Adam. Together, they had the same qualities that were previously contained within Adam alone.

I wish we could show you our "home-made Adam" that we use in our workshops. He was stitched from miscellaneous sewing leftovers: heavy muslin sheeting material and cotton bunting for a body that was about 36 inches long, with hazel-colored buttons for eyes, red embroidery yarn for hair, and a covering of artificial green leaves for his loins. On his left side, just under the "heart space" was a slit in our Adam's side. Yes, his neck was too long and his navel to high, but he looked just like his maker—me—and I love him. That is what creators do—they love their creations. I created him in my own image which is a hazel eyed, red-headed Jewish-German-born Christian whose grandmother saw the Messiah in Jesus the Christ.

Anyway, in all of the seminars we gave, we would reenact the first appearance of Eve on earth. We would lay our "sleeping Adam" on the table next to a femininely decorated box. The box was dressed in white netting and white satin ribbons: denoting a pure, innocent, emotional, first-time surroundings from which Adam's bride would come. The white sparkly bells hanging everywhere on the box would not mistake this occasion for anything but that a wedding was about to begin. Then "the hand of God," poorly played by Bev Bentley, would reach into the side of Adam and pull out a "volume" and put it in the decorated box. Meanwhile, "the voice of God," inadequately portrayed by Larry Bentley, would call out a "characteristic" and explain why that specific feature was taken from Adam. After the withdrawal of several handfuls of "volume" taken from Adam's side, which were described in full detail and thrown into the "Bridal Suite," the members of the class would catch on. They were experiencing from visual drama, the formation of Eve's body from the body of Adam. The uniqueness of the characteristics that were call out loud, now made sense to them as they individually compared the presence of some features in females but almost absent in males, and the presence of other features in males that were absent in females. They were beginning to understand the differences in male versus females, and yet more importantly; it was God who made the differences.

The time came in the seminar when I would go into the femininely decorated box and pull out a beautiful red-headed Eve clothed in a negligee of fine silk and lace. Her hair was long and curly, winding around her neck and shoulders. I would join the two together (Adam and Eve), and ask the members of the class if they could understand what went on here. The class would spontaneously laugh, and call out, "God did better with Adam's parts than anyone could have done." And although that is true: God does better with all things (even all things we give Him) than we could ever do by ourselves, there is a "higher understanding" here. In all the volume He took out of Adam, He returned this volume *back* to Adam in the most beautiful form: a wife—his other half! A bonding marriage was formed. They were "one flesh" and could not exist well without each other. When Adam needed some of the volume God took from him, he turned to his wife. When Eve found herself lacking in strength or another virtue, she turned to Adam. They were *complete* in and with each other, fully knowing that God was their center.

Eve's "Volume" from Adam

1. Nurturing

Eve will need the majority of nurturing for:
- The children who need to be raised and trained in development
- The home and garden that provides a pleasant environment
- The family pet that needs feeding and training
- The nursing of illnesses, colds, bruises, and fevers

While Adam needs a little nurturing, we will leave a little for:
- His job of "rancher," "farmer," "doctor" or "chemist"
- Being the Priest and Prophet of the family
- Teaching football to his sons or being a model husband for his daughters

2. Emotional

Eve will need the majority of emotions, which compose most of the contents of the right side of the brain. The major emotion is *sensitivity*, which Eve will need a bundle of:

- Sound judgment, wisdom in the ways of being a helpmate
- Sensing, supporting, and attending to comforts, discomforts, and needs for love for all family members
- A reflection of God's concerns in the presence of her tears
- Enthusiasm for play —for the husband and with the kids!

3. Relationships: Eve

Eve needs lots of skills for making and keeping *relationships*. She needs to *like people*, because most of her home and family care includes dealing with people:

- Shopping for clothes and food
- Household, creature comforts
- Making Super-Bowl snacks!
- Extending the family: School, church, and neighborhood.

Relationships: Adam's "Share"

Now, Adam is going to be busy:
- Hunting and fishing
- Providing for family needs
- Making money
- Instruction in God's plan for marriage

For Adam's benefit, we'll leave a little *emotion* in the right side of the brain—enough to help him understand his wife and children and to keep him from kicking the cat. Let's leave him the majority of the left side of the brain. After all, one of them has got to be factual, logical, and able to make decisions in a timely fashion.

We selected only a few characteristics for purposes of illustration. This list is by no means complete. We need to understand that what God took from Adam and what he left behind in Adam, does generally shape the different behaviors we can expect from ourselves and our spouses. When we say that certain attributes were taken from Adam and given to Eve, we are not speaking in terms of the entire attribute and that Adam was left without some of his original possession of it. By no means, Adam was left a portion of each attribute, but for a different reason.

> *... and He brought her to the man ...* (Genesis 2:22b ESV)

Adam recognized her immediately as being one of his own kind and there was no shame or confusion between them. Another point worth considering is the attitude of Adam toward God. Adam and God had walked in the garden together. They had fellowship. God saw that Adam was alone. This is not to say that Adam was lonely. There is a lesson, here, about the character of our Heavenly Father. God, in His infinite wisdom, knows our needs even before we identify them. Adam received his mate with joy! Why? Not because He was lonely, but because Adam so trusted his Father that he knew whatever God would bring to him, would be *good*. Even though Adam named his helper "woman," God called them "man."

> *Male and female He created them, and He blessed them and named them Man when they were created.* (Genesis 5:2 ESV)

There was no division between the two of them. They acted as one flesh in body, spirit, and soul. The woman got her value from Adam, and Adam got his value from God. There was no need for "self-worth" or "self-image"; God was their source. When Adam was first created the main responsibilities assigned to him by God lay within the activities of the garden. After woman was formed to be a helper to Adam, God assigned man bigger things to accomplish such as " ... filling the earth, subduing it and ruling over it ... "

> *God blessed them and said to them, "Be fruitful and increase in number; fill the earth and subdue it. Rule over the fish of the sea and the birds of the*

air and over every living creature that moves on the ground."
(Genesis 1:28 NIV)

"One-flesh" Marriage: What Purpose?

Marriage is far more important than you may have thought. Marriage affects God's reputation. In Matthew 19:4-6, Jesus makes the statement that what God has joined together, let no man separate. Marriage is not just for today, but for all the tomorrows of our life on this earth. There is *real purpose* for our "one-flesh" marriage. Part of our purpose is to be, the earthly function that shows "being in agreement with God's will." In the statehood of our "one flesh," there are three important reasons why we must understand our "oneness."

1.   We are to mirror God to the world, for the sake of others

After all, we were created in His image. That means we are to be a living example of what God is really like in all His character. When we obey and understand God's words and ways, we are God's representatives. As we act out God's meaning of the "one-flesh" marriage, we are up-holding His holiness, passing it on to our children, which in turn pass it on to their children. Our marriage is God's smallest battle formation! We are a living generations of mankind, with a living hope for the original covenant of "eternal life." In conducting ourselves in obedience to God's plan, we are showing the world that desperately needs Him, what He is really like: a loving covenant God who always keeps His promises. We are to be ambassadors to His world.

> *Therefore we are ambassadors for Christ, God making His appeal through us.* (2 Corinthians 5:20 ESV)

Jesus has commissioned us to spread God's message—the Gospel or "Good News"—of reconciliation between a sinful world and a righteous God that cannot look upon sin. Remember it was sin that separated God from walking and talking in person with His creation.

There is no way we can live our one-flesh covenant marriage without God's presence in our marriage. Only in Jesus can we receive all that God has planned for our marriage because Jesus is the only one who has purchased back for us that which Adam and Eve abandoned. Due to sin, we operate as separate identities and our spirit needs to be "born again"; we need a "new breath" of life from God.

> *Jesus answered, "I tell you the truth no one can enter the kingdom of God unless he is born of water and the Spirit. Flesh gives birth to flesh, but the Spirit gives birth to spirit."* (John 3:5-6 NIV)

The "new breath" is the revival of the dead spirit we are born with. When we are "born again," we receive the Holy Spirit from God. He, the Holy

Spirit, begins to form a new work in our hearts and souls. It is God who does the changing.

> *For it is God who works in you both to will and to do for His good pleasure.* (Philippians 2:13 NKJV)

2. We are to mutually complete one another

God formed Eve out of the "rib" of Adam. This must have left Adam incomplete. He now existed without the fullness of God when He was created from the dust. God separated the "Eve part" from Adam and molded it into a "walking," "talking" form that later acted independently from its main source. Adam had an indescribable emptiness; and that is the true condition of man to this day.

However, when God presented to Adam, the results of what He had formed from the missing volume, he became happy. It was a beautiful person, one like himself. Adam later named her "Eve." God gave her to Adam for his lost volume, and Adam's "emptiness" was filled again. Adam recognized Eve as part of himself formed out of his familiar "wholeness." Hence, Eve was created in Adam's image. It's no wonder that Adam received his future bride with joy.

> *Then the man said, "This at last is bone of my bones and flesh of my flesh; she shall be called "woman" for she was taken out of Man."* (Genesis 2:23 ESV)

God had virtually created something together that does not exist alone! Preferring each other totally is the wholeness and unity of one flesh. It is a power greater than just two people side by side. Think of your oneness as a "three-legged race." To get to the finish line you must run in unison, working together, using each other's talents to win the race.

3. Keep God's legacy alive through family instruction

Even after the flood, God continued to press forward in renewing the lost relationship moments He had with mankind in the Garden of Eden. Remember we said that all God's promises (covenants) are a blessing, and they are to be passed on to others around us. One of the ways to mirror God's image is through a line of godly descendants, our children, who carry a reflection of His character to the next generation. We are taught to regard God highly in all His laws and in His love.

God has called us into the positions of "husband" and "wife" where we have different roles and responsibilities, which were meant to nurture each other. We actually hold a position of service. We function as an act of worship, performing various duties of kindness, love, and help. In the role of husband and wife, our children observe us as an extension of God. Husbands must honor their wives in front of the children. It is only through

38

the demonstrated one flesh between the husband and wife in the home that children can understand unconditional love, and appreciate their own sexual identity. Women are not made emotionally, spiritually or physically to raise children by themselves. We should be better at being a husband and wife than being a father, a mother, or grandparent. It is through the office of our "one flesh" that brings all the others into God's order of authority for the family.

"One flesh" or "oneness" is a major theme in Christianity. "Oneness" as explained by Webster's New World College Dictionary (Webster's, *oneness*) means, "singleness in unity: unity of mind, feeling or purpose, and sameness in identity." Ponder, for a minute "the Trinity." There are three *persons* in one God. Ponder the "the Body," also known as "the bride of Christ." This is composed of the assembly of *all* believers, each unique in its individual function.

Unity functions in achieving a common purpose. Within a unity there are different levels of activity. These levels of activity need to be assigned according to the ability of the members of the union. God made man and woman quite different from each other. We have different abilities and character. It only stands to reason that we as husband and wife have different roles to contribute. Husband, you have the role of leadership and that means the final responsibility for the outcome of your family is on your shoulders, while your wife, whom God referred to as a "helper," surrounds you with support. She makes available to you all the godly qualities that God has placed within you enabling you to lead as God directs.

Even though God has assigned different levels of role authority to our office as Husband and Wife, He still holds them both equal in importance before Him.

> *There is neither Jew nor Greek, slave nor free, male nor female, for you are all one in Christ Jesus. If you belong to Christ, then you are Abraham's seed and heirs according to the promise.*
> (Galatians 3:28-29 NIV)

God designed marriage to be interdependent, not co-dependent. Jesus gives us the greatest example of service. Christ served the Church. It is an exciting fact that when you enter into the marriage designed by God, you also are entering into a personal ministry that will witness to others.

You enhance, in a very special way, all that you do in the name of Christ and in the way you serve the Lord. It's your love for each other that shows Christ's love for all.

God's "One Flesh" Altered by Sin

As sin entered the garden, the order of creation was altered; division began to appear in God's appointed "oneness for man."

> *Then the eyes of both of them were opened, and they knew that they were naked. And they sewed fig leaves together and made themselves loincloths.* (Genesis 3:7 ESV)

Adam and Eve, even before they hid from God, were aware that they needed to cover up parts of their body in the presence of each other. A person might ask why? They certainly, up to this point, and in the act of eating the "forbidden" fruit, had felt no need to cover anything.

The weather was comfortable; no other creature adorned their body with anything except what their creator had provided. Why did they cover what they covered? Why didn't they, for example, cover their eyes? Their eyes were the part of the body that saw the fruit and "it was good." Why, then, didn't they just cover their mouth? It was the part of the body that "lusted" after the taste of the fruit. Further, why didn't they cover their ears? It was the part of the body that heard the temptation, compelling them to act on their own will and judgment instead of consulting God.

It wasn't any of these commonly body characteristics that we all have and use in every day life that they felt the need to cover. It was something entirely "different" between the two of them. Sin had opened their eyes to the only physical difference between the two of them, and because of this difference, Adam and woman used fig leaves to hide these parts, not only from each other, but from God, as well.

Genesis tells us that Adam answered God's question of "Where are you?" with, " ... I heard the sound of you in the garden, and I was afraid, because I was naked and hid myself." (Genesis 3:10 ESV)

This newly married couple had lost their innocence. They were about to experience many differences, among them being the emotion of "fear." God had not meant for man to have fear, yet sin brought a lifetime of different fears. Secondly, Adam and Eve had only known "one-flesh" unity, yet now they became aware of "self," and that difference led to fears of rejection. Sin had robbed them of the glorious freedom of utter acceptance as they were. The word "self," used for the first time in the Bible, now became more important and isolating. Instead of being "selfless," they became "selfish." Although the image of "covering up" in scripture is physical, it also depicts a "covering up" of our emotions and feelings. When Adam and Eve lived in moral innocence before the fall, nakedness was not wrong nor did it bring a feeling of shame.

However, after they sinned, the awareness of nakedness became associated with sin and the fallen depravation of mankind. Because of the evil that nakedness would cause in the world, God Himself made garments and clothed them. This is the first account of blood being shed for mankind. God slew an animal and used its skin for clothing.

The first account of man protecting his "self" is seen in Adam and Eve's statement to God about their disobedience.

> And He said, "Who told you that you were naked? Have you eaten from the tree that I commanded you not to eat from?" The man said, "The woman you put here with me – she gave me some fruit from the tree and I ate it." Then the Lord God said to the woman, "What is this you have done?" The woman said, "The serpent deceived me and I ate it." (Genesis 3:11-13 NIV)

The division was complete. Here we see Adam blaming woman, and the woman blaming the serpent instead of admitting to their own sin. Their unity of spirit and soul had been divided through sin. Each one was more concerned for "self" than about the other. As man was falling away from the image of God he was created in, so his tending to his wife became less and less protective, and her completeness became more insecure. Protecting the "self" and fear of rejection are two strong barriers to overcome in becoming a "one-flesh" couple.

Every Wife Has One Basic Need: To Be Loved by Her Husband

God gave her that desire right in the garden after the fruit-eating incident.

> To the woman He said, " ... your desire shall be for your husband and he shall rule over you." (Genesis 3:16b ESV)

God saw a developing autonomy in Eve, a "moving up the ladder," declaring ability to make independent decisions concerning the unity with God and her husband. In Genesis 3 we see the serpent confusing and tempting Eve about the rule God had set on the "tree of the knowledge of good and evil." In her confusion, did she discuss the content of the serpent's challenge with her husband? No! Who was second in command for the marriage anyhow? The Bible doesn't tell us everything but this we know Satan; had to lie about God's words in order to get Eve to taste the fruit.

> "You will not surely die." the serpent said to the woman. "For God knows that when you eat of it your eyes will be opened, you will be like God, knowing good and evil." (Genesis 4-5 NASB)

She acted independently and wrongfully on her own. God is now going to make sure that she understands her role of authority to be "under" her husband's lead. The "desire" for her husband guarantees that she will be dependent on him. And that is why every woman has the need for love! God added to the characteristics He took from Adam, "a desire" that could only be satisfied by her husband. It is a God-given need in every female. After her need is satisfied through her husband, she will be able to find fulfillment in the other details of her wifely role.

Eve's Temptation and Her Deception

Eve's temptation is not a unique experience to anyone, not even Jesus. Jesus suffered the same temptation approach from Satan when the "Spirit" took Him to the desert for forty days. In fact, every worldly temptation that is known to man comes in this structural form; lust of the flesh, lust of the eyes, and the pride of life. Let's reread Eve's temptation, only this time we will divide it into the three targeted weaknesses of the human body that Satan is so aware of in his desire to destroy all mankind.

> *When the woman saw that the fruit of the tree was* [1] *good for food, and* [2] *pleasing to the eye, and* [3] *also desirable for gaining wisdom, she took some and ate it. She also gave some to her husband, who was with her, and he ate it.* (Genesis 3:6 NIV; numbering added for discussion below.)

We shall assign human weakness to these three parts.

1. "Lust of the Flesh"

For Eve, it was food. Anything that makes the flesh feel good can go in this category—drugs, alcohol, or categories of deviant sexual behavior.

2. "Lust of the Eyes"

For Eve, it was a delight to look upon it. Many human sins are caught-up in this category: things, materialism, self-indulgence, and covetousness.

3. "Pride of Life"

For Eve, it was to be wise. For others, it could be power, greediness, being in control, ownership, money, uncharitable attitude, lying etc.

Please, note that the temptation to sin is introduced in the first of 39 books in the Old Testament, in Genesis 3:6, as we have already reviewed. Let us compare Jesus' temptation with Eve's temptation. In the first book of 27 books in the New Testament, Matthew 4:1-11 gives us a written account of Jesus' temptation. Now, note how Satan uses the same temptation sin-targets he used on Eve. Satan zeros in on the same weaknesses he knows is in all of mankind. He should be susceptible to the same weaknesses—the satisfaction of fleshly desires. So, why shouldn't the same approach used on Eve have the same outcome on this man called Jesus? After Jesus' forty days of fasting, Satan was sure that if he "upped the rewards" he could lure Jesus into committing a sin, although the offerings were on a much higher scale. Satan would compensate Jesus with the highest of earthly positions and treasures.

> *Now when the tempter came to Him, he said, "If You are the Son of God, command that these stones become bread."* (Matthew 4:3 NKJV)

Lust of the Flesh

With Jesus, Satan tried to tempt His human flesh by enticing Jesus to use His godly powers to satisfy His human hunger after His forty day fast. How did He resist temptation? *By quoting the word of God*:

> *But He answered and said, "It is written, 'Man shall not live by bread alone, but by every word that proceeds from the mouth of God.'"* (Matthew 4:4 NKJV)

> *Then the devil took Him up into the holy city, set Him on the pinnacle of the temple and said to Him, "If you are the Son of God, throw Yourself down. For it is written: 'He will Command His angels concerning you, and they will lift you up in their hands, so that you will not strike your foot against a stone.'"* (Matthew 4:5 NIV)

Lust of the Eyes

He was not confused by Satan's offer. How did He resist temptation? *By quoting the word of God*:

> *It is written again, thou shall not tempt the Lord thy God.* (Matthew 4:7)

> *Again, the devil took Him up on an exceedingly high mountain and showed Him all the kingdoms of the world and their glory. And he said to Him, "All these things I will give You if You will fall down and worship me."* (Matthew 4:8-9 NKJV)

Pride of Life

With Jesus, Satan appeals to the fleshly feeling of pride. After all Satan knew "pride" very well. It was his own feelings of pride that got him kicked out of heaven when he caused a rebellion in heaven with a multitude of angles he was hoping would elevate him to the level of God, his creator. How did He resist temptation? *By quoting the word of God.*

> *"Away with you, Satan! For it is written, 'You shall worship the Lord your God, and Him only you shall serve.'"* (Matthew 4:10 NKJV)

It is comforting to know that Jesus was attacked in the same areas of our flesh with the same temptations that each one of us experience daily. Through Satan's temptation, Adam, the first created man brought sin into the world. But only the God-Man, Jesus, sinlessly resisted Satan's temptations to sin. In that desert, the fate of all mankind laid in the response of the fully-God fully-man, Jesus. Jesus in His fleshly manhood proved that He was a worthy sacrifice for all mankind. And, thus salvation was born. We can go to Jesus with confidence. He understands temptation!

Adam's Conscious Reply to Temptation

After examining Eve's behavior, it would appear that it is "she" who brought sin into the world. But wait just a moment. Where was Adam while this conversation with the serpent was going on? Well, again, just after the serpent spoke to Eve in Genesis 3:4, the very next verse tells us that:

> ... *she took its fruit and ate; and she gave also to her husband with her, and he ate.* (Genesis 3:5 NASB)

Aha! Adam was with her! What was he doing—pruning the hedges? We learned in chapter 1 that God had a responsibility and accountability leader for marriage. The man is to be the covering for his wife. He is head of the marriage, and therefore accountable to God for the actions of the entire family.

Why, then, was Adam just listening to the conversation—which in fact is just what he was doing? Why didn't he assert his authority and rebuke the serpent's advances? Did Adam fail in his duty to protect his wife and marriage? Yes, not only did he fail in advising his wife the best action to take, but when Eve offered him some, Genesis 3:5 states *"and he ate."* Adam ate what he knew to be forbidden! God had already told him so.

Did Adam forget what God had said to him when they were walking and talking in the Garden of Eden, even before Eve came into his life?

> *The Lord God took the man and put him in the Garden of Eden to work it and take care of it. And the Lord God commanded the man, "You are free to eat from any tree in the garden; but you must not eat from the tree of the knowledge of good and evil, for when you eat of it you will surely die."* (Genesis 2:15-16 NIV)

It's true: Eve was deceived, but Adam deliberately disobeyed God.

Eve's Weakness and Adam's Submission to Eve

God straightened out Eve and her confusion about "the chain of command" by giving her a desire (a need for love) that could only be satisfied by her husband. Again, we know the outcome was to create dependence for her on her husband. God, in His wisdom of confining her "subject to her husband" gave a warning to Adam not to take advantage of this wife's weakness. God felt so strongly about this that He gave a very clear word for husbands on this matter.

> *Husbands, likewise, dwell with them with understanding, giving honor to the wife, as to the weaker vessel, and as being heirs together of the grace of life, that your prayers may not be hindered.* (1 Peter 3:7 NKJV)

God is serious. If a husband mistreats his wife, God is putting the husband on notice that his prayers may be stalled, or even postponed.

Peter, the apostle, points out three things in this verse that husbands must be concerned about.

Adam's Three Admonitions Regarding Eve's Weakness

1. Husbands are to live with their wives in an understanding way

Understanding here means to see her as she really is: different from the male. After all, since God took so much volume from Adam to make Eve, he may not recognize or even have an understanding of her behavior. Some of the original temperaments may be absent, or marginal, within his own structure. The "understanding" goes even deeper; it implies that husbands are to accept the difference, to live with that difference, and *to submit to that difference*. In fact, husbands are to work with the difference according to God's words. It does not mean a husband may think that his wife's irritating characteristics such as her talkativeness, or her mood swings, or those unexpected tears are a "woman thing," and that he can fling up his hands and leave her to solve her own dilemmas. It is quite the opposite.

Ephesians says a husband is *responsible for the mental, emotional, and physical welfare of his wife,* even as he is responsible for his own body. This is the total submission of the husband to the wife.

> *Husbands, love your wives, just as Christ loved the church and gave Himself up for her to make her holy, cleansing her by the washing with water through the word, and to present her to Himself as a radiant church, without stain or wrinkle or any other blemish, but holy and blameless. In this same way, husbands ought to love their wives as their own bodies. He who loves his wife loves himself. After all, no one ever hated their own body, but they feed and care for their body...* (Ephesians 5:25-29 NIV)

As Jesus submitted to death and the Cross for his bride the Church, He also nurtured her, cleansed her, instructed her, made her radiant and took away her stains, making her holy and blameless. Note verse 28: "In this same way, husbands ought to love their wives as they love their own bodies ...." Husbands, you are *commanded to submit to your wife* those things God has told you?

> *The husband should fulfill his marital duty to his wife, and likewise the wife to her husband. The wife's body does not belong to her alone but also to her husband. In the same way the husband's body does not belong to him alone but also to his wife. Do not deprive each other except by mutual consent and for a time ...* (1 Corinthians 7: 3-5 NIV)

This tells us that the commitment of marriage means that each partner relinquishes the exclusive right to his or her own body and gives the other a claim to it. Therefore, neither marriage partner should fail to submit to the *normal* sexual desires of their spouse. Such desires within marriage are natural and God-given. Refusal to carry out the responsibility of fulfilling the other" needs is to open up the marriage to Satan's temptation of adultery.

2. Husbands are to grant wives honor as a fellow heir of the grace of life

Peter first tells husbands to live with their wives in an understanding way. Then he tells them that their wives are fellow heirs and that they are to honor their wives. And, in fact, they must treat their wives with respect as equal heirs of God's grace and salvation. If the wife is a fellow heir with her husband in the kingdom of God, then it follows that as God has placed the husband over the wife, the husband is to *help* his wife as she seeks to fulfill *her role* as God defines it.

The role model God has given us for our marriage is the example of Christ and the Church. How much does Christ love the Church? So much that He gave His life for her. Although Christ is in the Godhead of all creation and of the Church, He also *serves* the Church by giving His very life for her. God has assigned the same responsibility to the husband: to serve his wife and be the head of the marriage. As Jesus cares for His Bride, purifying her for presentation to His Father, so does the husband have the command to do so unto his own wife. God's "line of authority" is inherent within this command.

You first note that God is sovereign. He has full authority over everything on earth and Heaven. God the Father is the highest "figurehead" of the triune God, and is therefore above His Son, Jesus The Christ. Jesus, being the essence of God and the essence of man is delegated by His Father to be in charge of all creation—heaven and earth. It is only through Jesus that we know all about God. Jesus is the model for how all mankind should love and behave. We have already heard that God put Adam (man) in charge of Eve (woman) and the entire family. But what about Church work, gainful employment and society as a whole? Where do they fit in the order of attention?

Let's start from the beginning. God is the ultimate authority. Jesus is "the Word of God." Use His words and guidance in every decision you encounter. If God says "no" to stealing, then *don't steal*. Since Jesus says, "Give unto Caesar that which is Caesar's," then pay your taxes! God, in His manual for life, the Bible, has an answer for every situation. Study it.

God put man in charge over all He had created, allowing Adam to name the animals and birds. God put husband over the wife as we learned in Genesis, chapter 3. Life was good! God "walked" in the garden with Adam and Eve.

The presence of God lent itself to an environment of love, peace, and unity. No quarrels. God was sovereign. Oh, there were a few trees and shrubs to tend, but there were no "food chain" to be satisfied, even the animals were vegetarians.

After sin, as man multiplied, other activities had to be mastered for survival. Places of worship and learning of God's word were needed. Man was now to earn his food by the sweat of his brow, physical labor—working!

Insight: *The Order of Role Authority*

God, Jesus, and Holy Spirit are the ultimate "three-In-one" authority
↓
Jesus Christ, the Son of God
|
Husband cares for, covers and protects...
↓
Wife, children, and family
↓
Husband and wife together make decisions in the following priority order:
- First, decisions involving *church*
- Next, decisions involving *work*
- Finally, decisions involving *society*

Families grew, morals, manners, and behaviors had to come into play for men to exist in peace: a society grew and needed attention! How do we successfully manage all this? By following "The Order of Role Authority," above, we can settle most of our scheduling conflicts between church, work, and society. If the wife and children want to go to a potluck at church, but the husband wants to go to a party at work, which comes before the other on the list. Church should come before a party at the job. If the job demands that one of the parents will have to work on Sundays, severe attempts should be made to find a non-Sunday job, or at least an alternating Sunday job. If the husband wants to go to church on Sundays, but the kids want to take bowling lessons on Sunday, the kids must find another day to bowl on. Church is more important than a social event at the local bowling alley. In our complex society, some of us have so many different involvements that it can often be a tough decision as to what to do first. While this list may not provide the final answer for some specific issues, it is useful as a yardstick. But always remember to *first pray* for God's wisdom on all your situations requiring decisions.

3. **Much of the husband's prayer life depends on how he treats his wife**

Peter now gives all husbands a good reason for obeying the first and second part of the passage. He says, " ... so that nothing will hinder your prayers." This implies that *much of your prayer life depends on how you treat your wife.* A husband can actually create a wall between God and his prayers by willful mistreatment of his wife.

> *In the Lord, however, woman is not independent of man, nor is man independent of woman. For as woman came from man, so also man is born of woman. But everything comes from God.*
> (1 Corinthians 11:11-12 NIV)

God has initiated two realms of behavior for man: an earthly behavior and a spiritual behavior. In earthly behavior there has to be order, an order of authority for continuity and accord. This is where God has designated the husband to be the top authority for the family. It is the man who reports to God, and has accountability to God for the affairs of the earthly domain. Someone has to give the orders while taking responsibility for the action, and someone has to follow the orders for the work to reach completion. In the family unit, the husband is the "boss" and the wife and children are the "workers." Submission is needed for harmony. Yet, in His word, God says there has to be *interdependence* between husband and wife for the marriage to exist in intimacy and harmony. However, they are to be mutually dependent upon God for all their needs.

In the spiritual realm, it is clear that God will hold individuals responsible for their own actions according to His written word. God has been clear in His word: "The Father is the Head of Jesus, Jesus is the head of man, and man is the head of the woman, children and family." In this spiritual reign of authority, there is no question of who is to submit to whom!

Wife's Submission to her Husband

While we've just reviewed in the Bible the only example of where a husband should be submissive to his wife, the Bible does states, in six different verses, that the wife is to be submissive to her husband. Here is just one of them:

> *Wives, submit to your husbands as to the Lord. For the husband is the head of the wife, as also Christ is the head of the church; and He is the Savior of the body. Therefore, just as the church is subject to Christ so let the wives be to their own husbands in everything.* (Ephesians 5:22-24 NKJV)

There it is, God's word on the matter of wifely submission. Although we could review other five verses, this one reference is sufficient.

Three Important Clarifications of Ephesians 5:22-24

1. Paul says, "Submit to your husband," indicating that your submission is *not* to *all* men! The actions between submission and obedience are not the same behaviors. In this text, as we will explain later, submission is voluntary where obedience is always a "must." We must all obey the law of the land. There are men and nations that believe that all women should

48

be submissive to all men. Not true! Wives, be submissive to *your* husband only, and let your husband deal with the other men.

2. The New Testament verb does not immediately carry the thought of "obedience." The apostle Paul probably intended something like "should submit" when he used the Greek words "hupeiko" and "hupotasso," which are thought to translate into English as *a surrendering,* or *to be under* (Strong's, *submit*). It a voluntary action, a voluntary act of love. All wives are to submit to their husbands in recognizing his leadership in the family.

   God says "a suitable helper" (Genesis 2:18 NIV). To be a helper or "help-meet" was God's special intent and purpose for a wife. God designed woman to help their husbands to be all that God intended them to be! The wife's main responsibilities are (1) to *submit* to the husband's leadership, and (2) to *show* him respect. As a result of her voluntarily submission to her husband, the wife submits in obedience to God and thus completes her husband, as well as glorying God. This is one of the greatest tributes to a "triune marriage."

3. Paul has given the "what" (submission) and to whom (the husband) now, he clarifies it by defining the scope of the submission. He accents it by adding "in everything." The wife is to be submissive to her husband in everything!

   "Surely," you wives are asking, "He didn't mean everything, did He?" And that is an important question. We believe that Ephesians was written in the context of giving advice to a godly marriage where the husband is a godly man. We must not forget the overall message for marriage in the Bible is to lead a godly life, setting an example for our children and their children.

   We realize that there are some of you wives out there in book land that are striving to be godly, but your husband has not quite made the break from worldly temptations. If that is the case, and a husband asks his wife to do something that is *ungodly,* say "to act out pornography in the home or on the phone, I am willing to stand on God's word, and refuse."

   I can still hear my husband offensively say, in a playful mood that righteously defended all manhood, bark from across the room to the audience in our seminar classes, "Hey, let's just stop right here. This all seems to be "one-sided." The husband has to take on the authority for the family by being in charge of the family" life itinerary, he has to be responsible to his family and to God for the choices he makes, he has to be a student of the Bible so as to fulfill his role as priest to his family and a prophet of leadership. He is the defender, protector, feeder of the family, and, then, he has to nurture his wife so she can come to the fulfillment of her role as a wife and mother, but all the wife has to do is be submissive, and that's voluntary!" We all had a good laugh out of that, but there are times when it does seem unbalanced.

Nevertheless, it all goes back to the original sin and how God punished it.

We remember the "timing" of the command. Before Eve was made a suitable helper for Adam, God had already ordained Adam to be in charge of everything.

The first temptation by Satan was to show God how His precious creation would disobey Him. Eve offers Adam a bite of the fruit. Adam eats of the forbidden fruit, and now we read how God reacted to Adam's sin.

God says to Adam, "Because you listened to your wife and ate from the tree about which I commanded you, 'You must not eat from it,' "Cursed is the ground because of you..." (Genesis 3:17 NIV)

God blamed Adam for the alteration of all earthly creations. Adam's willingness to disobey God's command brought down curses on nature, as well as all mankind. He did not use his God given authority to cover Eve in her confusion. In her confusion she repeated God's words wrong. Yet it was Satan who did confuse her. However, Eve doesn't get off completely free! We know that Eve's attempt to liberate herself from God and act independently from her husband was not over-looked by God? God's restraints on her desires would always, from now on, rest for her husband only. Any future attempts to act on her own would be counteracted by a strong desire for her husband. Her deep attraction toward Adam and his headship over her would bring her trouble and suffering, along with joy and blessings. Yes, *trouble and suffering,* if she rejected the natural laws that God put into effect in the Garden; or *joy and blessings,* if she willingly submitted to his authority.

One-Flesh Submission in Troubled Times

Now the question comes up, "What if I submit and my husband does something that is the wrong thing, and his decision hurts a member the family?" Are you still to submit? Yes! We will discuss more about this in the next chapter on "The Presence of The Holy Spirit," and in chapter 7 on "How to be In Total Agreement." But for now, take your concerns to God in prayer. Entrust yourself to Him and believe.

For there is one God and, one mediator between God and men; the man Christ Jesus. (1 Timothy 2:5 KJV)

We must draw near to God through Christ Jesus, relying in faith for strength and mercy to help us with all of our needs. Also, we cannot respond to areas of responsibility that God has not given us. We, as women lack the abilities. We must not take on those areas God has assigned to our spouses. God is the center of your covenant marriage, and as such He is concerned with the business of making and molding of you both. God knows what's going on and He has great plans for you. God promised.

> *And we know that all things work together for good to them that love God, to them who are the called according to His purpose.* (Romans 8:28 KJV)

We must release our husbands and let God lead their growth. Seek out, in your prayers, the abilities that God has given you, and let God do a good work in you.

The act of submission, whether on the husband's part or the wife's part is a very hard concept to "just do." The selfish state, of which we now live in, due to the inheritance of a sinful nature, does not lend itself to this major change. "What? Live for another person when I have needs of my own?" our inner self screams. You know the old saying, "God helps them who help themselves!" By the way, you won't find that statement in the Bible. Listen, husbands and wives, the act of submission of one spouse to another is *as unto God*—it is your ministry to God.

The Fracture of "One flesh": Divorce

When we truly understand the "covenant" of marriage—a spiritual bonding of God with us in our "triune" marriage, and the reality of husband and wife being "one flesh"—it reinforces the terms of any marriage, "til death do us part." Yet time and time again we always come to the issue and question of separation and divorce in marriage.

God puts limits on who should marry whom. He draws a "line in the sand." He calls it "being equally yoked."

> *Do not be yoked together with unbelievers. For what do righteousness and wickedness have in common? Or what fellowship can light have with darkness. What harmony ... What does a believer have in common with an unbeliever?* (2 Corinthians 6:14-15b NIV)

In God's eyes, He sees only two groups of people: those who believe in Him and those that do not. To be equally yoked, simply means that you do not go into any contracts or agreements (marriage, partnership, etc.) that binds pledges or connects you with an unbeliever. At the very first marriage, Adam and Even were "equally yoked." They could and did make vows that bound themselves to each other because they both were believers in God. That is what God intended marriage to be for all of us.

God did not intend for either of the marriage partners to even separate.

> *But to the married I give instructions, not I, but the Lord, that the wife should not leave her husband but if she does leave, let her remain unmarried, or else be reconciled to her husband, and that the husband should not send his wife away.* (1 Corinthians 7:10-11 NASB)

51

We are quoting God. He is saying that neither a wife nor a husband should separate in a marriage. God addresses the woman's part, but if she does, she must not marry. Under this condition, part of the covenant marriage is still being fulfilled. That is to say that, if a believer is content to marry a non-believer anyway, then there are still some blessings that are bestowed on the marriage; and because of that, the believer must not separate from the non-believer.

Divorce is an unremitting wound. Its hurt is worse then that of death. There is no such thing as a civilized divorce. God says that we should not divorce the spouse we made promises and vows in the presence of God.

Remarriage is defined as marriage to another spouse when the first spouse is still alive. Jesus says that when we divorce and remarry, we are committing adultery. It is not the having of a sexual union with another person that is primary to God. God uses that word to explain how He feels when we do not keep *our word* to Him! In the act of remarrying, we are committing adultery on Him. When we remarry, it involves making a second covenant with God, calling Him, again, to hear our vows as a witness when we didn't keep the first one we made in His presence.

Out of divorce comes a sin: adultery. Therefore divorce in itself is a sin! Okay, then another question comes up: what about divorcing a non-believing spouse? Let's see what God has to say about that.

> *And if a woman has a husband who is not a believer and he is willing to live with her, she must not divorce him. For the unbelieving husband has been sanctified through his wife, and the unbelieving wife has been sanctified through her believing husband, otherwise your children would be unclean, but as it is, they are holy.* (1 Corinthians 7:13-14 NIV)

Even when a believer is involved in a marriage with an unbeliever, there should be no divorce because the marriage and the children born to that union are legitimate before God, and God holds the believer to the covenant promises.

God's Reasons for Divorce

Is divorce ever allowed? There is a lot of confusion in the body of Christ about divorce today. Some churches strictly forbid any divorced person to hold an office or position of any kind in the church. Even though divorce was not in God's original plan for a covenant marriage, Jesus gives us a reason or two for divorce.

When Jesus discussed divorce with the people of the New Testament, He spoke the heart of His Father when he answers the question.

> *Have ye not read that He which made them at the beginning made them male and female, and said, for this cause shall a man leave father and*

mother, and shall cleave to his wife ... therefore what God has joined together, let not man put asunder. (Matthew 19:4-6 KJV)

Yet, Jesus, in just a few verses later said:

He said to them, "Because of your hardness of heart Moses allowed you to divorce your wives, but from the beginning it was not so. And I say to you: whoever divorces his wife, except for sexual immorality, and marries another, commits adultery." (Matthew 19:8-9 ESV)

Let's highlight some of Jesus' remarks in Matthew 19:8-9.

- Jesus said, "Moses permitted you to divorce." Did God tell Moses he could institute divorce to the Israelites? The Bible doesn't tell us.

- Whether Moses did it on his own, or not, Jesus said it was because of their "hardness of heart." If you do a word study of "hardness of heart" you will find it is a compound word meaning *a fierce destruction of spiritual perception.*

To understand this, we must go back and evaluate the generation that Moses lived with, the generation that wandered in the desert for forty years. They were no sooner across the Red Sea than their cries of misery became loud grumbles and complaints that could not be satisfied. As their fleshly needs grew, their faith and ability to discern God's word withered. This difficult group of people lack faith in God and were very fearful of God. In essence, they became spiritually bankrupt. They were unable to apply God's words to their obedience. Their perception, or ability to demonstrate spiritual insight to the meaning of God's word, was dead! At one time, back in Egypt, they had heard that marriage, in the beginning, was one man and one woman forever. Yet, sin was now gaining ground to the point that anything fleshly they craved was perceived as a *need.* Idolatry, the building of their own idols, sexual sin, and drunkenness were running amok. Their faith was so dead that they were destitute of any spiritual perception of God's word: they had "hardness of heart." In light of the continual sin that now pledged even marriage, Moses granted them divorce, with or without God's permission.

However, because we live in the time of the New Testament, the eighth covenant is the "New Covenant," the final covenant. When we commit sin we are to be remorseful and ask God for His forgiveness, because divorce is a sin. Yet if we are sincere and "born again," He will forgive us. In my presumption of knowing the heart of God, I believe there is another reason why divorce should be accepted in the body of Christ by all believers. *Sexual immorality* is the number one reason for divorce.

Violent Behavior of Spouse

Violent behavior in divorce cases involves unresolved attempts to resolve destructive and aggressive physical abuse. It may border on life or death of the one being abused. Although there is not a direct verse in the Bible that speaks to physical or emotional abuse, it is our belief that God does not support this kind of behavior from man. Repeated physical abuse by any spouse toward any member of the nuclear family is a sign of mental disturbance. Many a pastor has counseled battered women to not seek a divorce or separation because divorce/separation is a "sin." For those of you who have divorced outside the above reasons, this teaching is not meant to put anyone under condemnation.

> *Therefore, there is now no condemnation for those who are in Christ Jesus.* (Romans 8:1-2 NIV)

For us who are now in Jesus, it is better to recognize sin and repent than to defend our actions and justify our mistakes like Adam and Eve. Jesus promises to forgive us for all sins. Jesus cannot enter into a sinful union. We must repent through prayer and humility, receiving the forgiveness that cost Christ so much on the Cross. Once we have done this, we can have peace in our second marriage, knowing that God will be the "third strand" to uphold us and protect us.

> *If we claim to be without sin, we deceive ourselves and the truth is not in us. If we confess our sins, He is faithful and just and will forgive us our sins and purify us from all unrighteousness. If we claim we have not sinned we make Him out to be a liar and His word has no place in our lives.* (1 John 1:8-10 NIV)

Let God purify us. There are those of you who have suffered divorce that was not of your own choosing. You may have even sacrificed everything just to keep "things going." Prayers to God for intervention seemed to go unheard. God, who forever loves you knows your pain and will heal your hurts. Whether your divorce is recent or in the past, rest assured. God has released you from the vows you spoke because your spouse sinned against you (as well as against God).

Let God Purify Us

Does anyone want or need to confess and receive forgiveness for the past sin of divorce: a breaking of their marriage covenant with God? Maybe some of us knew about the "covenant" part, or maybe some of you have just learned of it through this book. Maybe you only divorced once, or maybe there were many marriages that ended in divorce for you. We have spoken to women who have been married four times. Yet, when they submitted their prayers of repentance to God and asked forgiveness; they received an absence of guilt that renewed their relationships with their present husband and they felt secure in their role as a godly wife.

It makes no difference, no matter the reasons or circumstances for divorce, God looks at this as a "heart" matter. And it really is a matter of the heart— the "hardness of the heart" of those who seek divorce. We would like to give you an example of "hardness of heart" in Beverly's testimony on her two divorces before our marriage:

"When I became unhappy in each of my past two marriages, I really wanted out of those relationships. I was in such a hurry to get another chance at worldly love that I choose the easy way out: divorce. I blamed my ex-husbands for the split-ups for the ways they treated me. In my first marriage I committed adultery with a married man. Neglecting my own sin, I continued to blame my ex-husband for all my unhappiness. Was I a "born again Christian" then? I thought so; I was in church every Sunday! I taught Bible stories in Children's Sunday school. I was on all kinds of Church committees. In my "hardness of heart" I had neglected to pray and rely on God for change in my unhappy heart. I had forgotten the words of promises I'd made at God's altar, promises like " in good times and in bad." I overlooked the help of God. I was unhappy! I'd made a mistake in choice of marriage partners! I didn't love them anymore! I deserved love. God wants me to be happy, doesn't He? In the years that followed I learned that it was my own selfishness that doomed both marriages—the same selfishness that caused Adam to blame Eve as he sinned against God and took a bite of the forbidden fruit. So it was the same selfishness that causes quarrels in the marriage, the same selfishness that yells secretly in every heart! Me! Me! Me!

When I caught on to the disease called "selfishness," I was humbled and broken. After going to an ever-forgiving God for His mercy and grace, I called up both of my ex-husbands (one already had remarried) and humbly apologized for the hurts I'd caused them. I repented and ask for their forgiveness, of which they readily gave me. God knew that I was sincere and sorry for deserting the last two marriage covenants I vowed to Him. I, then, ask God to select a future husband for me. It was seven years later that God brought Laurence Robert Bentley into my life. When we got married, we requested the pastor to play the song "Majesty" as we recited our promises of love to each other and to God: in our one-flesh, triune, covenant marriage. We have kept that marriage covenant and we always will, until death do us part."

It is good to publicly repent for any known sin we have committed. At this point in the seminar we would ask all people who were divorced at one time or another to join us in a confessional prayer of repentance. For you who haven't broken this will of God, you're still in your first marriage, and God is so pleased! For you readers who need this prayer, let us use the following prayer.

Closing Prayer

Dear heavenly Father, please forgive me. I recognize that divorce is not your solution to marital problems and that I was not in your will when I divorced. I repent of the sin of divorce and my failure to keep the words of the marriage covenant I ask you to witness. I recognize that remarriage was also against your word and your will for me, and I repent of the sin of committing adultery when I remarried. I praise your name and humbly receive your forgiveness. And my testimony to you will be that I never again allow the enemy to speak, or condemn me on this matter." God, grant to all of us a marriage of enrichment as we apply Your principles and truths in our lives. Amen!

Summary and Applications for Marriage

- Adam was created perfectly by God, in God's image. Adam's own body and substances was used by God to fashion Eve. The two "halves" now become "one flesh" that contains all attributes we know as male and female.

- God's plan for "one flesh" in marriage has real purpose: (1) to mirror God's image, (2) to mutually complete each other, and (3) to multiply a godly legacy.

- God calls us into the offices of "husband" and "wife" where we have different roles and responsibilities for the purpose of nurturing each other. Let the different roles be complementary to each other. God holds them both equal in importance to the marriage.

- We often attempt to take on role responsibilities (those of our spouse) that are not in our area of abilities. Concentrate on God's plan for you. He will be responsible to move your spouse into his/her own roles.

- We must place our marital relationship as a priority over all other earthly relationships.

Visit our website for this book, at **www.NotYourEnemy.info**, where you will be welcome to ask questions or make comments. Enjoy!

Chapter 2: One Flesh
Thinking It over...

God see us as one flesh in our marriage. God fashioned Eve from Adam. He intended for the differences of our roles to flow closely together. For example: Where one spouse may be impatient, the other uses their strength of patience to support the team's effort for victory in godly circumstances. Answer the questions together. Read Philippians 2:3-4 and claim this for your marriage. Look up this verse frequently, in all situations. You will be blesses!

How are you and your spouse doing in regards to fulfilling God's purpose for marriage? Rank yourself on a scale from one to five, one being weakest, and five being strongest.

1. Purposes for "one-flesh" marriage   Husband   Wife

a. To mirror God's image   _____   _____

b. Mutually complete each other   _____   _____

c. To multiply a godly legacy   _____   _____

How can you help each other improve? _____

_____

_____

2. Spending time together alone, enhances the knowledge of your one flesh. How much time each day do you spend together? Discuss this together.

_____

If this is not enough time, make plans here and now to satisfy this need.

3. What "*same* traits or strengths" do you share in common? Talk this over and write the answers together. Start out with "We both..."

_____

_____

3. What "*opposite* traits/strengths" do each of you have that complement the other spouse? Meaning that when one of you has a tendency to be late the other is usually earlier. If this information is used wisely, then you both are covered due to a possession of a strong character trait in one of you.

Weakness	Strength
Example:	
Husband: *"Generalizes"*	Wife: *"Is detailed"*
Wife: _____	Husband: _____
Husband: _____	Wife: _____
Wife: _____	Husband: _____
Husband: _____	Wife: _____
Wife: _____	Husband: _____

4. Reread 1 Peter 3:7. What two main responsibilities are required of every husband?

(1) _____

_____

(2) _____

_____

5. Wife: Read Proverbs 31:10-31. These verses describe the ideal wife and mother. Do not be threatened—all those qualities are not in one single woman, because of sin. From the list, seek out the abilities that God has given you. Share with your husband.

A. _____

B. _____

C. _____

D. _____

6. Husband: Read 1 Timothy 3:1-16. Although these verses describe the qualifications for being a Church "overseer" (deacon or elder), they state moral qualifications that every husband should strive to attain. List three of the moral qualifications you feel you function most strongly in, and share them with your wife.

(1) _____

(2) _____

(3) _____

Chapter 3
Role of the Holy Spirit

Godly Principle 3:
God gave us the Holy Spirit to dwell within us.

God gave us His Holy Spirit—the same Holy Spirit that gave Jesus power and victory over the grave—so that we, too, could have that same power in our lives to carry out our victory for a marriage that God intended for all of mankind.

Spiritual growth (going from glory-to-glory revelations) *is a process* (by the Holy Spirit) *of being molded into the image of Christ* (that of the new Adam) *for the sake of others!*

Cooperating with the Holy Spirit in our marriage produces character qualities that will benefit all other persons who surround us. It is a byproduct of being "born again."

The Abundant Life

Is there an abundance of happy times in your marriage? Do you enjoy being in the company of your spouse day in and day out? Do you wake up most mornings excited about what the day will bring? Have you ever experienced one of those special moments of peace "that passes all understanding'? Are there times in your life that take you to "mountain top experiences" where the very essence of your being races with ecstasy and happiness? It's a feeling that overwhelms your concentration and you are aware that this is a special time. You know what I mean; you've heard other people try to express it. But words often fail them, because those "once in a lifetime" events happen deep within our souls exercised as a result of our spirit communicating with God's Holy Spirit!

We must ask you another question, if you answered "yes" to most of the above questions. Do you believe the resources of those experiences were determined solely by *you* or your actions? In part, of course, we have the right of choices to use our will and determine life's outcomes. But we must always be aware of the interactions between our human pursuits and the activity of the God given spirit that dwells within us.

For our soul purpose is communication with Him. We must know who and what is "the Ultimate Authority" in our lives and in the universe. God says He is the ultimate authority in the universe. He is, also, the giver of all good things, and the provider of justice, mercy and grace. If peace and joy are the by-products of your lifestyle then what Jesus said: is clearly true, He has granted His promises to you!

... I came that they might have life, and might have it abundantly.
(John 10:10 NASB)

The Human Race—a Triune Creation

Each one of us is a "triune" being—body, soul and spirit. "Triune" simply means being "three-in-one." We know that God is a "triune" God: the Father, the Son, and the Holy Spirit.

> *As soon as Jesus was baptized, He went up out of the water. At that moment heaven was opened, and He saw the Spirit of God descending like a dove and lighting on Him. And a voice from heaven said, "This is my Son whom I love; with Him I am well pleased."* (Matthew 3:16-17 NIV)

Although we are viewing this scene in Matthew as part of History, the people of that time and event saw and heard the presence of the triune God. And in our mind's eye, we, too, can "see" three distinct actions going on at the Baptism. We can "see" *Jesus, the Son*, standing in the Jordan River. We can imagine seeing the descending dove, *the Holy Spirit*, as it lights on Jesus signifying the beginning of His three years ministry, a ministry that could not have taken place without the power of Holy Spirit. And if our spirit is alert, we can "hear" the voice from heaven proudly proclaiming His Son to the world—"This is my Son whom I love; with Him I am well pleased" as *God the Father*. They were all present at that baptism although in different forms, thus allowing us to understand the only true living God is three distinct persons in one God.

In chapter 1 we learned that our marriage, through a covenant, is a triune marriage: husband, wife and God. In chapter 2 we learned that our one flesh is a spiritual unity with God in which the souls and hearts of both partners are joined before and with Him in a "three-fold cord."

Now, let's look at our individual selves as a "triune" being. We see that the body is the only part of the human that dies and that is due to the sin of disobedient in the Garden of Eden. God meant what He said. If they, Adam and Eve, ate of the tree of the knowledge of good and evil, they would surely die. And, so the earthly body returns to dust at its death. However, the body when resurrected at Christ's second coming is renewed into a "spiritual body" like that of Christ after His resurrection. The soul and the spirit live on eternally. God is spirit and therefore when God breathed life into Adam, it was a "spiritual" life. He gave him a spirit, a source of communication. This we know that God is first a Spirit, according to the book of John.

God does not exist in a physical body. We believe God clothed the spiritual part of Adam with flesh, something that God isn't in His original state except when He came down in the flesh of Jesus Christ.

You know your Spirit is living, and not dead; when you pray, when you enjoy reading the Bible, when you get pleasure from your Bible study classes, and when you sing songs of love, that is called *worship*. The communication to God is open, and your spirit is alive and flourishing.

What if your spirit is not flourishing? Do we mean that the spirit can be dead? Yes. Every one born from Adam's seed is born with a dead spirit.

Again, back in Genesis, that old serpent tempted Eve to disregard God's *only* restriction in the Garden. Hence, she and Adam disobeyed bringing sin into the world. What did sin do to Adam; it caused separation between the three of them. God is holy and cannot look upon sin. Therefore there were no more walks with God in the Garden. Adam and Eve were thrown out of the garden, and from that day forward, they only heard His voice. Because they believed in God and His promises, they continued to hear His voice. Their Spirit was still alive only because of *faith*.

However, what about their children and the condition of their spirit? They were conceived while their parents were sinners. Therefore, they, as are all children now born today, are born spiritual dead. No one is born believing in God, and His Son Jesus. They have to be taught about God. If not taught, they will not have any expression of faith. And where there is no belief in Jesus Christ, the spirit continues as a dead spirit. When parents teach their children about the presence and power of the triune God: faith is born anew. Then a person can declare that they are a sinner in their flesh, and invite Christ into their heart. They will begin to seek a relationship with Jesus, proclaiming that they believe in God and all His promises. This is what being "born again" is all about.

The Human: One Body, One Soul, and One Spirit

1. **Body**
   Our earthly body is the mechanism by which we sense the world around us. Our body does: returns to dust and is resurrected as a "spiritual body" at judgment time.

2. **Soul**
   * Our soul does not die
   * For believers: at body's death, soul goes to Heaven
   * For non-believers: at body's death, soul goes to hell

   Soul is "life," "inner life of man," "seat of emotions and desires."

   The Lord God formed the man from the dust of the ground and breathed into his nostrils the breath of life, and the man became a living being. (Genesis 2:7 NIV)

   And do not fear those who kill the body but cannot kill the soul. But rather fear Him who is able to destroy both soul and body in hell. (Matthew 10:28 NKJV)

When he opened the fifth seal, I saw under the altar the souls of those who had been slain because of the word of God and the testimony they had maintained. They called out... (Revelation 6:9 NIV)

3. **Spirit**

The "Spirit of God" and "the Holy Spirit" are equivalent terms

God is spirit; and those who worship Him must worship in spirit and truth. (John 4:24 NJKV)

When the Spirit of God awaken our dead spirit that makes us one with God.

References to the spirit of "human beings":
Do you not know that your body is a temple of the Holy Spirit, who is in you, whom you have received from God? (1 Corinthians 6:19 NKJV)

But Steven, full of the Holy Spirit, looked up to heaven and saw the Glory of God, and Jesus standing ... (Acts 7:55 NKJV)

The Spirit of the Lord came powerfully upon him [Samson] *so that he tore the lion apart with his bare hands ...* (Judges 14:6 NIV)

References to good and evil spirits other than humans:
- Good spirits: *His messengers* (Psalms 104:4 NKJV)
- Bad spirits: *He rebuked the evil spirit.* (Mark 9:25 NKJV)

In the realm of this covenant marriage relationship we have with God: there are three main areas that must be occupied and practiced by both covenant partners. How would you answer the following questions?

1. Do you, as an individual, in your marriage, reflect (to others) active membership (so all can see) in the family of God?

2. Is your "one-flesh" marriage dependent on the absolute reign of Christ?

3. Are both of you continually seeking the Holy Spirit to direct your lives?

Unless you can answer yes to all three questions, you will lack the power to build your home with the oneness God intended. You will find it impossible to follow all the practical advice this book offers you, because you will be attempting to achieve it under your own power. We have said it before: God provides the blueprint for our marriages, and He also gives us the power we need to follow the plan. God's ideal plan is to bring each individual partner in a covenant marriage, into a personal relationship with Himself, sealing their adoption into His family before they try to build a family of their own.

Membership in the Family of God

So, we ask the first question: Do you, as an individual, in your marriage, reflect (to others) active membership (so all can see) in the family of God? At the end of chapter 1, we gave you "the Sinner's Prayer." If you have forgotten it or your heart wasn't in it, go back and review it. Within that prayer is the power that puts us in the family of God. Among other requests and repentances, we said, "thank you for bringing us into the family of God." If we sincerely prayed that prayer to God, we became "born again" and now have all the promises of God that belong to those who proclaim Jesus as Savior and Lord of their lives! One of God's promises is that He will give us the power to live the Christian life in our marriages because He knows we can't do it by ourselves.

> *I am the vine; you are the branches. If a man remains in me and I in him, he will bear much fruit; apart from me you can do nothing.*
> (John 15:5 NIV)

Without the presence of the triune God in our lives, we can do nothing— nothing good! It is only God's power that can bring us to the place where we can utter in bold faith, saying, Jesus Christ is our Lord *and* Savior.

Here's a way to test yourself if you are a part of the family of God. Ask yourself these questions:

* Would my life be any different if Jesus were not real?

* To whom would I go when I am concerned with life's problems?

* Who can I trust when I need a different perspective on my problems?

* What do I do with my confusion and helplessness in those desperate moments of loss over loved ones?

We have questions to ask of you: Would Sundays have a different meaning in your life? Would your life have any meaning or purpose? And if so, what would that be? Consider this: if Jesus the Christ *is* the absolute source of your life, then you would be incredibly different if He were gone. Bewilderment and loneliness would be your constant companion. You would be confused, cut off from your supply of guidance, wisdom, and power. You would feel an unbelievable emptiness in the pit of your existence that Christ had once filled.

However, if you feel that Jesus is a part of your upbringing that hasn't become a reality to you, and that your words, thoughts, actions and attitudes would be no different, then you need to consider the fact that Christ may not be *Lord* of your life! If your church attendance is on-again off-again due to your need of "open" Sundays so that you can include "other pleasures" at the sacrifice of weekly worship, then you surely do not have Jesus as the *Lord* of your life.

The word *Lord* has various meanings in the Hebrew and Greek language. There are many language translations, but let's stick with Hebrew, as it was the language of the day. In Hebrew, the word *J^{e}hovah* (Strong's, *Jehovah*) has been translated into the English word "LORD." Jehovah (LORD) is the proper name of the God of the Hebrews. *LORD's* meaning describes a God that is self-existent and eternal, and is used 6,394 times in the Old Testament.

A second meaning of Lord in Hebrew is *adonai,* which means *one possessed of absolute control* (this can be divine or human). It indicates a master, or a ruler of His subjects, or even a husband to his wife.

> Sarah laughed to herself as she thought, *"After I am worn out and my master is old, will I now have this pleasure?"* (Genesis 18:12 NIV)

Of course Sarah's questions were addressed to the angel who announced that she would have a child.

Wives, has your husband ever asked you to call him "lord"? It would not insult God if he requested it in the human meaning of the second translation. My point is, how is he going to qualify as "one possessed of absolute control?" (Remember the translation can be a divine or human being.) Husbands did have that control in the Old Testament society. Today, a husband is commanded to be a godly man, treating his wife respectfully, including her opinion on all family matters. Absolute control? We don't think so.

Absolute Reign of Christ

Now, consider the second question: Is your "one-flesh" marriage dependent on the absolute reign of Christ? The operative words are "dependent on" and "absolute reign of Christ." Again, the word we are looking for is the Hebrew word *adonai,* one who possesses absolute control.

Do you consult Him: asking His will in all the decisions you make in your life and marriage? When you involve Him in the daily ups and downs of your life, then, He is the *Lord* of your life as well as the *Savior.* Is He that for you now? Or are you asking the question: "How do we make Jesus Christ Lord *and* Savior of our lives?" Most Christians do not have any problem with the "Savior" part of that question. Even the world knows the Cross is symbolic for "doing away with man's sins."

This is one of the "elementary" teachings of the gospel. Elementary means it is a stepping-stone for further understanding. The Bible calls it "the milk of infants." It is taught in Sunday school programs and preached from the pulpit; a necessary foundation for building our faith. We must accept Jesus Christ as our "personal Savior," knowing that He gave His life for us, that He died on the Cross, making Himself an acceptable sacrifice to Father God so that we may be forgiven for *all* our sins. Even in our understanding of the gigantic importance of this belief, many Christian couples stop with this foundational truth. Jesus is my *Savior.* Amen! Jesus takes away all my sins! Amen! I'm saved. I'm going to heaven when I die. And they are on with their lives.

Many Christians *stop at the Cross.* In their true sincerity, they humbly accept Jesus, God's only Son, as God's gift for blotting out their sins. They repent and desperately try to keep their lives from more sin. Many build altars in their homes and attempt to never forget what Jesus did on the Cross. This is pleasing to God. However, Jesus did get off of the Cross; His work for mankind was not finished! The Cross is not "the end of the story." In essence, we need to understand just who God is and what He desires for His Children. We need to grasp what "getting off the Cross" means.

For this very reason, Christ died and returned to life so that He might be the Lord of both the dead and the living. (Romans 14:9 NIV)

Here, we see Jesus as wanting to be more than the sacrifice; He wants to be "Lord" of our lives. But you might say, "I don't know how to do that. Even though I want to, how can I remember to give control to Christ in *all things* when I have trouble remembering a grocery list?" The good news is you don't have to do it by yourself!

Now it is God who makes both us and you stand firm in Christ. He anointed us, set his seal of ownership on us, and put his Spirit in our hearts as a deposit, guaranteeing what is to come. (2 Corinthians 1:21-22 NIV)

Paul outlines four major steps of God's work in believers through the power of the Holy Spirit, and they all point us to Jesus.

1. The Holy Spirit establishes and preserves our faith in Jesus Christ.

2. He anoints us with the power to witness about Jesus Christ.

3. The Holy Spirit claims us as God's property and produces godly character in us that conforms us to the image of Christ

4. He indwells in all believers, guaranteeing a greater life with Christ now, here on earth, and in our future home in Heaven.

So, if God does it all, what is our part if any? The answer is in the following verses:

For you were once darkness, but now you are light in the Lord. Live as children of light for the fruit of the light consists in all goodness, righteousness and truth, and find out what pleases the Lord. (Ephesians 5:8-10 NIV

... do not be foolish but understand what the Lord's will is for your life. (Ephesians 5:17 NKJV)

These two verses say it well:

1. God tells us to live as children of light and find out what pleases God. Living as children of light denotes that we are already in the light, and that it is a commandment to do what we already are: *Live* as children of the Lord.

2. There is a choice that requires the using of the "will" God gave to us! In our will, we are to direct our decisions, attitudes, and actions in accordance with the word of God. In the light we are visible, always being a model to the world. Scriptures does not say we have to tread this path alone. The last half of verse 18 says, "be filled with the Spirit." God's will for us is to

desire the activity of the Holy Spirit in our lives. We get there by first getting familiar with the Scriptures. As we read the Bible, it is the Holy Spirit that strengthens our faith for us to see how much Jesus loves us and wants to be our Lord and Savior. Once we understand Christ's commitment to us, it comes very easy to take the second step. And that is: to allow God's Holy Spirit to guide and empower our life.

Seek the Holy Spirit to Direct Your Lives

Which leads us into the third question; Are both of you continually seeking the Holy Spirit to direct your lives?

> *You, however, are controlled not by the sinful nature but by the Spirit, if the Spirit of God lives in you. And if anyone does not have the Spirit of Christ, he does not belong to Christ.* (Romans 8:9 NIV)

Scripture is telling us that all believers from the moment they accept Jesus Christ as Lord and Savior have the Holy Spirit living in them. This Holy Spirit is described in the Bible as having the divine nature, united with the Father and the Son, and has the *same characteristics:*

1. He is *eternal*, meaning that He is everlasting throughout all of the future, and even *beyond* time.

   > *... God has made it plain to them. For since the creation of the world God's invisible qualities, His eternal power and divine nature have been clearly seen, being understood from what has been made, so that men are without excuse.* (Romans 1:20 NASB)

2. He is *omnipresent*, meaning that the Holy Spirit has the ability to be everywhere at the same time—as do Father God and Christ Jesus.

   > *"Am I only a God nearby," declares the Lord, "and not a God far away?" "Can anyone hide in secret places so that I cannot see him?" declares the Lord, "Do not I fill heaven and earth?" declares the Lord.* (Jeremiah 23:23-24 NIV)

3. He is *omniscient*, meaning that He has the ability of endless knowledge, knowing everything—past, present, and future.

   > *I make known the end from the beginning, from ancient times, what is still to come.* (Isaiah 46:10a NIV)

4. He is *omnipotent*, meaning He has unlimited power and authority.

   > *Why should any of you consider it incredible that God raises the dead?* (Acts 26:8 NIV)

   Jesus tells us, *"But I tell you the truth, it is to your advantage that I go away; for if I do not go away, the Helper shall not come to you; but if I go, I will send Him to you."* (John 16:7 NASB)

The "Person" of the Holy Spirit

Romans 8:9 tells us that all believers from the moment they accept Jesus Christ as Lord and Savior they have the Holy Spirit living in them. This very Holy Spirit is described in the Bible as having the divine nature of God. He is united with the Father and the Son, and possesses all the same characteristics, such as: being eternal, is present everywhere, is all-knowing, and has great powers.

The Holy Spirit was Active in the Life of Christ

- Conceived Jesus in Mary's womb
- Filled Jesus from conception
- Anointed Jesus
- Gave Jesus the power of ministry
- Led Jesus into the wilderness to be tempted by Satan
- Gave Jesus the power to cast out demons
- Was the power in the resurrection
- Was the Spirit of Christ

At a glance, the Bible reveals to us the Holy Spirit shared in the life of Jesus from the cradle to the grave. We can see that it was the Holy Spirit who did all these things.

The work the Holy Spirit did in Jesus' life; is the same work He can do in us. The Holy Spirit is what controlled the flesh of Jesus: all God and all man. We can give ourselves over to the Holy Spirit the control of our lives.

The Role He Plays in our Fleshly Lives

- He indwells us
- He convicts us of sin
- He regenerates us and gives us *new life*
- He gives us the power to witness, and even what to say
- He teaches us all things
- He brings Christ's presence to us
- He prays for us
- He encourages us and gives us joy and peace
- He enables us to live the Christian life
- He wonderfully controls us, if we let Him
- He experiences grief and He can be resisted

Finally, the Holy Spirit was there when the world was created.

- He was in the Old Testament
- He has been around ever sense "time" was
- He is a person in the triune God

We can give over to the Holy Spirit the control of our lives by surrendering our will. Let's review the role He plays in *our lives*. Reread those sentences, substituting the first person words "me," "my," and "I" for the word "us":

- He indwells *me*
- He convicts *me* of *my* sin
- He regenerates *me* and gives *me* new life
- He gives *me* the power to witness and the words to use
- He teaches *me* all things
- He brings Christ's presence to *me*
- He prays for *me*
- He encourages *me*
- He gives *me* joy and peace
- He enables *me* to live the Christian life
- He controls *me*
- He can experience grief from *my* behavior
- It is possible for *us* to resist Him

The Essence of the Holy Spirit

> *You, however, are controlled not by the sinful nature but by the Spirit,* **if** *the Spirit of God lives in you. And* **if** *anyone does not have the Spirit of Christ, he does not belong to Christ. But* **if** *Christ is in you, your body is dead because of sin, yet your spirit is alive because of righteousness. And* **if** *the Spirit of Him who raised Jesus from the dead is living in you, He who raised Christ from the dead will also give life to your mortal bodies through His Spirit, who lives in you.* (Romans 8: 9-11 NIV; bold added.)

The Holy Spirit, who lives within believers, is a Person who experiences intense grief and sorrow just as Jesus himself did when He wept over Jerusalem. Believers can cause the Holy Spirit grief or pain when they ignore his presence, his voice, or his leading. In fact, to keep on sinning deliberately after we have received the Spirit, is to insult and rebel against the Spirit.

> *And do not grieve the Holy Spirit of God, with whom you were sealed for the day of redemption. Get rid of all bitterness, rage and anger, brawling and slander, along with every form of malice.* (Ephesians 4:30-31 NIV)

Grieving the Holy Spirit is to offend or cause sadness to Him, particularity in the area of your relationship with Jesus Christ. Grieving the Holy Spirit is a mind-set against our creator. If we have persistent anger against someone in our life, we are grieving the Holy Spirit. Grieving the Spirit leads to our resisting His work in our character and lifestyle.

The English word *malice* comes from the Latin word that means "bad." The dictionary (Webster's, *malice*) says malice is "an active will or desire to harm another or to do mischief; a state of mind shown by intention ... " This definition shows us what "paybacks" look like. When we are in this state of mind, we tend to dwell on our intentions.

70

Our intentions may not always be in our conscious mind, but they are ready to be put in action when called up to review. For instance, when we unexpectedly encounter a person involved in an unresolved conflict from our past, and we begin thinking about the incident, feelings usually surface—whether of anger, hurt or pain—and ideas of what we'd like to say or do start stirring our awareness. Anger (as well as hurt or pain) and malice are close cousins—if not actually two sides of the same coin. Whichever way we flip the coin, the other emotion is often brought in to play.

Constant attention on anger and rage, in turn, leads to putting out the Spirit's fire.

> Do not put out the Spirit's fire; do not treat prophecies with contempt. Test everything. Hold on to the good. Avoid every kind of evil.
> (1 Thessalonians 5:19-22 NIV)

In our flesh we can grieve and resist the workings of the Holy Spirit. It is in this battle, between our flesh and the prompting of the Holy Spirit, that a final insulting of the Spirit can lead to God's judgment and a loss of our inheritance in the Kingdom. If we do not live by those words in 1 Thessalonians, a final insulting of the Spirit of grace can occur: leading to blasphemy against the Spirit.

Blasphemy against the Spirit is a continual and deliberate rejection of the Holy Spirit's witness of Christ, and His words, and His convicting word against sin. Those who reject and oppose the voice of the spirit remove themselves from the voice of conviction that can lead them to their Salvation through Christ the Messiah. The process that leads from grieving the Spirit to blasphemy against the Spirit is:

1. Grieving the Holy Spirit with offenses. This can cause us to…

2. Resist the Spirit. This can cause us to…

3. Put out the Spirit's fire. This usually causes us to…

4. Harden our hearts. This creates in us…

5. A mind that leads us to be our own "umpire" as to the *goodness* or *evil* of our sinful behavior

   > Woe to those who call evil good and good evil, who put darkness for light and light for darkness, who put bitter for sweet and sweet for bitter. Woe to those who are wise in their own eyes and clever in their own sight.
   > (Isaiah 5:20 NASB)

6. This process in our lives leads God to the following response:

   > And just as they did not see fit to acknowledge God any longer, God gave them over to a depraved mind, to do those things which are not proper … and, although they know the ordinance of God, that those who practice

71

such things are worthy of death, they not only do the same, but also give hearty approval to those who practice them. (Romans 1:28, 32 NASB)

When this hardening of the heart reaches a certain fullness of development, determined only by God, the Spirit will no longer strive to lead that person to repentance.

How much more severely do you think a man deserves to be punished who has trampled the Son of God under foot, who has treated as an unholy thing the blood of the covenant that sanctified him, and who has insulted the Spirit of grace. (Hebrews 10:29 NIV)

Dear friends, this is not the "elementary teachings" we talked about earlier, the so-called milk of infant faith; it is the meat of the growing maturing bondservant of the Messiah, the Lord Jesus Christ.

Anyone who lives on milk, being still an infant, is not acquainted with the teaching about righteousness. But solid food is for the mature who by constant use have trained themselves to distinguish good from evil. (Hebrews 5:13-14 NIV)

The weak and immature in the faith lack spiritual sensitivity and discernment with regard to what is good and what is evil in this life, and what honors God and what dishonors God.

Mature believers, on the other hand, have trained their senses to carefully distinguish between good and evil through the continual practice of righteousness and obedience. They have learned to love righteousness and hate wickedness, renewing their minds according to principles of righteousness, and being enabled by the Holy Spirit to see things from God's point of view. They are able to receive the solid food of God's word and grow toward the full stature of Christ. It is the discerning mature adult child of God that understands the scripture.

The fear of the Lord is the beginning of wisdom. (Psalms 111:10 NIV)

The Two Main Areas of the Holy Spirit's Work

We are going to study the two main areas the Holy Spirit works in our lives. We will focus on "the fruit of the Spirit" (Galatians 5:22-23) and "the gifts of the Spirit." (1 Corinthians 12:7-11).

In our seminars, there were always some people who were confused concerning parts of the scripture that silhouette "gifts" from God. In their uncertainty, they grouped all "gifts" as being from God in which all believers could participate, and that non-believers do not receive. This is not true. In a broad sense, all things that flow from God are "gifts," but not all the children of God are granted full access to all of the gifts. *Example:* God gives gifts to certain people that are called "ministerial gifts" (Ephesians 4:11-13) and "motivational gifts" (Romans 12:6-8).

72

1. Ministerial Gifts

And He gave some as apostles, and some as prophets, and some as evangelists, and some as pastors and teachers, for the equipping of saints for the work of service to the building up of the body of Christ until we all attain the unity of the faith and the knowledge of the Son of God ...
(Ephesians 4:11-13 NASB)

The gifts in Ephesians are called *ministerial gifts*. The gift of being a pastor or teacher is truly a gift to specific individuals, given by God only, for the purpose of edifying the bride of Christ, the Church. Not everyone can participate in this appointment of godly service. It is the work of God alone who selects individuals to equip the body, the Church. Those selected individuals are anointed by the Holy Spirit to: (1) work toward the unity of the faith; (2) acknowledge the son of God (the faithful message of the New Covenant); and (3) to mature the body to the fullness of Christ. Again, this gift is not given to everyone.

Shall we then blindly trust every word from a pastor, a Sunday School teacher, a home Bible study leader, or elder who is anointed by God? No! We are to observe the actions and words of all God's servants. We should question where his/her authority comes from. We must ask ourselves, was he appointed by God, or is he serving by his own aspiration? Scripture sends many warnings about false prophets.

But the goal of our instruction is love from a pure heart and a good conscience and a sincere faith. For some men, straying from these things, have turned aside to fruitless discussion, wanting to be teachers of the Law, even though they do not understand either what they are saying or the matters about which they make confident assertions.
(1Timothy 1:5-7 NASB)

We are to be in dutiful examination of all individuals who preach God's word, whether they stand in the pulpit, are on television, or teach a home Bible class. We must be convinced that the "robe of righteousness" they adorn is appointed by the one true living God and not by their own selfish ambitions.

2. Motivational Gifts

And since we have gifts that differ according to the grace given to us, let each exercise them accordingly: if prophecy, according to the proportion of his faith; if service, in his serving; or he who teaches, in his teaching; or he who exhorts, in his exhortation; he who gives, with liberality; he who leads, with diligence; he who shows mercy, with cheerfulness.
(Romans 12:6:8 NASB)

The gifts in Romans are called *motivational gifts*, and like ministerial gifts are given to specific individuals. However, the motivational gifts, unlike the ministerial gifts, are given by God not only to believers, but also to non-believers. Gifts may be given to non-believers, yet they never fully mature due to their lack of faith and trust in God. After reading Scripture, it is our opinion that these gifts—ministerial gifts and motivational gifts—are incorporated into our being while we are being formed within the womb. In other words, we own these gifts, having them perhaps from conception. They are a part of us whether active or inactive. We have these abilities given to us by the one true, living God, and not for self-glorification.

Here's a little quiz to see which gift you have. We've listed the usual reaction to a specific situation. After reading the situation, below, first look at each of the "usual reaction" descriptions and select the one (or two) that most fits you. Do not select what you *hoped* you'd do, but what you would actually *feel* like doing. Then check out the related gift. And do not be ashamed of who you are. God gives each of us gifts as he sees fit.

A Situation to Illustrate Typical Differences in Reaction

During the middle of the Sunday night service, a tattered old man stumbles into church, smelling of alcohol, and appears to be very sick.

Well, what would you do? You would do what God has given you to do. Not all of us will have mercy and serving gifts. Not all of us will have all of the gifts, but most of us have at least a gift or two. Some people simply can't stand up in front of a group and give a lesson or message to even a small group of people. They shrink from things like ushering or working on committees. The people who don't like this situation are usually people who possess gifts of prophecy and teaching. It bothers them to see people be drunken, needy, or have a lifestyle of bad decisions. The encourager and the leaders have to make the situation work out, be okay. They are the ones that get things started in the church. So who are you? Would you do something in this situation? What is it?

Usual Reaction	Gift
Predict his future	Prophet/perceiver
Give him something to eat or drink	Server
Ask him "Why?" or "Don't you know…"	Teacher
Calm him "It is okay, let's take care of some things"	Encourager/exhorter
Go buy clothes, pay for a motel room	Giver
Cry with him, feeling his pain	Mercy
Organize the above people	Leader/administrator

Born with Given Gifts

Two particular passages address the possibility that we are born with God-given gifts. God told the prophet Jeremiah, that He, Himself, was active in the shaping of Jeremiah's future.

Before I formed thee in the belly, I knew thee; and before thou camest forth out of the womb I sanctified thee... (Jeremiah 1:5 KVJ)

This very sanctification and a future already planned are gifts given at birth! Our own sin causes us not to recognize them. Our own self-centeredness spotlights temporal things rather than spiritual manifestations. It is when we are "born again" that the Holy Spirit uncovers them and brings them to fruition. When we spend time in Prayer, Bible Study, Worship, and in Christian Fellowship, the gifts become more visible through the developing work of the Holy Spirit.

In the act of pursuing the Holy Spirit to influence our lives so that we can destroy sin's power, we must be able to discern the difference between gifts given only to specific individuals and those that are available to all of us!

But the Comforter, which is the Holy Ghost, whom the Father will send in my name, He shall teach you all things, and bring all things to your remembrance, whatsoever I have said unto you. (John 14:26 KJV)

Gifts Given to All Believers

The promise of the Holy Spirit's activity is given to all of us in the fruit of the Spirit and in the gifts of the Spirit. And for what? For the building up of the Body of Christ, the Church. And where do we get the power and authority to perform and bring these gifts to realization?

Power and Authority

1. Power is the Holy Spirit!

- To walk in life as Christ did
- To see what the Father has said to us in His word
- To resist temptation!

2. Authority Comes from Christ!

a. Christ Crucified

- We actually hung on the Cross with Him
- We were judged with Christ
- We also died with Christ

b. Christ Resurrected

Satan forever lost his authority over the humanity of Jesus and everyone who claims union with Him.

And having disarmed the powers and authorities, He made a public spectacle of them, triumphing over them by the Cross..
(Colossians 2:15 NIV)

Satan now knows that he has no legal right to any ground in the life of the believer.

c. Christ Ascended

God's redemptive plan was to place Christ on the throne at His right hand. Because of my total identification with Christ in the mind of God, whatever is true of Christ is true of me. He has delegated to us, committed believers, the use of the same authority He has and the power to use it over our enemies while we are here on earth.

The Fruit of the Spirit

We are first going to look at "the fruit of the Spirit." This is only for believers, for the Holy Spirit does His work only in believers. Non-believers are spiritually dead and cannot respond to spiritual activity. The Holy Spirit's target is to the inner man to produce *inner works*—meaning to change our *character*. We are to cultivate these because they *control the flesh*.

These are gracious dispositions and spiritual habits the Spirit produces in those whom He indwells and works through. God must change the inner man so that he will be equipped to fulfill the plans God has for his life. First let us read Galatians 5: 22-23 (NKJV): *"But the fruit of the Spirit is..."*

Insight: *The Fruit of the Spirit*

Scripture Word	Biblical Definition	Bible Reference
Love	Unconditional love	1 John 3:16
Joy	Deeper than happiness	John 15:11
Peace	Security, safety, and tranquility	John 14:21
Patience	Endurance and steadfastness	James 1:4
Kindness	Gentleness and integrity	Proverbs 19:17
Goodness	Uprightness in heart and life	Psalm 97:11
Faithfulness	Covenant keeping	Revelation 3:10
Gentleness	Strength under godly control	Psalms 18:32
Self-Control	Mastery of desires, passions	1 Peter 1:13

The fruit of the Spirit works within us to produce character qualities and spiritual maturity. It is for relationships, both with God and each other. It is a molding toward the image of Christ. All relationship problems begin with the heart. We often look elsewhere for improving our marital affairs but the Lord

76

wants us to look at our own heart. When we yield ourselves to the work of the Holy Spirit, He brings about the harvest.

Actually, marriage is the best relationship to test the fruit of the Spirit. We often appear to have the fruit of the Spirit when we are with friends. We do even better when we put on our "spiritual masks" at Sunday church. But if the fruit is not real, meaning that the work of the Holy Spirit is not in our lives, we cannot fake it with our spouse, who knows us best.

We have an obligation to live according to the Spirit's instructions. We have to take responsibility for the deeds of the flesh, and be active in putting to death the works of the flesh. We cannot do this by ourselves.

> *For if you are living according to the flesh, you must die: but if by the Spirit you are putting to death the deeds of the body, you will live.* (Romans 8:13 NASB)

We all have attributes and attitudes that God needs to change in order for us to get on the right path for His plan in our lives and marriages. These changes often come in the form of trials and tests, whether they be illnesses, loss of job, death of a family member, great disappointments, whatever; and they work for the good of those who love God and *who are called according to His purpose.* (Romans 8:28 NASB)

Herein lies a *hidden "mystery" of marriage*: God provided a source of earthly comfort for all of us in the trials He knew would come. This is *part* of what our marriages are all about; the covenant marriage provides security and a safe place for us as individuals, and as a couple, during this process of change, healing, and maturity. A covenant marriage partner is one who supports the other partner while the potter's wheel is molding, or I should say "remolding" us toward the image of Christ. It's a partnership with God in that we are sharing God's heavenly changes in our marriage. Our part of the partnership is to provide earthly comforts in the form of support, love, understanding, and just being there as we grow spiritually. The potter's wheel is easier to bear when there is someone who is near to help us with our tears when the pain gets severe. And have no doubts, we all go to the potter's wheel, now and then, for a tune-up!

For a strong healthy relationship, don't look for what is wrong with your spouse but yield to the work of the Holy Spirit within you. We must not attempt to be the Holy Spirit for our spouse by nagging, controlling, or manipulation. We can only be obedient to the Holy Spirit for ourselves. The fruit that will come forth from us is a natural result of the indwelling of the Holy Spirit. It begins at our salvation, and we will exhibit the fruit to the extent that we yield to and are obedient to His work in us. Remember, our *spiritual "maturity"* is the goal of the fruit of the Spirit. Yes, there is a constant battle that rages between our flesh and the Holy Spirit, but the same Holy Spirit that empowered Jesus to resist the desires of the flesh, dwells within us today and empowers us in the very same way. We do not have to struggle in the natural; it is the power of the Holy Spirit within us that transforms our hearts in a supernatural work to produce a change in our lives.

The Gifts of the Spirit

We will now look at the gifts of the Holy Spirit. These gifts are specifically directed toward our "outer works." What we mean by that is they are gifts of grace that leads us to acts of behavior that benefits others, mainly the body of Christ. Not only is it the Holy Spirit's desire to work within us, but He also wants to work through us in *power and might*. Just as He anointed Jesus in His ministry and enabled Him to cast out demons, so the Gifts of the Spirit is a direct outflow of the power of the Holy Spirit in our lives. The gifts we are about to study are intended for the building and sanctification of the church and may occur in various combinations.

> *Now here are diversities of gifts, but the same Spirit. And there are differences of administrations, but the same Lord. And there are diversities of operations, but it is the same God which worketh all in all. But the manifestation of the Spirit is given to every man to profit withal. For to one is given by the Spirit the word of wisdom; to another the word of knowledge by the same Spirit; to another Faith by the same Spirit; to another the gifts of healing by the same Spirit; to another the workings of miracles; to another prophecy; to another discerning of spirits; to another divers kinds of tongues; to another the interpretations of tongues.*
> (1 Corinthians 12:4-11 KJV)

These gifts are *not based on natural* knowledge, that is: we do not know them by our own thinking, learning or experience. We are not born with them. These gifts are of a spiritual nature, yet NOT a spiritual index of the believer. However, because the gifts are of a spiritual nature, Satan can counterfeit them, so we are not to believe all manifestations of the gifts. Again, we are told to test the spirits.

> *Dear friends, do not believe every spirit, but test the spirits to see whether they are from God, because many false prophets have gone out into the world.* (1 John 4:1 NIV)

What is a believer to do? To trust or not to trust? But here is hope:

> *This is how you can recognize the Spirit of God: every spirit that acknowledges that Jesus Christ has come in the flesh is from God, but every spirit that does not acknowledge Jesus in not from God ...*
> (1 John 4:2-3 NIV)

When we read 1 Corinthians 12:4-11, we catch sight of nine gifts of the Spirit. In order for us to better understand this passage we have divided these nine spiritual gifts into three categories. This configuration is commonly acknowledged by most Bible teachers as a way to clarify the nine gifts. The gifts of the Holy Spirit are given according to the Holy Spirit's will when a need arises and according to the believer's eager desire to be used of God. The Holy Spirit reveals to us our participation in any one of the nine gifts, in supernatural discernment given to us in specific settings. You will hopefully recognize them as we present them in three different spheres: (1) gifts of *revelation*; (2) gifts of *power*; and (3) gifts of *inspiration*.

1. **Gifts of Revelation**

   • *Word of wisdom:* A revealing of the mind and purpose of God in a specific area.

   • *Word of knowledge:* A revealing of the existence, or nature, of a person or thing or knowledge of some event, can connect with prophecy.

   • *Discerning of spirits:* Revealing the source of utterances, false prophets, etc.

2. **Gifts of Power**

   • **Faith:** Enable us to sustain an unwavering trust in God's healings and miracles.

   • *Gifts of healing:* Supernatural power to heal and cast out devils.

   • *Working of miracles:* Supernatural power to intervene in the ordinary laws of nature includes divine acts against Satan and evil spirits.

3. **Gifts of Inspiration**

   • *Prophecy:* Supernatural utterance of God's word and "will" for the future.

   • *Speaking in Tongues:* Supernatural utterance of an unknown language.

   • *Interpretation of Tongues:* Spirit-given ability to understand and communicate an utterance of tongues.

The role of the Holy Spirit operating in our lives through the *fruit* and the *gifts* of the Holy Spirit must be balanced for the development of a mature couple. These gifts were meant to be active in our homes as well as in and for the Church Body. Oftentimes we think these activities of the Spirit are given to "special people" or "those of great faith." Not true!

> *And these signs will accompany those who believe: In my name they will drive out demons; they will speak in new tongues; they ... will place their hands on sick people; and they will get well.* (Mark 16:17-18 NIV)

These are promises that Jesus made to us. They come from the New Testament, the New Covenant: Mark 16:15—the "go and preach" commission by Jesus—

says that Jesus instructed us go into all the world preaching the good news, and He would give us the power to perform signs. The Bible does not put a time restriction on the performance of these signs. In fact, scripture clearly teach that Christ wants His followers to perform these miraculous spiritual works until He returns. The failure of these signs to occur in the church today is not Christ's failure to keep his promises; rather the failure lies within the reluctant hearts of some in the Church. Christ has promised that his power, authority, and presence will accompany and occupy us to the end of time as we battle Satan's kingdom.

> *Then Jesus came to them and said, "All authority in heaven and on earth has been given to me. Therefore go and make disciples of all nations, baptizing them in the name of the Father and of the Son and of the Holy Spirit and teaching them to obey everything I have commanded you. And surely I am with you always, to the very end of the age."*
> (Matthew 28:18-20 NIV)

God's plan from "day one," at the creation of Adam and Eve, has never changed. He created man to possess a will, placed him in paradise, and devised a plan for salvation in the event of man breach of obedience. In His wisdom, even before the creation of the earth, God planned to preserve the world that He created. God is a loving Father who cares for what he has made, and He has given us the Holy Spirit to preserve us.

Begin to desire and anticipate the gifts flowing through both of you in your home. Invite the presence of the Holy Spirit into your home and hearts daily. Ask Him to reveal the gifts He has for you and then claim them. Even when only one spouse proclaims a gift, the other is often given confirmation of its true manifestation. Be more sensitive to the flowing of the Spirit and see how the two of you will be used: not only as an example to edify others, but to *edify* your mate. As a powerful "one-flesh" team with the fruit and gifts of the Spirit flowing through our marriages, we enter into partnership with Christ to change our neighborhoods, our church, and our workplace.

Closing Prayer

Show us your ways, O Lord, teach us your paths; guide us in your truth and teach us, for you are God our Savior, and our hope is in you all day long. Remember, O Lord, your great mercy and love, for they are from old. Remember not the sins of our youth and our rebellious ways; but according to your love remember us, for you are good, O Lord. Good and upright is the Lord; therefore He instructs sinners in His ways. He guides the humble in what is right and teaches them all His ways. All the ways of the Lord are loving and faithful for those who keep the demands of His covenant." Amen and Amen.
(Psalms 25:4-10 NIV)

- We need to learn to cooperate with the Holy Spirit in…

    - The fruit of the Spirit: the Holy Spirit develops character qualities in us

    - The gifts of the Spirit: He gives them to us for the edification of all

- We are commanded to know about the gifts of the Holy Spirit, and cannot excuse that we do not understand them, or prefer one gift over certain other gifts.

- We should ask ourselves, frequently, "Are we both allowing the Holy Spirit to guide and empower our lives?"

- We need to be sensitive to the leading of the Holy Spirit, always trying to understand and cooperate with Him.

- A constant battle rages between our flesh (sin) and The Holy Spirit.

- Marriage problems are usually related to issues of the heart.

- There are battles between our flesh and the Holy Spirit.

- In our flesh, we can "grieve" and even resist the workings of The Holy Spirit.

Visit our website for this book, at **www.NotYourEnemy.info**, where you will be welcome to ask questions or make comments. Enjoy!

To live in a dynamic "one-flesh" marriage, both covenant partners must practice being sensitive to the filling of the Holy Spirit. We must *daily* fill ourselves with the Holy Spirit, because we have a leak—it's called *sin*. To be filled with the Spirit, you must walk in the Spirit (read Galatians 5:25). You do this by faith, in a process called "spiritual breathing." When you slip or grow spiritually cold "exhale" by confessing your sins. Then "inhale" and claim the filling of God's Spirit by faith.

For class review, name the three godly principles we have studied so far. You may look back, if you like.

Principle 1: _____

Principle 2: _____

Principle 3: _____

1. Jesus wants to be both _____ and _____ of your life and marriage.

2. Review "the fruit of the Spirit," and record the character qualities you are most mature in, then give an example:

   Husband: One of my strong character qualities is _____

   Example: _____

   Wife: One of my strong character qualities is _____

   Example: _____

3. Review the following nine "spiritual gifts." Check the ones you think you may have experienced with the Holy Spirit:

Gift	Husband	Wife
Word of wisdom	☐	☐
Word of knowledge	☐	☐
Discerning of spirits	☐	☐
Faith	☐	☐
Gifts of healing	☐	☐
Working of miracles	☐	☐
Prophecy	☐	☐
Speaking in tongues	☐	☐
Interpretation of tongues	☐	☐

4. We are not to place more importance on one gift. However, if there is a gift you would like to have from Holy Spirit, pray for it.

Husband: _____

Wife: _____

If you "long" for a fruit or a gift of the Spirit, pray every day, for a week. Ask the Holy Spirit to reveal it to you. Ask Him to use you in it. Then, after a week of prayer, ask your spouse if they see any signs of the *gifts* or of *fruit*. Be honest with each other. Even if only one receives, the other most likely will be able to confirm the gift/fruit. What one receives, the other is also blessed because of it.

Chapter 4
Heaven on Earth

Godly Principle 4:
God has a plan for our "one-flesh" covenant marriage.

"The kingdom of God (the way things are in heaven; God's perfect rule) *is primarily a spiritual assertion* (acts of a spiritual nature) *of divine power* (gifts of the Holy Spirit) *in action."*

In other words, for the wonders of heaven to rule here on earth, it takes our allowing the Holy Spirit to act through us in words and deeds.

When we pray "Thy kingdom come, Thy will be done on earth as it is in Heaven" we are inviting "the kingdom of God" to reign in our lives. It is our obedience to His word that brings His plans to reality.

My favorite thing about marriage is—well, let me paint you a written picture. This is really for the husbands, but the wives will catch on.

Husbands, let us go back to your youth and singleness. Say that you are the only child of your father and that He owned all the wealth of the world. He sets you up in the best accommodations of what He has, an environment with all creature comforts you could desire. He is always there for you, to teach you and mature you in the ways of your growing life. Not only do you have time to roam the hills and swim in the rivers, but your father accompanies you, always being a great companion at your side. The fruit you find to eat in the lush green hills delights you, and adds to your roaming adventures. As you survey your surroundings, you observe that there is peace everywhere. All things around you are in perfect harmony. Your father is beside you with all the things He has provided, including naming all the living creatures that occupy the garden.

But as you look around, you don't see anything that resembles yourself. Day after day, it's the same, and soon the days began to get longer and longer. You've come to sense a warm cuddly feeling between some of the other creatures you have named. They enjoy romping together; they even have a language of their own. You've even seen some offspring come out of that warmth you witnessed.

Then one day your father comes to visit you after your afternoon nap, and to your surprise, another creature is with him. This creature looks a bit like you and stands upright, but has long flowing hair and eyes that sparkle. As it smiles at you, your father says, "It is not good that I've left you alone." Before your father has a chance to finish his greeting, you jump on your feet running toward the new creature, wondering what name you'll give it.

You yell out in a howl, "Wow, man!" You feel excitement as you sense that, of all the gifts your father has provided, this creature will bring you the greatest fulfillment. Just the sight of her makes you feel "completed." You hug her and declare to your father that she is bone of your bone and flesh of your flesh, and you willingly accept her as the greatest gift from your father and your promise to love and care for her always.

Does this romantic account of the "first date" sound familiar? Or does it merely sound like a "folklore" love story, something out of the past. It may remind you of a similar story you may have read—like maybe *the Bible*. And then you recognize its resemblance to the first book of the Bible, Genesis. It's a part of the Bible that we often skim over, especially the first five chapters, when we rush to chapter 6, the "Flood story." These first five chapters are where we can see the "real history" of man—at least the first *records* of man's history. (I say all this with tongue in cheek!)

But many of us tend to overlook those first five chapters because: (1) we know what God created because we live it; (2) Adam and Eve supposedly lived so long ago; (3) we hear about sin every Sunday, including the *first murder* in the Bible; we live with the consequences of it every day in our community; and (4) the "genealogy" of Adam to Noah—often disinteresting. And with that we're back to the Flood account in chapter 6. Yet, those first five chapters of the Bible are so enlightening! They tell us how to live our everyday lives together and they provide the basics for love and marriage between a man and a woman.

In my favorite story that talks about how God created marriage for Adam and Eve in the Garden of Eden, several parallels become apparent between this story and our own present-day marriages.

For the first similarity, as in Genesis when God brought Eve to her husband, ladies, it is *God* who brings us the mate He feels is just right for us, when we let Him lead us in the choice. How many times have you prayed for God to send the man of His choice into your life as a future husband? How many of you parents have taught this blessing to your children? How many of you grandparents have prayed this blessing for your grandchildren?

For those of you who are already married, it is not necessary to debate over whether God sent your spouse or not—it's a done deal. We married them in a covenant wedding, asking God to be our witness. We therefore live under the promises and terms of the spoken covenant, making God a partner who would manage the marriage. No, wives, your *husband* may not be "perfect"—but neither are us *wives*. A *triune* marriage has a much better chance of staying out of divorce court. You've heard the old saying, "Be patient—God is not finished with me yet." And so it is with each of us entering into a marriage. God has a special solution for us imperfect couples as we journey through this life. Again, we repeat one of my very favorite verses:

... I have come that they may have life, and that they might have it more abundantly. (John 10:10b KJV)

Here is the second parallel: Husbands, did you sense the way Adam reacted when he saw Eve? He was excited at the first sight of his new helpmate. He welcomed his wife with joy, proclaiming that this woman was bone of his bone and flesh of his flesh. So in this way he recognized their God-given marriage to be "one flesh." Husbands, do you see your wife as a source of joy? Men, just as Adam trusted God, you too should trust God that His choice of mate for you is a gift, a jewel, a very special gift from your heavenly Father. Do you let the world know that? Do you show her off by holding her hand in public or telling people that you will discuss things with your wife? Do you see, treat, and feel that your wife is a part of your own flesh? And wives, wouldn't you like to be greeted that way by you husband, knowing that when you are in his presence, he feels a great delight in the togetherness?

The joy related in this story, however, is truly how God meant our marriage relationship to be. Right now you are in the will of God and His plan for your marriage. You can have "heaven on Earth." In Ephesians we read that every family in heaven and earth get its name from the Father.

> *For this reason I kneel before the Father, from whom His whole family in heaven and on earth derives its name.* (Ephesians 3:14-15 NIV)

Because our earthly family can become a picture of God's heavenly family, the family is sacred to God. God wants harmony in your home because there is harmony in *His* home. For this reason, loving harmony becomes the responsibility of each member of our family. And the greatest responsibility for the welfare of a family falls upon the head of the home. "Heaven on earth" starts when the husband and the wife understand the main two responsibilities they have in marriage: to *leave* and to *cleave*.

> *Now, I want you to realize that the head of every man is Christ, and the head of the woman is man, and the head of Christ is God.*
> (1 Corinthians 11:3 NIV)

> *For this reason a man will leave his father and mother and be united to his wife, and they will become one flesh.* (Genesis 2: 24 NIV)

The Meaning of "to Leave"

To "leave" means that for the newly married couple, their relationship is their *first priority*, and that they are to establish independence from their parents, siblings and all other persons, including sons and daughters, cousins, "best friends" and "soul mates"—both male and female—and any members of their "blended family." This does not mean that you toss these dear ones out of your life altogether. Rather, it means that the two of you do not allow any other relationships to interfere with your covenant marriage vows to each other. *Your number one relationship is with your spouse.*

There are many reasons for this command:

1. When we leave our parents we are to look to a *new Father*—our heavenly Father—and to develop a trust in Him for all our needs. When a newly married couple keeps going back to their parents for money, or to borrow the car, or for constant baby-sitting, etc., they have not learned to transfer their material and practical dependence from their parents to God.

2. We must avoid the "multiple-master syndrome."

   No one can serve two masters. Either he will hate the one and love the other or he will be devoted to the one and despise the other.... (Matthew 6:24 NIV)

   To "serve two masters" may sound like an action of Bible times, and not for our day and age of "modern" ways. However, if we look deeply into the intent of the scripture passage above, we will see that it speaks of a very common occurrence in our everyday lives.

3. Many young people have what they call "soul ties." This relationship is often described as someone who has always "been there" for them; as a person they call when they need a friend or a companion to do something with. The root word comes from the word "soul" which is the seat of emotions, sentiment, and aspirations. It is the center of our moral powers. Although it may appear harmless and platonic, the basis of this relationship is a commitment to always "be there" for each other. This is a relationship of closeness that is often seen with a "lover" or "mistress." But in truth, this relationship is an intimate sharing of self that should only occur between a husband and wife. When a man and woman get married, the expression "soul-mates" should, from that day on, apply to *them only*. And for those not yet married, it is very wise that both partners agree on this principle *prior* to getting married, rather than having to deal with the consequences of later discovering that you disagree. The essence of your "one flesh" should become so apparent that when anyone sees one of you, they are instantly reminded of your strong relationship with the other!

Multiple Masters in Marriage: An Illustration

When Bob arrived home late one Friday afternoon, the den looked like a garage sale in the making. Deb and her mother were rearranging, sorting, discarding. It was every knickknack for itself!

"Hello, Dorothy, did you have a safe trip?" Bob asked Deb's mom.

"Hello, Bob. Yes, it was lovely. I got here just in time to help Deb start shaping up the house. Time for spring cleaning, you know! Deb, I'm going to take this load out to the garage, I'll be right back."

When they were alone, Deb looked at Bob a bit sheepishly and shrugged her shoulders.

"Well, Mom's here, as you can see."

"As a matter of fact, I can," Bob replied coolly. "What's going on, Deb?"

"Well, mom just felt like the house needed an overhaul and you know how hard it is to tell her "no." I decided it was easier to just go ahead and let her have her way than to argue. You're not upset, are you?"

"Not at your mom, Deb. That's just the way she is will always be, I guess. But I am wondering, did you go out to dinner with Tim and Tracy tonight? That's been planned for a couple of weeks, Deb."

"I remember, Bob. But I was going to ask you if we could go tomorrow night. Mom is so intent on getting this cleaning and reorganizing done tonight. It seems like it would be pretty thoughtless of me to let her finish this by herself."

"I see," Bob replied, turning away.

In this story of Bob, Deb, and her mother, we see confusion in Deb as to whom she should give priority to. Is it to her excited mother who really thinks she is helping Deb clean house, or to the commitments she has with her husband? What she is forgetting, or unaware of, is that *all other persons*—including children—are to be positioned in *second place* in the couple's family relationship priorities. It is of utmost concern that every marriage comes to the agreement that their one-flesh, covenant, triune marriage is the *top priority* in the circle of all their relationships.

Understanding Matthew 6:24

What husband or wife has not struggled with a parent who just will not let go? Parents who feel they still have the right to direct the life of their child. It's understandable. And it's wrong! Let's see why.

In Scripture, the kingdom of God is represented as a kingdom of choices. Christ said that no person can serve two masters as top priority. The failure to choose will eventually produce a negative choice. One contender will end up despised and hated while the other is loved. Spouses who do not keep priorities and loyalties clear will offend either a parent or a spouse. As for a spouse, God has already made the decision. Parents are the lower priority.

For the Heart

Can you recall a time when a situation similar to the one described here in your marriage? Or, are your parents reluctant to allow you or your spouse to run your own affairs, whether your decision is good or bad. There is perhaps a measure of this in every marriage.

Because this situation is predictable and understandable, you can prepare for it. Depending on your situation, and the sensitivity of the parents, action could be anything from a subtle hint to a more forthright conversation. Discuss and prepare now how to maintain loyalties. If offense is necessary, it is better to offend for what is right.

The Meaning of "to Cleave"

To *cleave* (Genesis 2:24 KJV) means to establish commitment to one another, to pursue, to be joined with and "keep fast" together—"oneness." It is the number one relationship in all of mankind. What a couple must do to experience this oneness in marriage is:

1. Leave everyone else out of your commitment to each other
2. Remain pure sexually
3. Love for the long term
4. Live within your standard of living
5. Work at your marital happiness
6. Forgive seventy times seventy
7. Keep God in the center of your marriage

> But since there is so much immorality, each man should have his own wife and each woman her own husband. The husband should fulfill his marital duty to his wife, and likewise the wife to her husband. The wife's body does not belong to her alone but also to her husband. In the same way, the husband's body does not belong to him alone but also to his wife.
> (1 Corinthians 7:2-4 NIV)

We've already given you examples of how to experience cleaving to each other so that "oneness" can be achieved in your marriage. But you may ask, "In the event of a loss of our cleaving in our marriage, how will I recognize the signs?" Here are some examples:

• Be aware of your manner of speech, especially when you are talking to others. The pronouns *I*, *me* and *mine* are terms of division. They bring attention to *self*, and they don't belong in a "one-flesh" marriage. Try using "we," "us," and "ours."

• Be aware of the amount of time you spend with other people, apart from the presence of your spouse. A good marriage enjoys the audience of the "one flesh." When you find gratification in other relationships—whether through sports, luncheons, and so forth—that leads to an excessive amount of time away from your spouse, Satan is at the door. There is a wedge in your marriage, allowing all forms of temptation to enter.

• Be aware of losing notice of your spouse's interests and desires and characteristics.

So often we think we know our spouses, when, in reality, we are quite "fuzzy" about our mate's likes and needs.

Now go to "Spousal Character" on the next two pages. We have enclosed a copy for both of you. Tear out the two pages and do them together—its fun!

Spousal Character

Husband's answers: My wife's character

My wife's three favorite foods:

1. _____

2. _____

3. _____

My wife recognizes I love her when I:

1. _____

2. _____

3. _____

Three things my wife likes about me:

1. _____

2. _____

3. _____

I recognize there are hurt feelings between us when my wife...

_____

_____

I know what to buy her on any special event: ☐ Yes ☐ No
Discuss it now, and be serious.

Spousal Character

Wife's answers: My husband's character

My husband's three favorite foods:

1. _____

2. _____

3. _____

My husband recognizes I love him when I:

1. _____

2. _____

3. _____

Three things my husband likes about me:

1. _____

2. _____

3. _____

I recognize there are hurt feelings between us when my husband...

_____

_____

I know what to buy him on any special event: ☐ Yes ☐ No
Discuss it now, and be serious.

_____

Men's Basic Threats to the "Oneness" of Marriage

Men have two basic fears, where women have only one basic need. First, men have a fear of *being subjugated* by a woman. Why? God ordained man to rule over woman as we have read. But even in the garden, Eve tried to usurp Adam authority by eating the fruit first. Hence, her punishment:

> ... *your desire will be for your husband, and he will rule over you.*
> (Genesis 3:16 NIV)

Do women realize that this stain put upon Eve was designed and instilled in all future generations of females? Prior to this first sin, Adam and Eve were in equal dependence upon God. But for earthly unity, Eve was a "helpmeet" to Adam—they both knew that!

We can't even imagine how Adam must have felt as he took a bite from the forbidden fruit that Eve offered him (discussion later on his part of the sin). But after the incident, Adam must have had a lot of hindsight thoughts about temptation to sin. At one time Adam must've wondered why she hadn't come to him asking about the fruit, and what the snake meant in what he was saying to her. He must have viewed Eve's attempts to liberate herself from God's word, and to act independently from her husband as an inherent trait of his helpmeet. Eve listened to another source, a source that encouraged her to defy the warnings of her God and her husband about the clear rule for respect for the tree with the forbidden fruit.

In today's world, we see the formidable striving of women—even "godly" women—to be equal. They have tackled the issue, without advice from God or their husbands, on the impulse of temptation. We women forget God's *order of authority*. Why did God place an *order of authority*? For earthly unity and peace, someone has to be accountable for "the buck stops here." It's no wonder that many husbands fear subjugation by wives. The first formed woman in creation, Eve, that set the example. And, ladies, we should not fool ourselves. Our world is filled with advertisements directed toward women alone, such as "be your own woman" and "get your own charge account." There are even "seven rules for moving in together" and many other articles that encourage women to be independent and on their own, without God or His word.

All around us, we wives see examples of the temptation to exert ourselves to the level of our own understanding, neglecting the advice and guidance of our Creator, and the husband God gave us to be our umbrella of protection. The result of such bombardment can be the beginning of a wedge in a marriage. However, when a woman's behavior is clearly submissive in godliness, the man is freed of this kind of fear.

Man's second fear is that of *being found inadequate*! Why? Because as the "head of the family" appointed by God, he has the ultimate responsibility for the welfare of his wife and family. A husband's need for *respect* is a God-given need, so that's why God gave this command to the wife:

> *Nevertheless let every one of you in particular so love his wife even as himself; and the wife see that she reverence her husband.*
> (Ephesians 5:33 KJV)

Other translations use the word "respect her husband" instead of "reverence her husband." Translators often soften the impact of the Greek word "revere," using a second or third root word of the same word. It is true that the word "respect" carries a lesser impending action (look up *respect* and *reverence* in Webster's dictionary). However, both words ultimately reach for the same behavioral action and are therefore interchangeable in a sentence. Both words render the following meanings: to be in awe of, hold in high esteem, to feel or show honor for, to be afraid or fear.

Husbands, flawed as they are from Adam's sin, instinctively realize the huge job of living up to what God demands of them. Often husbands will quote:

> *Wives, submit to your husbands as to the Lord. For the husband is the head of the wife as Christ is the head of the church, His body of which he is the Savior. Now as the church submits to Christ, so also wives should submit to their husbands in everything.* (Ephesians 5:22 NIV)

Often when things go wrong in a family, the husband may feel: "If she would just let me do it my way!" "If she would just submit like the word says." Most people fail to see that submission is not subjection. Man in all his fears, is not commanded to make his wife submit. We know that Submission is a choice on the woman's part, a choice to obey or to disobey God. The bottom line is that husbands and wives are to be *witnesses to each other* in their behavior, obedience, and attitude toward God's word, and in the ways they honor God. Whatever a husband or wife's purpose for pleasing their spouse, they are really doing *the work of the Lord*.

Basic Threats to the "Oneness" of Marriage: Women's Need

Women have one basic need: to be *loved*! Since we thoroughly covered this topic in chapter 2, we won't go into a repetition of this very needful subject. But one point does bear repeating: if this God-given need is genuinely fulfilled by her husband, she will be able to find fulfillment in her role as a dutiful wife, and submission will come more effortlessly for her.

Considering these fears and needs, that are genuine, it would appear to be obvious that every married couple understands them and are more than willing to work in that arena to bring about a godly marriage. Since God has given the husband the starring role in the marriage, he can start the road to success by loving his wife so dearly that she willing give him the respect by allowing him to be head of the house, which makes him love her more. And so the cycle becomes a hedge of protection around a blissful marriage. Sounds simple, huh?

If we do that, the threats to marriage are diminished—right? So, what's the problem? The problem is we cannot do it by our own power! We are wrapped in sinful flesh—flesh that functions on a "for self" level. So, what is a marriage to do?

There is an answer: each partner should first seek *the kingdom of God and His righteousness*. Rest assured, that the God who cannot lie, will add to you all the other things a man needs for his family: food, clothing and shelter.

> *But seek first His kingdom and His righteousness and all these things will be given to you as well.* (Matthew 6:33 NIV)

> *Love the Lord your God with all your heart and with all your soul and with all your strength.* (Deuteronomy 6:5 NIV)

We have looked at these verses back to back because they tells us if we first seek His Kingdom, and if we love Him with all our hearts and souls, all things will be taken care of. In other words, God must be our priority! When God becomes our priority, our lives come into order. We will have divine direction from the God the Father. He will enable us to confront and handle the pressures of life His way. Then, husbands will fulfill God's will as a provider, as a mate, and as a parent. Wives will become true "helper" to their husbands.

Unfortunately, our marriages are "on the job" training, and society lends very little knowledge to the instruction of how we are to go about living in a "one-flesh" state. Only God's word gives us direction.

> *You shall therefore impress these words of mine on your heart and on your soul; and you shall bind them as a sign on your hand, and they shall be as frontals on your forehead. And you shall teach them to your sons, talking of them when you sit in your house and when you walk along the road and when you lie down and when you rise up. So that your days and the days of your sons may be multiplied on the land which the Lord swore to your fathers to give them, as long as the heavens* remain *above the earth.* (Deuteronomy 11:18-19, 21 NASB)

We have intentionally left out the words that address the Hebrew Nation because ALL scripture is valid for mankind through all the ages. Just as these verses were meaningful to the Hebrews four or more thousand years ago, so are they meaningful for this generation. One cannot separate the Old Testament from the New Testament as God's message for all seasons. In these words God is saying that heaven comes to earth when we have the word of God in our heart and soul, and when we teach it and live it out before our family.

The next step for every man of God who brings heaven to his home is to help bring heaven to the rest of the world. As your marriage improves through your learning of spiritual truths, God wants you to apply them everywhere, in all of his creation! In fact, Jesus told the apostles that in the world to come, they would be assigned responsibilities in His kingdom on Earth.

And I confer on you a kingdom, just as my Father conferred one on me, so that you may eat and drink at my table in my kingdom. (Luke 22:29 NIV)

Jesus tells us we should pray for the kingdom of heaven to be on earth. In fact, He tells us how to pray.

This, then, is how you should pray: "Our Father who art in Heaven, hallowed be thy name, thy kingdom come, thy will be done, on earth as it is in heaven...." (Matthew 6:9-10 KJV)

You will recognize it as "the Lord's Prayer" that is said in all Christian churches across the world. This prayer is concerned with the kingdom of God on earth now and with its fulfillment in the future. This includes asserting God's power among his people in order to destroy the works of Satan, heal the sick, save the lost, promote righteousness and pour out the Holy Spirit on his people. Didn't we study in chapter 3, that all the above can be accomplished because we have the Holy Spirit in us? The kingdom of God is primarily a spiritual assertion of divine power in action. The essential evidence that one is experiencing God's kingdom here on earth is in a life that reflects "righteousness, peace and joy in the Holy Spirit."

For the kingdom of God is not a matter of eating and drinking, but of righteousness, peace, and joy in the Holy Spirit. (Romans 14:17 NIV)

It is the responsibility of every believer to unceasingly seek God's kingdom in all of its power that rests in the "gifts of the Holy Spirit." We should have hunger and thirsting for God's presence and power both in our own lives and within the Christian community.

We first bring the kingdom of God into our marriage by loving each other. In our love for each other we should be transparent with each other. Do not cover yourself like Adam did in the Garden of Eden when he covered himself with fig leaves and would not come before God! Be truthful with your spouse, this is the first step of love.

Let us review reasons why love is so important in our marriage relationship. It is God's priority command. We are "commanded" to love one another 55 times in the New Testament.

God doesn't just say, "It would be nice if you loved one another" or "Hey, try loving one another!" No, it is a command! The *act* of "loving," or the *lack* of loving, colors all the actions of the heart. When we looked up the word "love" in our Bible concordance at the back of our Bible; the word "love" is referenced in 519 verses. The only other category references larger than love are "God" and "Lord." One can see God's priorities in reading the concordance alone. Here are a few references on *love*:

... if God so loved us, we also ought to love one another.
(1 John 4:11 NKJV)

... but through love serve one another. (Galatians 5:13 NKJV)

... with lowliness and gentleness, with longsuffering, bearing with one another in love ... (Ephesians 4:2 NKJV)

And now abide faith, hope, love ... the greatest of these is love. (1 Corinthians 13:13 NKJV)

Above all, love each other deeply, because love covers a multitude of sins. (1 Peter 4:8 NIV) [It's a permanent virtue!]

Love never fails ... [everything else] will vanish away. (1 Corinthians 13:8 NKJV)

If we are going to love others as ourselves and as Christ loved them, we must put others before our selves. The love of God has its focal point the interests and the welfare of others. This we find in:

Do nothing out of selfish ambition or vain conceit, but in humility consider others better than yourselves. Each of you should look not only to your own interests, but also to the interests of others. Your attitude should be the same as that of Christ Jesus. (Philippians 2:3-5 NIV)

In verse 5, we are told "to have this attitude in ourselves which was also in Christ Jesus." It was the "servant attitude" of Christ, an attitude of submission and obedience that would go so far as to lay down His own life. The servant attitude of Christ is further explained in Philippians, chapter 2, verses 6-11—a very good reading, if you would like to stop here and read it.

The servanthood of Christ in this passage is *in relationship to his Father*, not as a servant to *man*. If we realize that we are to love others in submission to the Father rather than in submission to man, we see just how critical submission is. Simply put, it is *submission to our Father*. All commandments, or any biblical indications of actions like a "command," or a "must," or a "shall" are not just "suggestions." God is saying for us to *do* them—and He is saying *do them as unto Him!* He is asking us to empty ourselves and do all things for Him, just as Jesus did all things for His Father.

Basic Threats to the "Oneness" of Marriage: Blended Families

Let us focus on blended families for a moment. Inter-relationship problems occur within "blended families," often due to the consequences of divorce. We said, before, that divorce was a sin. And we, in chapter 2, have repented of our sin of divorce—those of us who needed to. Now, we are forgiven for breaking our covenant with God in the vows we spoke at the marriage ceremony! However, we are still left with the consequences that came about because of the divorce. That is the main "thorn in the side" in blended families. God forgives sin, but He, often, does not remove the consequences of that sin. What is a repented person to do? Look to the Lord and His word for our solutions!

Blended families, as well as first marriages are to serve the Lord in the same ways. We would like to look at three areas pertaining to blended families: child discipline, identity, and pre-nuptial agreements.

Child Discipline

We first want to remind you that Jesus was a stepchild; He had a stepfather.

> *Children, obey your parents in the Lord, for this is right. Honor your father and mother, which is the first commandment with a promise that it may go well with you and that you may enjoy long life on the earth.* (Ephesians 6:1-3 NIV)

Did Jesus know of this commandment? Of course He did. Children must submit to the authority of the parents by obedience. Small children must be taught to obey and honor their parents, real parents or step-parents, by being brought up in the training and instruction of the Lord. There are biblical instructions for parents on how to use discipline when raising children.

> *Train a child in the way he should go, and when is old he will not turn from it.* (Proverbs 22:6 NIV)

> *Do not withhold discipline from a child; if you punish him with the rod, he will not die. Punish him with the rod and save his soul from death.* (Proverbs 23:13-14 NIV)

> *He who spares the rod hates his son, but he who loves him is careful to discipline him.* (Proverbs 13:24 NIV)

> *The rod of correction imparts wisdom, but a child left to himself disgraces his mother.* (Proverbs 29:15 NIV)

These verses direct discipline to be used for a "child." God is talking here about instructions to parents on disciplining their children with the rod during their formative years. We know that society has made this biblical principle difficult to apply, yet we also know that children who are not trained, disciplined, or restrained by their partners will later bring shame to them and harm to themselves. Spanking should be done only for willful disobedience or defiance. Many times words of rebuke alone are adequate; at other times the rod of correction must accompany them.

Parents are warned against excessive discipline.

> *Fathers, do not exasperate your children ...* (Ephesians 6:4 NIV)

Adequate parental discipline when administered in a wise and loving manner helps children to learn that wrong behavior carries unpleasant consequences and may involve suffering.

The area of child discipline is most difficult in blended families. The father of the family has the burden of leadership as appointed to him by God, and this includes the area of discipline. In a blended family where there are offspring from a former marriage, or relationship, it is critical that the husband listens and respects feedback from the wife, while making the final decision. However, it also takes the natural parent in a blended family to assume the responsibility to teach their child mutual respect for both marital partners. Just as husbands are to discipline children from a former marriage, so are the marital partners to treat all children in the home as if they were their very own.

Identity

Children *find their proper identity* in biblically administered discipline. The wife should find her identity in her husband, as the husband should find his identity in Christ. There are no hyphenated names in heaven. Often, for working reasons, a woman might think she needs to carry her maiden name. However, in all other family matter, as well as social situations, she should use her husband's name. It defines her role according to God's authority.

Pre-nuptial Agreements

Marriages of convenience, and open marriages are all distortions of the biblical marriage God ordained, and they are not to be practiced by Christians. God made marriage to be a lasting thing: "til death do us part." Pre-nuptial agreements are all about money and possessions, and for the most part are written out of fear and mistrust of the spouse. In the situation of widows and widowers, a pre-nuptial agreement might seem the best thing to do where age may not allow for the couple to build up financial assets. And since they have already obtained the majority of life's monetary blessings, it might seem more proper to write a trust and will to favor the children conceived by a previous marriage. However, when a person is confronted with widowhood in mid-life, and a future marriage is possible, a pre-nuptial agreement is a "red flag" that may indicate an unequally yoked relationship.

The Essence of Marriage: Heaven on Earth

The essence of marriage cannot be found in possessions or monetary goods. It cannot be found in the stresses or lack of strife in our life. It is not the good-looking spouse we selected to marry. It's not the beautiful ceremony we experience or the freedom of the honeymoon. It's not the great neighborhood we live in, or the wonderful relatives that came with the reunion. Marriage is a "testing" ground for our spiritual growth, among other things. The real nature of marriage is in its ultimate purpose to provide a protected arena where God hones and polishes each of us into the kind of people He wants us to be. Marriage should be a safe and forgiving field where we go through new changes accompanied by a loving, supportive spouse! A place where we're allowed to fail: in the face of someone seeing all our weakness. Marriage is very revealing about our spiritual growth because how we treat our covenant partner is in direct relationship to our obedience and relationship with God.

Personal Commitment to Marriage

Is time that we looked at what a personal commitment to marriage means! For the marriage, it should go this way:

Husband: *I commit to you that I will respond to God's call on my life to be the leader of this family, give protection and provide for you. I ask for your forgiveness for the times I have failed you and have not acted for you as the source God expected me to be. I hereby pledge to be an active leader, who will serve you with love, understanding and a gentle Spirit.*

Wife: *I commit to you that I will respond to God's call on my life to follow you as the head of my life. I ask your forgiveness for the times I have struggled against you and thereby have not pleased the Lord. I hereby pledge to give you my respect and follow you as the head of our household.*

Together: *We affirm today that God designed the husband to be the head of the wife. We willingly choose to submit to each other, as is your will for us. We pray that we will walk the path of righteousness: in your name. It will be our privilege to honor and bring praises to Your Throne. In the name of Jesus the Messiah. Amen.*

God's total creation begins with a wedding and ends with a wedding. In the beginning was the marriage of Adam and Eve. And when this earth as we know it, comes to an end, the new heaven begins with a wedding.

> *Let us rejoice and be glad and give Him glory! For the wedding of the Lamb has come, and His bride has made herself ready. Fine linen, bright and clean, was given her to wear. Then the angel said to me, "Write: 'Blessed are those who are invited to the wedding supper of the Lamb!' "*
> *And he added, "These are the true words of God."*
> (Revelation 19:7-9 NIV)

Fine linen stands for the righteous acts of the saints. The Bride, known as the Church, is making herself ready for her groom, Jesus Christ. Her "fine linen, bright and clean" is the righteous acts of the saints—you and me! Let us Praise God for His wisdom to provide a mate to help us through our "sainthood" under the protective umbrella of a godly "marriage."

Closing Prayer

Lord, God, let us remember that every family in heaven and earth derives its name from you. Seal in our hearts that we are to "leave and cleave" all others for the sake of the "one-flesh" marriage you have given us. Let us serve no master but you! Father, Thank you for the prayer that pleads, "Your kingdom come, on earth as it is in heaven," for you have enabled us to bring down you love in our marital relationship. Father, we know your priority command is to love! And when we love in our "one flesh," we start a ripple that travels through our family, into our neighborhoods and church and into the world at large. Lord, as you use our marriage as a testing ground, a protected area where we can grow, continue to give us your love to give to others. And, then, may we be counted among the saints at the greatest wedding feast of all in Heaven. Amen!

- To have a "heaven on earth" marriage, we must *seek the kingdom of God* and His righteousness.

- The kingdom of God is *spiritual assertion of divine power in action.*

- The "divine power in action" is the work of the Holy Spirit, love being a priority.

- *Love is a commandment of God*, with its focus on the welfare of others.

- Both spouses are instructed to "leave" and "cleave" in marriage:
    - *Leave*: To establish independence from other relationships.
    - *Cleave*: To establish commitment to each other.

- *Submission to each other* compliments itself, from a higher calling, to submit to the Father in heaven.

Visit our website for this book, at **www.NotYourEnemy.info**, where you will be welcome to ask questions or make comments. Enjoy!

God intended our marriages to be a vibrant, dynamic state of ever-deepening love and growth. We must see our spouses as they really are: a gift from God. Start right now accepting your mate and thanking God for his grace and goodness. He knows you better than you know yourself. He knows your needs better than you know them yourself.

1. Husband, can you look at your wife and welcome her as Adam did Eve? Plan to do something for her to let her know you welcome her as a wife.

   _____

   _____

2. Wife, do you know and accept that you were made for your husband, to do him good? What good thing can you do for him?

   _____

   _____

3. Leaving—the *role* of the couple

   A. We were successful in leaving our parents and/or grown children when we got married?
      Husband: ☐ Yes ☐ No   Wife: ☐ Yes ☐ No

   B. Both of us are free from manipulation of control by parents and grown children.
      Husband: ☐ Yes ☐ No   Wife: ☐ Yes ☐ No

   C. Our sense of emotion and well-being does not depend upon frequent visits or phone calls from our parents or children.
      Husband: ☐ Yes ☐ No   Wife: ☐ Yes ☐ No

4. Cleaving—the *responsibility* of the couple

   A. We are committed to each other for life. Divorce is not an acceptable option.
      Husband: ☐ Yes ☐ No   Wife: ☐ Yes ☐ No

   B. Both of us are being careful to avoid the establishment or maintenance of opposite-sex friends.
      Husband: ☐ Yes ☐ No   Wife: ☐ Yes ☐ No

C. We are both making an effort to prevent other people or activities from infringing on our time for each other.
Husband: ☐ Yes ☐ No   Wife: ☐ Yes ☐ No

D. Both of us are choosing to forgive hurts before walls are built between us.
Husband: ☐ Yes ☐ No   Wife: ☐ Yes ☐ No

E. We both guard against vengefully using past hurts to retaliate against our spouse.
Husband: ☐ Yes ☐ No   Wife: ☐ Yes ☐ No

F. Giving God His rightful place in our lives is our highest goal as a couple.
Husband: ☐ Yes ☐ No   Wife: ☐ Yes ☐ No

5. Men have two basic fears. This area of discussion is for both spouses.

A. Fear of being *subjugated by a woman*. Does the husband of the family feel this way? ☐ Yes ☐ No

If yes, discuss ways you can show your mate that you have submission in your heart to obey God's will for your marriage.

_____

_____

B. Fear of being *found inadequate*. Does your husband feel this way?

☐ Yes ☐ No

If yes, discuss ways you can make him feel better.

_____

_____

6. Do you use terms like "I," "me," or "mine"? If you do, especially if front of children from a former marriage; practice saying: "us," "ours," "dad" (if he is not the original father), or "mom" (if she is the children's step-mom). Refer to the grandchildren as "Your Grandma Jill" (or whatever her name is), and "Your Grandpa Bob" (or whatever his name is). If one of you has nationally that uses special names for grandpa or grandma, use those. Remembering always to say that we are a God-given brought-together family, and as such, we'll act that way. If you meet resistance, don't demand the usage. You be the role model and continue to declare the wisdom needed to bring the family together.

7. Love is the greatest gift of all, a permanent virtue, it lasts forever!

Both of you together define how you can bring "the kingdom of heaven" down into your home.

Chapter 5
No Intimacy? No Romance!

Godly Principle 5:
Submit to one another. (Ephesians 5:21 NKJV)

> *The closeness of intimacy involves a daily, private, and personal interaction that is committed and caring in action.*

> *Mutual commitment creates a mutual love response that exercises the romantic attitude of the heart.*

> *It is an exclusive commitment with an intense devotion that allows for no other courtship.*

Every marriage is moving in one of two directions —*intimacy,* or *isolation.*

We are going to look at *sex, love, romance,* and *intimacy* as they pertain to marriage *today,* and then how *God* defines these four words. In the real world around us, these words have lost much of their meaning and authenticity as God had intended for marriage. Physical sex and love is a sensitive subject to discuss in a mixed-gender group setting. We all know it is a subject that makes children giggle. Teenagers speak to the matter, in moments of privacy, among their own age group. Do you remember in high school, for some of us that was centuries ago, we would tolerate the macho males who bragged about "last night's conquests." And yes, we girls would spend hours endlessly revealing our interests and the experiences of our "date night." Later in life just when we as parents had gotten enough courage up to speak to our children about "the birds and the bees," they retorted with, "Yeah, we learned that in school."

Our subject for this chapter has always had a certain "mystery" about it, all through human history. They are, at the least, the foundational core of mankind's functions, communications, and family matters. The majority of our choices, and errors, we make in life come from how we view these four words. Our movies, books, plays, television, and social events embrace their presence. While we learn of their charisma early in childhood, it is in our adulthood that the effect of the wisdom, knowledge and application of the words *sex, love, romance, and intimacy* plays out their biggest role in our lives, shaping our very existence. What we believe about these words affects our daily lives in gigantic magnitude—regardless of whether it is *true* or *false* in reality.

Many Christians have confusion about physical sex and feelings of love. We often confuse romance and intimacy, habitually incorporating them within the separate arenas of sex and love. This repeatedly brings about individual definitions and varied experience in all four areas of life.

The best source of information and understanding about our topics are found in the word of God, the Creator of them all. It is our intent to bring your focus to the mind of God and catch sight of why He established these feelings in us. They are the foundation of every godly marriage that invites His presence within the marital unity. At this point we could explore the world's meaning of such words, but it would entail a vast explanation of various interpretations. It is not our intent to try to reconstruct the world's misconceptions. It is our intent to "renew your mind" with the word of God, and what better place to start than with the word *sex*.

Sex

Why did God create sex? There are five reasons why God gave sex to mankind. Let's stand in God's shoes, for a moment. If you were God and had created a wonderful Garden of Eden, and you wanted something equal to your image to be with, you know—someone who has the likeness of yourself, a resemblance of you that would provide a basis for interaction, a living being that could speak and communicate—you couldn't do better than to create "man." And, if in fact, you wanted *many* "men" to populate that garden, you would have to give "man" a means by which he could reproduce himself, thus fulfilling the commandment.

> God blessed them and said to them, "Be fruitful and increase in number; fill the earth and subdue it. Rule ... over every living creature ..."
> (Genesis 1:28 NIV)

So, here are five reasons in response to our question of why God created sex.

First Reason: So that man could fulfill God's Genesis command. God created sex and gave it to man.

In creating sex, God made it a very powerful feeling—as we will learn later in this chapter. God chose sex as a wedding present so that His creation could obey Him. The "act of marriage" is the *work* of the marriage; it is a function that produces intimate knowledge of our spouse. In his book *The Act of Marriage*, pastor Tim LaHaye calls the beauty of sexual love "the act of marriage." By the way, get this book (LaHaye); it is factual, loving and informative about why God did it His way.

Second Reason: God made sex to *provide mutual pleasure and comfort in marriage*. God meant for sex to give us pleasure. Solomon makes that point when he intimately describes his lover's body, suggesting it is a delight to him.

> How beautiful you are and how pleasing, O love, with your delights! Your stature is like that of the palm, and your beasts like clusters of fruit. I said, "I will climb the palm tree: I will take hold of its fruit." May your breasts be like the clusters of the vine, the fragrance of your breath like apples, and your mouth like the best wine. (Song of Solomon 7:6-9 NIV)

Is that sex, love, romance, or intimacy? Knowing God, it is probably all four. It shows a bridegroom that regards his wife as awe-inspiring; every part of her body pleases him. The sensuous love story between Solomon and his wife is an example of how God views the physical aspects of love in our marriage relationship. Sensuous delight comes from kissing, embracing, hearing, seeing, feeling, touching, and even smelling. These feelings are God's gift to us; He created them for us to enjoy to the fullest. For it is through these sensual feelings that love completes us as humans in the physical, spiritual and emotional arena of life.

Third Reason: God mandated that sex be practiced only in marriage, so as to reduce any sexual temptation outside the marriage union. The "act of marriage," the sexual part, the coming together of the physical bodies, is a gift that when properly practiced reduces to a manageable amount any temptations to share this gift outside of marriage.

> *Do not deprive each other except by mutual consent and for a time, so that you may devote yourselves to prayer. Then come together again so that Satan will not tempt you because of your lack of self-control.*
> (1 Corinthians 7:5 NIV)

When couples share commonly in gratifying sexual interactions, the satisfaction of their normal sex drive provides less vulnerability to Satan's temptations. Solomon of the Bible, who also wrote most of Proverbs, said this:

> *Drink water from your own cistern, running water from your own well."* ...
> *May your fountain be blessed, and may you rejoice in the wife of your youth. A loving doe, a graceful deer—may her breasts satisfy you always, may you ever be captivated by her love.* (Proverbs 5:15, 18-19 NIV)

At first reading, this sounds somewhat strange. Taken out of context, it isn't very clear. Like many other verses in the Bible, we need to read the chapter to get a sense of its content. We've already done that for you, so you can trust our future remarks. It starts out by saying, "drink from your own cistern." In previous verses Solomon is discussing ways to stay away from adultery, and is trying to make the point that a man's source of affectionate love should come from his own wife. The phrase "May your fountain be blessed" refers to the use of the males" sexual organs, and does, in fact, refer to the health of those sex organs. Solomon also lived in a time of sexually transmitted diseases. He is saying that if we keep our sex to our marital partner, there is health in this wisdom. And, lastly, the phrase "may her breasts satisfy you always; may you ever be captivated by her love" confirms the fact that there is love in the sexual act and that God has put his blessings on physical sex.

Fourth Reason: Sex gives mutual ownership, between husband and wife, to the covenant of one-flesh marriage.

The husband should fulfill his marital duty to his wife, and likewise the wife to her husband. The wife's body does not belong to her alone but also to her husband. In the same way, the husband's body does not belong to him alone but also to his wife. (1 Corinthians 7:3-4 NIV)

Paul calls the act of marriage a duty. The term "duty" in the Greek language means *to perform, to restore, repay, and to reward.* We will discuss more on duty later. First Corinthians 7:3-4 (KJV) says "render unto the wife due benevolence, and likewise also the wife unto the husband." The word "benevolence" means *kindness or goodwill,* it comes from the Greek root word meaning *to agree.* Sex is an act of kindness we perform together to show our love for each other. *Mutual ownership* is very important because it guarantees interdependency between the husband and wife.

Fifth Reason: God gave the gift of sex for intimate communion that is not possible on any other level. This sexual act of total exclusion, only in marriage, is a means of expressing love and commitment to one another. We are prohibited from communicating this kind of love, in any form, with any other person outside our marriage. Sex between a husband and a wife is a Divine imperative, an absolute necessity in fulfilling the will of God. In the Bible the books of Song of Solomon and Proverbs teach us that sexual love between a husband and wife is, in fact, *by God, and to the glory of God.* Sex in its highest form becomes *an act of worship.*

Sex is a wedding present from God as we have just discussed, and has a definite purpose for life. Sexual expression has been altered ever since sin entered the Garden of Eden. Today, the world views sexuality very different than God intended. You can tell how important the matter of physical sex, intimacy and love is to the heart of God by how much time the enemy spends perverting it.

Satan has fabricated physical counterfeits to imitate God's pure and honorable physical intimacy between marriage partners. He has deceived people into believing that pornography, adultery, incest, masturbation, homosexuality, fornication, and other sensual perversions produce sexual intimacy. No so! In reality, they are damaging counterfeits, and create a "spiritual warfare" for all marriages, especially for Christian married couples. It is in the best interests of all godly marriages that they do not practice any of these counterfeits. They all damage the unity of the covenant marriage. Again, go to God. Whoever suffers in these areas is to rely on God and His perfect word.

... who through faith are shielded by God's power until the coming of the salvation that is ready to be revealed in the last time. (1 Peter 1:5 NIV)

Any Christian sexual union that is without God's covenant covering permits greater vulnerability to pain, hurt, and shame and withers without God's protection. It takes away one's ability to be truly intimate with their spouse.

Instead of edifying and ministering to the loved one, it degrades and defiles the very act.

There are some couples that are not able to experience sexual intimacy in marriage because of wounds from sexual sin either by themselves or by another person. If any of you have fallen into that category, know that *right now* Jesus loves you! He knows you have come with a repentant heart and he loves you just as you are. We must deal with this area of spiritual warfare through prayer and in agreement with our spouses! In chapter 10, we will discuss the weapons we are directed by God to use.

Love

To many people, sex and love are the same thing. We have heard it said, "A person can have sex without love, but can't have love without sex." If that sentence is true, then it suggests that everybody we love must be sexually involved with us. Of course, that is pure rubbish. But it does help us make a point. We want to make a very important statement here: What a person believes about sex and love—whether it be true or false—will influence their behavior. The world talks of love, artists compose works of love, and authors write books on love. They can be true or false; in fact, fiction or myth. Whatever the source that molds us to our preconceived notions about the subject, it is important to understand that what we accept love to be, does effects us in many ways. It affects our marriage in totality—it shapes our behavior and responses to our spouse; it even affects our parental role for our children when it influences our teachings to our family. It determines the outcome of the future of our marriage. Although love is our primary emotional need, it is not our only emotional need. It takes a difference in shaping our other meaningful needs such as security, self-worth, and significance.

We humans have various expressions of love toward "the desired one" as well as, differences in the ways we feel we are loved. Why different expressions and responses to love? Of all the books on the bookshelves today, there is a certain one we would like to recommend for your reading. The author believes that we all have "emotional love tanks" that from time to time need refilling. The refilling time occurs when we show love to each other. And that's the "catch'— we all do not feel loved just because our marriage partner states they love us! We have said it before—love is an action!

As a side road to understanding how we perceive love, we would like to direct you to a book for your reading pleasure. In his book (Chapman) *The Five Love Languages,* Dr. Gary Chapman explains that every person during their childhood will develop a "primary love language" through the actions of their parents or significant others, in relationship to their own characteristics and personality dynamics. Dr. Chapman has put the love languages into five categories: *Words of Affirmation, Quality Time, Receiving Gifts, Acts of Service, and Physical Touch.* When we come to an understanding of how we

111

formed our perceptions of love via parental programming, it gives us a handle on how we recognize love from our spouse, and how we communicate love to our spouse.

A good overall definition for love is this: love is an unconditional commitment to an imperfect person.

In the following verses, God has told us four ways to love our spouse:

> *Husbands, love your wives just as Christ loved the church and gave himself up for her to make her holy, cleansing her by the washing with water through the word, and to present her to himself as a radiant church, without stain or wrinkle or any other blemish, but holy and blameless. In this same way, husbands ought to love their wives as their own bodies. He who loves his wife loves himself. After all, no one ever hated his own body, but he feeds and cares for it, just as Christ does the church.*
> (Ephesians 5:25-29 NIV)

1. We are to love *sincerely*! Verse 25 tells us " *... just as Christ also loved the church ... *" He loved us and went to the Cross when we were yet still ungodly. Sincerely means for real, no doubt or rejection of origin. He had no doubts about us; Jesus knew just what we are, full of sin and selfishness. Yet he loved us anyway, knowing all our flaws, and so, we too are to accept each other in the flesh.

2. We are to love *sacrificially*! The second half of Ephesians 5:25 says, " *... and gave Himself up for her.* " Some of us feel if we give 50-50, it's a good marriage. But unfortunately the trio of temptation—Satan, the world, and our flesh—are a constant danger to our marriages. In order to overcome the influences of evil, and have a marriage that is meaningful and righteous before God, each partner must give 100 percent. When we sacrifice for our spouse, we are transformed more into the image of Christ.

3. We are to love *deliberately*! Ephesians 5:26 and 27 says, " ... that He might sanctify her, cleanse her, and present her to Himself ... in glory, having no spot or wrinkle, but be holy and blameless." We need to become aware of our mate's spiritual life. To encourage them in the role God has for them. Husbands are to become the priest and prophet of the home, while wives are to respect, honor, and uphold their husbands in his God-given responsibilities.

4. We are to love *absolutely*! Ephesians 5:28 and 29 says " ... love their wives as their own bodies." Just as husbands nourish and take care of their own bodies, so should they nourish and cherish their wives, just as Christ did the church (His bride). Husbands, you really are one body with our wives, in a spiritual sense. When God took Eve out of Adam, it left him incomplete. God gave back to Adam his wholeness when He pronounced them "one flesh." When your own body hurts, you tend to its needs and healing. So

when your spouse hurts, it is most important to tend to his or her needs. In the real world of marriage, we *must* recognize the importance of love, with its accompanying emotions. That is why we recommend Chapman's book.

The action of love is very convoluted, and at times, very hard to describe and understand. When we consider various personality traits and different characteristics, we soon realize that each person, even within the same sex, is uniquely different in character makeup, emotions, physical and genetic determinations.

However, let us stay focused on the differences between the genders: male and female. For instance: men think of sex in biological terms rather than emotional terms. To a husband, sex is the fulfillment of his love for his wife, but its release is primarily physical – not emotional. To his wife, sex is the fulfillment of the totality of her relationship with her husband, which is dominated by the emotional. In women, physical release is minimal, next to the emotional fulfillment she experiences. Why do you think that she wants to talk all night after the lovemaking? Or why is foreplay so important to the woman? It gives her time to build up and express her emotional feelings. For her that's the best part. Differences between men and women really do exist. The individualities that exist between male and female, when accepted and respected, bring about an intimacy in the marriage that adds to its enjoyment.

In our attempts to see the differences in men verses women, it compares its self only with the warning statement: "You can't mix apples with oranges." They are simply different! This is the summation of the average man (there are always exceptions to every rule). Men are made to lead the family. They are career bound with a competitive attitude of a conqueror. They usually succeed at their vocation whether it is due to their body strength or their emotional detachment.

The metabolism of healthy men is higher than women, with the result of a constant sex drive. Men use the left side of the brain more, and rightly so; it encases the logical aspect of life's decisions in a factual, direct way. This is necessary due to the fact that men use only 12,500 words a day. Men have no trouble with "change" as they are moment oriented. They get the job done, now, its time to relax and watch that football game. They make good listeners. However, a drawback that needs consideration: men get angrier more often, but at *things*, not *people*, and this difference influences his life expectancy. Men express their anger in a physical way—by hitting the wall, kicking the tires, or maybe even the dog. (For you dog lovers, substitute the word "cat." For you cat lovers, don't worry, they always land on their feet!)

Insight: *Understanding our Differences*

Man	Woman
Protective	Nurture
Vocational/self-identity	Surroundings and relationships
Needs to lead	Better at discernment
"Moment" oriented	"Future" oriented
Activity oriented (sports)	People oriented
Competition oriented	Group oriented
Conqueror oriented	Shopping oriented
Change: logically deduces benefit	Needs time to adjust to change
Emotionally detached	Emotionally involved
Decides on "facts"	Sees, hears, feels, senses body language
Is "direct"	Is "indirect"
General	Details, often embellished
40% muscle, 50 % more strength	23% muscle
Sexual drive: constant	Sexual drive: cyclic
Visual	Verbal
Primarily physical	Emotional fulfillment
Metabolism higher	Metabolism lower
Deeper voice	Larger kidneys, liver, and stomach
B/P up, pulse down, lung capacity up	Prone to fainting
Weaker immune system	Lives longer (4-8 years)
Left brain is typically dominant	Right brain is typically dominant
• Typically logically centered	• Typically emotionally centered
• Linear thinking is typical	• Multi-tasking typically enabled
Gets angry 6x/week, at things	Gets angry 3x/week, at "people"
Expresses hostility *physically*	Expresses hostility *verbally*
Uses 12,500 words/day	Uses 25,000 words/day
Great listeners	Likes feedback

Now, the average female is quite different. Women are "people and relationship" oriented, an attitude that dictates their actions with life. They are more grounded in their surroundings and therefore have a tougher time with changes. They put their whole body and soul into every emotion they feel. Women embellish everything. To them, in the scheme of all things, life appears better, more romantic, and "cute"—if you will allow that cliché—than they normally are to a common-logic-sort-of-guy. Women use the *present* to plan

114

for the *future*. Even though the female sexual drive is cyclic, they readily respond to verbal pillow talk, which in turn stimulates their emotional fulfillment in the sexual arena. And women's metabolism is slower; they have a tougher time losing weight than men.

However, those larger kidneys, liver and stomach help elongate her life span. It is the kidneys and liver that removes the body toxins. They use both sides of their brain allowing the female to multi-task over men. Note: the emotional (right) side of the brain is larger in size than the left side of the brain. Due to a woman's "people orientation," her anger is often expressed toward *people,* because she is hurt, and feels vulnerable and betrayed. She has so many words to use that she tries to talk her way in and out of her feeling, looking for feedback that won't come unless she has a listening-kind-of-guy!

Multi-tasking is the action a mother takes, for example, when she is on her way to the laundry room to put the washed clothes into the dryer, while holding little junior in her arms and talking on the cell phone to her husband, who wants to know what is for dinner. On her way to the laundry, she picks up the dirty towels from the downstairs bathroom (they are the next load), stops to tie the shoes of her six-year-old who is screaming, "Where is my lunch bucket. The bus is almost here."

Let's do one more scenario in trying to blend these two very different, and often opposite human beings in marriage. The husband is offered a job promotion to another state. He has checked the school system, moving costs, the availability of medical care, and feels satisfied that it is a good family move to accept. Additional attraction is the increase in pay, which means more money for the children's college and their retirement. He goes home to give the good news to his wife.

"What," she questions, "We'd be leaving in a month? What will Mrs. Wilson do? I walk her dog for her everyday." She continues, "What about the children's friends, and our church family?" She is using both sides of her brain and can't decide to cry or try to talk him out of the move. Is this family stress? Sure it is! Could this end up in a big brawl? Sure it can—and often does. But it doesn't have to. We will find the solution in chapters 8 and 9.

It seems fitting, at this point and after such a scenario that we should expand and revisit the matter of *submission* discussed in chapter 2, just in case we lost some of you in the wordy pages of this book. Again, the Greek word used in the New Testament for submission (Strong's, *submit*) is *hupotasso,* which in English means *"to voluntarily complete, arrange, adapt, or blend so as to make a complete whole or complete a pattern."* The key concept, here, is *voluntary blending.* Love without affectionate submission often results in self-gratifying conquest. Selfishness began in the Garden of Eden — but where there is submission, selfishness dies.

Submission is not new to Christians.

Submit yourselves, then, to God. Resist the devil, and he will flee from you. (James 4:7 NIV)

First, we are told to submit ourselves to God.

Everyone must submit himself to the governing authorities, for there is no authority except that which God has established. (Romans 13:1 NIV)

Secondly, Christians are commanded to obey the state and federal authorities in our country. God says we are to do so because it is He who chooses the rulers in this world.

Submit to one another out of reverence for Christ. (Ephesians 5:21 NIV)

Mutual submission, by both husband and wife is ultimately an act of worship to God. As a married couple loves Christ, and in their allocation to Him as the third person in their marriage covenant, they progress to a higher spiritual principle that brings more of heaven into their earthly home. When there is a situation where the wife submits to the husband and the husband submits to the needs of the wife, an attitude of love and self-giving saturates the very fibers of the marriage, as well as the entire family unit. If this chapter sounds like it is talking mostly to men, you're right! God has set priority for His creation.

Now I want you to realize that the head of every man is Christ, and the head of the woman is man, and the head of Christ is God. (1 Corinthians 11:3 NIV)

Paul tells us that man's authority is just below Jesus Christ's authority. Man is the head of the woman, so it follows that God also holds man accountable in his responsibilities for the family.

Wives, we too are to love our "one-flesh" husbands *absolutely* and unconditionally. We are always to be there as his helpmeet. We too are to nourish and cherish him. And in particular, we are to support his plans for the family. We are practicing unconditional love at its highest level when our husbands fail at their intentions, and we suppress criticisms like, "I told you so!"

Romance

Romance means something different to every person. Have you ever tried to define "romance"? It has a multitude of meanings, an array of definitions. But none with the clarity that applies when we are seeking to describe how we feel. Not only is the word *romance* difficult to define, but its *feelings* are even harder to put into words. Most of us, at one time or another, have had a feeling of "romance." Do you remember ever saying "Wasn't that romantic?" Maybe it was during a movie, or the time your spouse brought home a gift or flowers for no reason. Maybe it was a location like the beach or on a high mountain. Romantic moments have an element *of something different from the ordinary.*

Sometimes, they just happen, while other times we can plan them, but they are different circumstances than our routine living.

The *intensity of romance varies* so that there are *quiet* times and *high energy* times. For some people it is hard to describe, for others it's like an invisible energy. A feeling that almost always creates a desire to be special and valuable to another person, as well as a desire for intimate, close companionship. It brings a sense of wanting to nurture and be nurtured; you automatically focus your entire being on the moment. There are peak moments of great romantic intensity, such as in erotic physical activity. But there are major portions of time when romance is no more intense than a quiet conversation, a smile or a gentle touch. *It is an emotional stirring shared enthusiastically by two people.* Examples might include: (1) creating a "secret signal" just between the two of you, and then signaling it back at an unexpected event or time; (2) a wife baking her husband's favorite pie with just the right amount of tartness; (3) the wife entering a room that has an unexpected big bouquet of flowers sitting on the coffee table, just for her; (5) sexy notes put in his lunch box; or (6) mushy notes left on her pillow just before he leaves for work. These actions keep the spark of romance in our marriages.

Here are some hints for you to make plans that differ from your routine lifestyles. Here are some hints for those of you who like to *plan* romance. Wives are more creative than husbands, but this is for both of you.

1. Do the *unexpected*
2. Make a *date*
3. Do something *impractical*
4. Romance involves *daily acts* of care, concern, love, speaking our partner's love language, and listening and giving each other your personal attention.
5. Romance involves *commitment*

Knowing that every day of your marriage will be full of both highs and lows, both joys and disappointments, feelings that both ebb and flow—having that understanding, and accepting it, will make your romance survive.

Such acts convey a message of acceptance and thoughtfulness to your spouse. You see, true romance begins *in your mind*, not "in your glands."

Intimacy

For true love and romance to exist in a marriage, *intimacy must be present.* Only 20% of married couples reach a level of intimacy that every soul cries out for. Intimacy is a special emotional closeness that allows an open communication of feelings, sensations, and motives. It is to "uncover" one's self without fear of moral condemnation or rejection. This intimate closeness describes a personal and private interaction between a husband and wife on a daily basis. The result of this mutual commitment creates a mutual love

117

response that produces a romantic attitude of the heart. It is an exclusive commitment with an intense devotion that allows for no other courtship.

The man and his wife were both naked, and they felt no shame.
(Genesis 2:25 NIV)

Insight: *Ways to Romance Your Spouse*

1. Put your spouse's name on your license plate	27. Carry a picture of her in your wallet
2. Start each day with a hug	28. Do the other person's chores for them
3. Serve breakfast in bed	29. Discuss, encourage, and relive each other's dreams
4. Say "I love you" every time you part	30. Commit a public display of affection
5. Compliment freely and often	31. Give loving massages with scent oils
6. Appreciate and *celebrate* your differences	32. Start a love journal and record your special moments
7. Live each day as if it is your last	33. Share and calm each fears
8. Write unexpected love letters	34. Don't accept a social engagement without asking the other spouse
9. Give your mate a giant poster of yourself	35. Ask her to marry you again
10. Go on a date once a week	36. Say "Yes"
11. Send flowers for no reason	37. Plant a tree together in celebration of a special event
12. Accept and love each other's family and friends	38. Be your spouse's biggest fan
13. Make little signs that say "I love you" and post them all over the house	39. Give the love your spouse wants
	40. Give the love you want to receive
14. Go for walks and smell the roses	41. Show interest in the other's work and hobbies
15. Kiss unexpectedly	42. Work on a project together
16. Seek out beautiful sunsets together	43. Go to bed early and take turns reading the Bible
17. Plan a "surprise" get-away for both	44. Seek out a moonlight night in your own backyard
18. Be forgiving, and apologize sincerely	
19. Respect each other	45. Have a picnic indoors on a rainy day
20. Hold hands when walking	46. Drink toasts to love and commitment
21. Never go to bed mad	
22. Flirt with your partner at a social event	47. Put your partner first in your prayers
23. Let her cry in your arms	48. Kiss each other good night
24. Make the bed together	49. Do something arousing at an unexpected moment
25. Bless your spouse in a prayer	
26. Laugh at his jokes	50. Sleep like "spoons"

To be truly intimate is scary and leaves us feeling vulnerable. It sets us up for possible rejection of the person we reveal ourselves to be. It lowers our protective defenses as we reveal our "real and intimate secret self," including our weaknesses and faults. The blessings of intimacy for couples that have worked at it, brings an accomplishment of fully accepted feelings about each other that could only be gained through exposing their emotional nakedness. Does intimacy come with the marriage ceremony? Yes, it does. In the embodiment of the covenant vows and promises we spoke to each other, there were unspoken boundaries for behavior and actions that applied only within the marriage arena. But as we mentioned before, the covenant words spoken in a state of high excitement can often leave insignificant impressions on most couples. Intimacy, for them is not automatic. Although intimacy is a deep-seated need in our physical make-up, it still needs to be a learned behavior for most people. We must work at it as a painter does to create a thing of beauty.

Prayer is the first step toward marital intimacy. It has been said that the level of your prayer relationship to Jesus will be the level upon which you will function in conversational intimacy with your spouse. Learning to pray together, out loud, as we will discuss in chapter 8, becomes a blessing. For when you pray together, communication barriers are broken down, our own wills are made more pliable, and our heart reach out to our spouses. When couples become sensitive to each other's needs through prayer and discuss the differences openly, adjustments are made and each partner achieves satisfaction. We begin to touch each other's lives with the gift of emotions and trust. We begin to really know each other, and that one-flesh separation gap starts to close. We do become "one." As long as two people remain married they will need to define and redefine their styles of loving because our needs change over the years. The safeguard that protects us as we open ourselves to one another is God's love. God can fill the needs that are lacking in our lives, and free us to love in a biblical way. The vehicle for creating and maintaining intimacy is communication. The act of communication is the means by which we get to know another person.

Learning communication skills is of utmost importance when we are sharing facts and information with others. We need to practice balance in sharing ideas and opinions, particularity when we enter into an area of our own beliefs, concerns, and personal experiences. Maturity tells us that we don't talk to our bosses like we talk to our children. And, just as important, a spouse should not share intimate moments of flirtation with the office secretary in the absence of his wife. When we share our innermost feelings outside the marriage, confusion happens between our heart and mind, especially if the content of the conversation is intimate. Intimate conversation is reserved for your marriage partner only. This requires that all conversation be adjusted according to the person or persons to whom the conversation is directed. Oftentimes we fail to set needed limits on the intimacy of our words when we are talking to persons other than our spouse. While there is a proper conversational setting for friends, there is a deeper quality reserved for our mates.

We must keep intimacy between our spouse and ourselves! We must strive hard to protect it, because intimacy can occur outside of a marriage commitment and without the element of physical love. When we start sharing our hearts with another person outside our marriage, this kind of intimacy leads to what we often call "soul ties." Soul ties such as: our children, family members or even our pastor is an acceptable relationship as long as they don't interfere with the needs of your spouse. A "soul" tie that binds you mentally or emotionally to *any other relationship* is ungodly and needs to be broken. This includes relationships with previous spouses or children and other family members of blended families. For example, you may need to deal with a previous spouse regarding children, or you may continue family ties after a divorce, but any emotional and mental ties that place your marriage in second place will have to be severed. Severing soul ties does not necessarily mean ending the relationship, it means placing boundaries, building a hedge around your marriage relationship that prevents and excludes outside influences on your behavior toward each other.

If you and your mate aren't living according to God's Plan, you're destined to experience the disease that causes intimacy and romance to die. That disease is *isolation*! Every marriage is going in one of two directions: either toward *intimacy* or toward *isolation*. Your marriage will naturally move toward a state of isolation from any or all of the following: "a busy calendar," or tending to the wants of your children, or from just plain "neglect." Our marriages can be crippled by boredom and apathy. But when we begin to touch each other's lives with the gift of emotions and trust, we begin to intimately know each other, and that one-flesh separation gap starts closing. As long as two people remain married they will need to define and redefine their styles of affection because our needs change over the years. The safeguard that shields us as we open ourselves to one another is God's love. God fills the needs that are lacking in our lives, and free us to love in a biblical way.

Love + Intimacy + Submission = Romance

This formula is just for "one-flesh" covenant marriage. It does not apply to other relationships, because "intimacy" and "submission" have boundaries that are biblically specific to marriage.

For your homework we are going to do something different. We are going to have each of you, write a love letter to your spouse. All the paperwork is included in this book. Let's make a memory!

Here is a little something, precious ones, to read to each other before you actually start to write your love letter.

120

Once in a Lifetime

Once in a lifetime, you find someone special. Your lives intermingle and somehow you know this is the beginning of all you have longed for. A love you build on, a love that will grow...

Once in a lifetime, to those who are lucky, a miracle happens, and dreams all come true...

I know it can happen—it happened to me—for I found my "once in a lifetime" with you!

With all my love.

Closing Prayer

We offer up to you, dear Father, a heart full of thanksgiving for your love, commitment, and mercy to us, that you would care enough to design a covenant one-flesh marriage full of joy and dignity. Marriage is a wedding gift from you, placed in the hearts of all man, and considered by you to be pure and chaste in wedded love. Renew our minds and soul to the beauty of married bliss. Holy Spirit, teach us how to show intimacy and romance to our spouse as you intended. We thank you for all these marital feelings and we give all praise and honor and glory to you. Amen.

Chapter 5: No Intimacy? No Romance!
Summary and Applications for Marriage

- Sex is a wedding present that honors and glorifies God when practiced as worship.

- Sensual love—"sex"—between a husband and his wife is, in fact, designed by God and to the glory of God. Many Bible commentaries even call it "an act of worship."

- What we *believe* about "love," whether *true* or *false* in reality, greatly affects the outcome of the marriage.

- Love + Intimacy and Submission = God's formula for true romance in the marriage.

- Intimacy was designed by God to produce life for our spirit, soul and physical unity.

- Every marriage is going in one of two directions: toward intimacy, or toward isolation.

- Intimacy when practiced is another form of "bonding" for a married couple.

- The level of your intimate prayer relationship to Jesus will be the level upon which you will function in intimacy with your spouse.

Visit our website for this book, at **www.NotYourEnemy.info**, where you will be welcome to ask questions or make comments. Enjoy!

Let's Make a Memory!

Husband's Instructions on the Night of Love Letters

Remember you are making a memory wife, something that is just between you and her. Women know men don't really care to sit down and write out their feelings, but when you do this for her, it will touch their heart. This can become a "bonding" experience for the both of you.

Things to Do

1. Be fresh for the evening you have selected to write your love letters. Discuss with her what evening would be best. Then come home early to show your eagerness to share this time with her alone.

2. Offer baby-sitting money if you handle the budget. Discuss with her where to do the letter writing, home or someplace else.

3. Keep the letter writing directions hidden from your wife until the night you both have selected to do the writing. Women love surprises.

4. On the night of the letter writing, bring home some flowers. Have a flower vase tucked away and fix the flower arrangement, yourself. She'll love it.

5. On the night of the reading, get into some comfortable clothes and slippers.

6. Remember you are the "priest" of your home appointed by Jesus Christ. This is a moment of intimacy to be remembered.

7. Know that God is pleased with the gift He has given you—sex.

Let's Make a Memory!

Wife's Instructions on the Night of Love Letters

It is important that you show your husband how much you love him at times such as this! Make this evening "special"—just between you and him.

Things to Do

1. Find a baby sitter. Give yourselves a couple of hours alone. Suggestions: go to a motel, send the kids to the show, or have the kids stay overnight elsewhere.

2. If you stay at home, pick a comfortable room you both like where you can sit together. Discuss before hand, with your husband, where he would feel most comfortable! If you really want to make a memory, and this pattern leads to sex try the kitchen table, the living room floor (take a bunch of pillows), or if you can, go out on the patio or grass area where the wonderful feeling of flesh against your skin, feels the grass.

3. Buy "scented" candles and use them as soft lighting in the room.

4. Turn off the phone, and the front/back lights. Turn off all other lights in the house. Close all drapes and blinds (keeps visitors away).

5. Prepare liquid refreshment and snacks on a table close by where you two have decided the letter writing will be.

6. Get into something comfortable, you can be creative with your apparel— remember you are making a memory.

Thinking It over...

Let's Make a Memory!

Marriage Takes Three

If tomorrow never comes,
Will you know how much I love you?
If my time on earth were through,
Would the love I gave you do,
If tomorrow never comes?

Love Letter to My Wife

_____

_____

_____

_____

_____

_____

_____

_____

_____

_____

_____

Thinking It over...

Let's Make a Memory!

Marriage Takes Three

If tomorrow never comes,
Will you know how much I love you?
If my time on earth were through,
Would the love I gave you do,
If tomorrow never comes?

Love Letter to My Husband

_____

_____

_____

_____

_____

_____

_____

_____

_____

_____

Chapter 6
The Bread You Cast

Godly Principle 6:
The Spiritual Law of Sowing and Reaping will ultimately determine the out come of the longevity and quality of our marriage relationship.

I've found a poem, and thought you'd enjoy it as well.

The Clock of Life

> *The clock of life is wound but once and no man has the power*
> *to say just when the hands will stop—the year, the day, the hour.*
>
> *To lose your wealth is bad enough. To lose your health is more.*
> *To lose your soul such tragedy that no man can restore.*
>
> *Today, alone, you call your own to do with as you will.*
> *Don't count upon tomorrow, friend, the hands may then be still.*

Our words, attitudes, and actions will return to us.

My grandmother used to say, "The bread you cast upon the water comes back three fold!" It was a stern statement meant to get my attention. At the age of twelve, I used to try and picture what that would look like. I could imagine myself at the water's edge as I broken off pieces of Grandmother's home baked bread and threw it out onto the waves. The bread would toss here and there by the waves, often breaking off into smaller pieces. And even though some of the bread would get watered-logged, the "tide of time" would bring most of it back and it seemed more abundant than before as it splashes on the shore. So as a child, I figured out that if I acted in kindness to other people, that same kindness, though now scattered and broken into smaller pieces would surely come back to bless my life many times over. However, if I caused hurt to others; that too, would come back into my life somewhere. There was so much more to grandmother's wisdom than I realized at the time. I've come to know it was her way of telling me about the "good old" spiritual law of sowing and reaping. Let's read it the way our Lord said it through Paul:

> *Do not be deceived: God cannot be mocked. A man reaps what he sows. The one who sows to please his sinful nature, from that nature will reap destruction; the one who sows to please the Spirit, from the Spirit will reap eternal life. Let us not become weary in doing good, for at the proper time we will reap a harvest if we do not give up. Therefore, as we have opportunity, let us do good to all people, especially to those who belong to the family of believers.* (Galatians 6:7-10 NIV)

A man reaps what he sows. That's the "sowing and reaping" law Grandma talked about. We all walk in that law everyday of our lives. Galatians indicates that we *will reap a harvest*, and goes on to say that it is a direct result of what we sow. It doesn't matter if we are unaware of what we are planting, or even if we don't understand it, the *natural law* does not go away or fail to operate.

Memories! All we do, say, and participate in, is recorded in our brain. Good actions toward us are recorded in the pleasure department of our brain bank, as well as the painful words said in "the heat of a moment." I remembering the lengthy periods of strife Larry and I used to have in our earlier years of marriage. I recall that some of those "periods of strife" lasted as much as 3 days; that is what we did on our weekends, or at least once a month! In between those periods of strife, we had wonderful times of sharing and intimacy that made us wonder what were we doing wrong that got us into those moments of strife and general warfare. After a while, it became very apparent that in the midst of the strife, the same issues always came up.

How many of you reading this book, believe that a marriages can be strife-free? Do any of you have a strife-free marriage? Larry and I have many strife-free relationships. But a strife-free relationship within our marriage, nope!

Let's look at a couple of verses in the book of Proverbs to see what God's word says about strife.

> *Better is a dry morsel with quietness than a house full of feasting with strife.* (Proverbs 17:1 NIV)

> *It is to a man's honor to avoid strife, but every fool is quick to quarrel.* (Proverbs 20:3 NIV)

> *Drive out the scoffer, and contention will go out; yes, strife and abuse will cease.* (Proverbs 22:10 NKJV)

> *For as churning the milk produces butter, and as twisting the nose produces blood, so stirring up anger produces strife.* (Proverbs 30:33 NIV)

These verses tells us that there are various ways strife can enter our lives: a quiet sober life has less strife than feasting, foolish men love to quarrel, we shouldn't walk with mockers for their conversation leads to insults, and participating in an angry environment will bring about strife. Even if we tried to lead a quiet life, and didn't walk with foolish or mocking men, I'm afraid reality tells us that periods of strife would still enter our marriage.

Conflict is universal to mankind, and common to all marriages. Being at odds with your spouse extends from individual views of life that are "learned behavior" formed during our formative years. Call it the "anatomy of the flesh." The flesh is self-concerned with its assumed greatness. It readily defends its opinions, striving in any disagreement to restore its prominence as an intelligent being.

Therefore, the goal of marriage is not to be conflict free, but to handle strife correctly when it occurs. All marriages suffer from various degrees of pain and anger brought on by a partner's offense. The choices we make during conflict will either drive you apart or bind you together. When we are hurt by our mate, our flesh-centered natural tendency is to respond in one of two ways: (1) rejection and withdrawal, or (2) anger and aggression that often leads to some form of hostility. For many of us, *anger* is the most common response when conflict occurs because allowing anger usually feels like it *empowers* us. Anger makes us less vulnerable than admitting our hurt which is at the root of our feelings.

Anger that quickly rises up in one's own behavior is usually from *unresolved conflict*. Frequent unresolved issue can cause burnout. When one of the spouses feels that they are explaining, over and over again, why they are bothered by a past action that has not been resolved according to their satisfaction, they feel a failure in expressing themselves. Hence, they keep their hurt feelings at a conscious level that explodes every time the subject comes up. Burnout brings about a sense of dissatisfaction with life, and eventually with our spouse. Unresolved conflict does two things: (1) intensifies future conflicts; and (2) its festering leads to isolation in the marriage. We carry around unresolved conflict either through poor communication skills, or through denial and avoidance of confrontations. The Bible gives us good advice on how to addresses conflict or strife that goes on too long.

> *Be angry, and yet do not sin; do not let the sun go down on your anger.* (Ephesians 4:26 NIV)

This warns us not to go to bed with our mate when there is anger in our hearts, and don't let the sunset find you still in anger. Uncontrolled anger and hurt can lead to bitterness and depression, which leads to conflict, sin, and resentment with God.

In fact, in the beginning of time, when God encountered Cain's act of anger toward Abel, God questioned Cain's anger.

> *If you do what is right, will you not be accepted? But if you do not do what is right, sin is crouching at your door; it desires to have you, but you must master it.* (Genesis 4:7 Amp)

Notice that God Himself instructed Cain, "you must master it [his anger]"!

Blessing-for-Insult

We can handle strife in two ways. The first way is called the "blessing-for-insult" attitude. This attitude comes to us as an example from our Lord Jesus.

> *When they hurled their insults at Him, He did not retaliate; when He suffered, He made no threats. Instead, He entrusted Himself to Him who judges justly.* (1 Peter 2:23 NIV)

Remember, some chapters ago, we learned that through the Holy Spirit, Jesus could do anything in the flesh? It's the same here. All of God's power through the Holy Spirit is available to us when we entrust ourselves to the Father, just as Jesus did. Our trust in the Lord gives us the courage to respond with a *blessing* when we are ill-treated; "a gentle answer turns away wrath" (Proverbs 15:1 NIV). The "blessing-for-insult" approach is based on an attitude of *forgiveness*. Forgiveness is the benefit of the Cross released and applied by our own repentance. Its focus is based on God and His word.

Insult-for-Insult

The second approach for dealing with strife is the "insult-for-insult" attitude, and it is defined as hurting someone with words or actions. This relationship is rooted in an attitude of unforgiveness—a hardened heart. The destructive results of hurtful words and actions are that they cannot be taken back. Words have a way of burning the heart and searing the soul and memory. The insult-for-insult attitude has its focus on "my rights" and "my feelings." It is an outworking of emotional immaturity that behaves by "hiding" (that is, by being non-responsive), or by "stuffing it" (simply running away), or "hurting the other person" (hurt comes from anger).

> *Do not repay evil with evil or insult with insult, but with blessing, because to this you were called so that you may inherit a blessing.*
> (1 Peter 3:9 NIV)

> *Wherefore, my beloved brethren, let every man be swift to hear, slow to speak, and slow to wrath.* (James 1:19 KJV)

This bears repeating. Here, James gives us three good principles to practice in the midst of communicating with one another: (1) be quick to listen; (2) be slow to speak; and (3) be slow to become angry.

Principles of Sowing and Reaping

A principle, as we all have learned in a high school Science class, tells us that there are certain natural elements that have a predictable outcome. So, as we study the principles of sowing and reaping, it is helpful to apply these principles to our own behavior.

In order for us to sow anything, we must have seeds. Examples of *seeds* in our behavior are: words we speak, tone of voice, attitudes we display, and actions we choose to take. There are really only two kinds of seeds.

1. **Good seeds:** Good seeds bear good fruit and come from the word of God. It is the work of the Holy Spirit to bring us into alignment with His gifts of mercy, grace, forgiveness, and love.

2. **Bad seeds:** Satan is always willing to offer us seeds of hate, anger, death and destruction from his weed bag.

But we have a choice. We can sow seeds that can be a blessing or a seed that can become a weed! There are no neutral seeds.

Principle 1

This principle says that the place where our seed falls is on "the soil of the heart." The condition of the heart is a very serious matter. Let's listen to one of Jesus' parables.

> Listen! A farmer went out to sow his seed. As he was scattering the seed, some fell along the path, and the birds came and ate it up. Some foil on rocky places, where it did not have much soil. It sprang up quickly, because the soil was shallow. But when the sun came up, the plants were scorched, and they withered because they had no root. Other seed fell among thorns, which grew up and choked the plants, so that they did not bear grain. Still other seed fell on good soil. It came up, grew and produced a crop, multiplying thirty, sixty, or even a hundred times. (Mark 4: 3-8 NIV)

Jesus explains the parable:
1. The farmer is the word of God
2. The scattering of the seed represents the world
3. The various kinds of soil are the conditions of the heart

You can read this for yourself in Matthew 13:18-23. It can be understood this way: A sower went forth to sow the seed. He was sharing the gospel, the words of God, and he comes upon the first person, who has a hardened heart and doesn't believe; thus the birds came and ate up the seed. The sower comes upon a second person with a heart than doesn't have much faith. The faith stayed a little while but when the sun came up the next morning, they burned and withered away. The third person the sower encountered had the soil filled with thorns, or better said, "a heart full of the cares of this world." The thorns sprang up and choked the seed. Ah, but the forth person had the soil of a good heart. The seed fell on good soil, and they heard and understood. Their deeds brought much spiritual fruit. The crops will yield thirty, sixty, and a hundred more than what was sown.

Principle 2

We must prepare the soil (heart)...
- For *ourselves*: Prayer and reading the word
- For *others*: Intercession prayer and spiritual warfare

As we discussed before, there is no neutral seed. Seeds are either good seeds or bad seeds. This principle involves the act of sowing two kinds of seeds.

> Keep my decrees ... "Do not plant your field with two kinds of seeds ... " (Leviticus 19:19 NIV)

Leviticus says that we are not to plant our fields with two kinds of seed. What does God mean by "two kinds of seeds"? Here is a hint:

> *Do not ... put tattoo marks on yourselves, I am the Lord.*
> (Leviticus 19:28 NIV)

Now, You must be wondering, at this point, what does one verse have to do with the other? Bear with me.

The Leviticus verse clearly tells us not to tattoo our bodies, yet how many times do we see children at fairs or even school events wearing tattoos? We may know this verse, and in wanting to obey God's word, we forbid our teenagers to tattoo their body. Yet some parents and grandparents see no harm in letting their children display "washable" tattoos on their body. There is a mixed message here that is sent to the children. Two different seeds are being planted, producing a harvest that is the beginning for children to feel either confused about the word of God, or the beginning of accepting permanent tattoos.

Principle 3

The Law of Sowing and Reaping is that *you will always reap in kind what you sow*. Since our living is accomplished through the use of words, actions and attitudes, it is imperative that we become aware of what kind of seeds we are planting. We are always sowing into someone's life—our children, our spouse, our in-laws, our families, and all people around us. As we become more aware of the seeds we are planting, we will realize that we plant good seeds and we plant bad seeds.

Principle 4

This principle tells us that *the harvest always come in a different season than the sowing*. We know that from farmers. They plant their tomato bushes in spring and harvest them in summer, and they don't expect to harvest the crop any earlier than its time. We, too, should not be too eager to dig into the soil to see how the seeds are doing. The seed comes to life from a protected environment that has had its soil prepared. What we can do while the season is in progress, is water it with God's word. We can even fertilize the crop with our actions.

> *As the body without the spirit is dead, so faith without deeds is dead.*
> (James 2:26 NIV)

Sow some *seeds of action* upon your seed of words. They go together, as God's words are practical and of good use in all situations.

As your planted seed began to appear, keep watering them. In the early sprout stage, your seed may not appear to be what you expected to see. Don't lose hope when it does not appear as what you have sown. Give it time to mature. There may be times that you don't recognize the harvest because you expected something "different." *Example:* The expected harvest from planting seeds of love may not appear in harvest form as we might expect because "love" comes in so many different colors. However, you are guaranteed a harvest of love when you plant a seed of love.

Principle 5

This states that *the harvest will produce more than we sow*. This preserves the selective choice of future crops of the same kind. With each seed that is sown, the crop springs up with the same kind of seed. The new self-planted seeds now continue to harvest the same crop. One poppy seed when replanted produces thousands of poppy seed plants. This principle works with bad seeds as well as good seeds. Bad seeds such as gossip, harsh words, or unkind acts don't just die at first exposure they multiply and ripple the landscape.

As we examine these principles of sowing and reaping, it is easy to see why *there are areas* in our marriages that have spiraled downward through the years. If we have been ignorantly sowing seeds of discontent, reaping the harvest, re-sowing the same seed, and reaping greater destruction. It is no wonder things that once were small areas of irritations have become major areas of contention. Satan, the old peddler of bad seeds, has blinded us to the cause of our hurt and unresolved conflicts. So, in self-defense we sow seeds of pride, arrogance, and self-righteousness that are rooted in envy and selfish ambition. Satan will give us as many seeds to sow as we are willing to receive.

In conclusion, we must pay attention during the growing season of the good seeds, and accept the fact that there will be weeds growing amidst the good plants. In recognizing the source of those weeds, we can call them for what they are: "unresolved conflicts." We know they originated from the festering conflicts of the past that just doesn't seem to go away. Those persistent strong weeds can choke out the new seedlings" growth. We must resolve to "burn" them so that they will lose their power of intensity when any new conflicts arise. To resolve old conflicts requires *loving confrontation*.

A loving confrontation is an arena of seed planting, good seed planting. Those of us who still have some unresolved conflict from the past, must step into that arena of mutual conflict and scratch up the soil until all the weeds are gone. Speak seeds of love. Show seeds of action by carefully considering the right timing, setting and other pressures. Spare nothing to resolve past conflicts.

As we recognize areas where we have sown poorly, we must be very careful not to come under Satan's condemnation. Instead, we should recognize those areas of bad seed plantings and simply repent. *Repentance* is the "number one weed killer." Spread that repentance everywhere a poor harvest crops up. Do not be discouraged. Eventually the undesirable crops will be choked out and replaced by the new crop of good seeds that are coming up beside them.

Peacemakers who sow in peace raise a harvest of righteousness.
(James 3:18 NIV)

God can change a lifestyle of strife. Our Lord will restore those areas where the bad crops were. Discover what seeds you sowed to produce those good crops, and carefully select more of those seeds of the same type so that you can continue to produce a good harvest. Patrol your marriage garden everyday. Nourish and water everyday. If anything begins to grow that is not of God, repent.

> He replied, "Every plant that my heavenly Father has not planted will be pulled up by the roots." (Matthew 15:13 NIV)

See examples of "good seeds" in "Husband's Seeds to Grow" and "Wife's Seeds to Grow" on the next two pages.

Closing Prayer

Dear Father in Heaven, we give praise and glory to you for showing us your Spiritual Law of Sowing and Reaping. We thank you for showing us how to respond when we are ill-treated, as was your Son, Jesus Christ. Who did not give Insult-for-Insult, but gave His blood, a great blessing, for the insult of our sins before you. By your power, Holy Spirit, work in our hearts a desire to follow in Christ example. Bring our focus down the path of the Cross where the forgiveness that was granted to us, flows in repentance to others for the strife we have and do cause others. Give us a hunger and a yearning for a strife-free marriage. Amen.

Husband's Seeds to Grow*

Think of your wife as a beautiful flower, who needs a specific amount of sunshine, nutrient and water to flourish. You need to discover who she really is, especially as she changes from year to year.

1. Your wife needs to feel that she is very valuable in your life, more important than your mother, your children, your friend, your job, and even your secretary.

2. When your wife is stressed out and hurting, she needs to know that you are willing to share an intimate moment of comfort without explanations or giving lectures.

3. She needs open and unobstructed communication.

4. She needs to be praised so she can feel a valuable part of your life.

5. She needs to feel free to help you without fearing retaliation and anger.

6. She needs to know that you will defend and protect her.

7. She needs to know that her opinion is so valuable that you will discuss decisions with her, and act only after carefully evaluating her advice.

8. She needs to share her life with you in every area—home, family, and outside interests.

9. She needs you to be the kind of man her son can follow and her daughter would want to marry.

10. She needs to be tenderly held often, just to be near you, apart from times of sexual intimacy.

*Points 1 through 10 are taken from *If Only He Knew* by Gary Smalley, © 2012 by Gary Smalley and used by permission of Zondervan. www.zondervan.com.

Wife's Seeds to Grow

Trust God that He has brought you the most perfect man. A man that God will lead in protecting you, a man that God will train to be the priest and prophet of your home and family. This man will love you and receive you as a fine jewel from his God.

1. Do you as the woman consistently seek to be a helper to your man?

2. Is your husband secure in his role a leader because you are not trying to fulfill that role yourself?

3. Have you voluntarily placed yourself in submission to your husband?

4. Is one of your highest priorities an awareness of and familiarity with your husband's dreams?

5. Do you boast about your husband to others and consistently portray him in a positive fashion?

6. Do you frequently ask what kind of help your husband needs?

7. Do you make your husband aware of your delight in discovering how you can blend your strength with his in order to aid him significant ways?

8. As the wife, have you learned to submit to your husband even if he is wrong?

9. Do you pray for your husband regarding all matters?

10. Even though your husband is an imperfect man, do you still show him respect in his role and office as the husband and leader of the home?

Chapter 6: The Bread You Cast
Summary and Applications for Marriage

1. Conflict (strife) is common to all marriages. The goal is to handle it correctly when it occurs and not let it drive a wedge in the marriage.

2. Two ways to handle strife: blessing-for-insult, or insult-for-insult.

3. Both partners must work at correcting "unresolved conflicts" of the past.

4. The spiritual law of sowing and reaping is real. We may be ignorant of its operation, but nevertheless, the law prevails, and its operation determines the outcome of all our relationships.

5. Principles of sowing and reaping.

    - The condition of the soil of the heart

    - To prepare the soil of the heart

        - In my own heart: Pray and read the word

        - In the hearts of others: Intercessory prayer and spiritual warfare

    - Examples of seeds: *words*, *attitudes*, and *actions*

    - Seeds are *not neutral*; there are "good seeds" and "bad seeds"

    - Do not plant *both* good seeds and bad seeds

    - You and I always reap "in kind" (in the same kind of seed we plant)

    - Harvest comes in a different season than planting

    - Harvest always produces more than we sowed, in good soil

    - Repentance is a weed killer

6. Only God can change a lifestyle of strife—with His power.

Visit our website for this book, at **www.NotYourEnemy.info**, where you will be welcome to ask questions or make comments. Enjoy!

We discussed the various ways we can plant seeds, *good* and *bad* seeds, by our *words*, *attitudes* or *actions*. The *harvest* is in direct relationship to what we've *planted*. Good seeds result in a good harvest. Bad seeds result in a bad harvest. There are no neural seeds. Take the time to examine one of each. As you are doing the following exercise, think of situations between you and your spouse.

1. Wife: I remember a good time when my husband: _____

_____

The "seeds" my spouse was planting were in the form of
☐ *Words* spoken
☐ An *attitude*/body language
☐ An *action* done

The harvest was: _____

2. Husband: I remember a good time when my wife _____

_____

The "seeds" my spouse was planting were in the form of
☐ *Words* spoken
☐ An *attitude*/body language
☐ An *action* done

The harvest was: _____

3. Give examples of "bad seeds" planted.

Husband: I remember when I _____

My seeds were _____

I reaped _____

Wife: I remember when I _____

My seeds were _____

I reaped _____

The seeds of strife and conflict come from the crops the enemy planted in our minds and find their way into our *words*, *attitudes* and *behaviors*. Discuss with your mate the answers you both have filled in.

•   The offender needs to seek forgiveness.

- The offended needs to grant forgiveness.

In seeking and granting forgiveness, pray your own prayer together, or this prayer:

> *"Lord God, Heavenly Father, giver of all good gifts, ever faithful to receive repentance and grant forgiveness, I offer up to you my sin of wrong against my spouse and you. I am sorry for the hurtful feelings I have caused in my spouse. I know that I have hurt my mate deeply, and I do not wish to hurt my spouse, again, in this manner. As I ask my loved one for forgiveness, I so do ask you, Lord. Change my life, my attitude and action so that we may walk the path you've set before us. Grant that all unresolved conflicts from the past are dead, and we are free to be honest and open before each other. Amen."*

Continue to remember the harvest of the "good seed." Thank God for the "good seeds" and ask His continued blessings on the planting.

4. Write down areas in your spouse's garden that you intend to plant good seeds. Discuss with each other the areas you need *uplifting and positive feedback.*

Husband fill in for your wife: Wife fill in for your husband:

1. _____   _____

   _____   _____

   _____   _____

2. _____   _____

   _____   _____

   _____   _____

3. _____   _____

   _____   _____

   _____   _____

Chapter 7
Repentance, Forgiveness, and Reconciliation

Godly Principle 7:
Forgiveness is a command from God.

This is the very heart of God. Our Heavenly Father set the standards, and His Son, Jesus Christ paid the price for the way of all reconciliation, weather it be your marital spouse, or another person. The Holy Spirit witnesses to and helps us conform to the standards God Himself met at the Cross.

Forgiveness is the benefit of the Cross, released and applied by our own repentance!

A Mother's Day Crisis

I can see myself a few Sundays ago, sitting in church on Mother's Day. It was 8:30 AM in the morning, on a chilly windy morning, unusual for the month of May in California. I yawned and realized that we have become, somewhat, accustom to this early Sunday morning service time. It was the first of three morning worship and sermon presentations, and the singing always started promptly at 8:30 AM sharp. We had started going to this service due to the large membership that was growing in our community. The whole purpose of our attendance at this early timeslot was to leave empty seats in the later services for newcomers. Hence, we were always rushing to get to church even earlier, to have extra time to spare so we could socialize with new people or old friends we saw only once a week.

To accomplish this, we had to get up around 6:30 AM—a time almost too early to be quite wide awake—and leave the house before 8:00 AM. I can still hear Larry yelling up the staircase to my bathroom, "You've got five minutes!" and myself, yelling back sharply, "I will be ready when I am ready!"

However, this Mother's Day morning, I was wide-awake, anticipating from my husband a "Happy Mother's Day, honey," along with flowers and a cheery greeting card.

When I had arrived home from a three-day Christian women's retreat at Mount Hermon, in the beautiful redwoods near Santa Cruz, I felt convinced that my husband had missed my presence, and that in his own sweet way he would celebrate my homecoming by preparing an "early" Mother's Day surprise. Larry and I always worked hard at being "one flesh," and "hammered home" that God-given principle in our marriage workshops. Living a covenant marriage was important to us. I was so sure that he would surprise me when I got home from the retreat. During the ride home, I almost bragged out loud to my two closest retreat friends what I was expecting when we get home.

As Linda drove toward my home to drop me off, I was mentally "smelling" the flowers that would be on the dining room table, waiting just for me. I was the first one in the car pool to be dropped off, and as we drove up the driveway, I saw my husband working in the garage with the garage door wide open. He looked up, smiling from his work and walked out to greet each one of us cheerfully. He helped get my luggage from the trunk, and remarked that he wanted to be home to welcome us because the "other" husbands were still at work. I thought "isn't he wonderful!" I rushed into the house to see my flowers. I stopped short—there was nothing on the dining room table. A little disappointed, I shrugged it off, thinking he might have been so busy that he was saving the "cheer me up routine" for the real Mother's Day.

The next day as we were driving to church I felt a cloud of gloom coming over me. Larry hadn't even said, "Happy Mother's Day, honey." Let alone presented me with flowers and a card. The children, who lived quite a distance, hadn't called either. As my expectations began to flatten, I became more and more melancholy. I was feeling sadness and depression in my spirit. My thoughts began to wander in search for reasons why Larry had neglected me. Soon my thoughts were accusing me of being a "bad mother" and a "bad wife" or why else would anyone be so spiteful as to neglect honoring any mother on this of all day—Mother's Day. What had I done as a mother to my sons that they would choose to show such neglect of my "motherly position" on this day? And my husband, what had I done to him? The fear of their rejection was growing. I could hear my heart cry, "God, please help me. My lack of joy on this day is failing me and it is growing into bitterness."

I knew my two grown boys were very busy with their own lives. I also knew that if I would hear from them at all, it probably wouldn't be until later in the day. Rarely would they call, but once in a while I'd get an e-mail or two. My daughter, who lives six states away, had sent me a wonderful book by Bruce Wilkerson yesterday. She always was prompt and on time—never left me waiting to see if she would remember me. My daughter-in-law, Larry's only child, had never sent me anything since Larry and I had been married, so there were no expectations there. In past years I shrugged it off as "just kids" behavior, even thought my "mother's heart" missed their attention. My husband had always taken their place by comforting me on these "special" days. He knows my past hurts. He'll make up for it; he always has! Thank God for sending me such a good husband!

As the worship time of singing praises to God came to a close, and before the day's sermon began, our pastor gave call for us to bring our concerns to the altar. This act of physically walking up to the altar and prayerfully giving my cares and woes to Jesus, trusting in Him for all things, was my favorite time during the whole service. We walked up to the altar to pray in our customary manner. I listened closely to every word my husband prayed for us as we directed our pray to God in our one-flesh unity. I would always feel joy when

144

Larry gave "a thanksgiving prayer" to God for me as his wife. But these words were absent today.

What was going on? I had been on a spiritual "high mountain top" for three wonderful days and now I was thrown into a valley that seemed worse than death. Not hearing my own husband pray for our marriage was the last straw—that's all it took. I could feel my whole being plummeting into desolation. I withheld my words of thanksgiving to God for our marriage. I groped for words in my prayer. I kept crying in my heart, "Jesus, Jesus, forgive me. I don't know where this is taking me, but I'm so hurt, I can't pray for anyone close to me." And finally, after a long period of silence, the only thing I could mumble was to ask God to bless all the mothers in our church who feel the hurts and pain I am feeling at this moment. There was no joy in me.

I was so busy with feelings of desertion, and recalling all the other times this had happened to me in some form or another that I didn't even hear the sermon. Feelings of isolation grew, not only against my children, but against Larry too. How could he ignore me like that? No flowers, no card, no happy Mother's day. I felt a pity party coming on, and I wasn't about to forgive anyone of them for all I've been through these last twenty-four hours! It's embarrassing to expect love and receive nothing, even if it is in your mind and heart. My embarrassment and guilt over expecting my family to honor me on this Mother's Day, had lead me to anger over my own expectations. The anger turned into real resentment toward each one of them. I could feel my anger turning into bitterness and rejection, now, heading their way. I didn't recognize the hardness that had set in my heart until Larry invited me to a "Mother's Day brunch" after church, to which I responded with a hollow, "No." Somehow I sensed I was headed toward "marital strife" and I was beginning to embrace it.

"The Morning after the Day Before"
After a long, silent breakfast, I knew a discussion with Larry about my hurts was needed in order to prevent any future unresolved conflict. I began slowly by asking him, in a self-pity way, almost begging tone of voice, "Why didn't you give me a Mother's Day card?"

The look on Larry's face was one I didn't expect. Shocked, holding his surprise, he questioned, "Don't you remember? I gave it to you while you were going through the mail when you got home yesterday from your retreat. You even said it was a wonderful card."

I was taken back. I had forgotten. Wow! Well, I'm sure there weren't any flowers on that dining room table—at least, I didn't remember seeing any flowers. Am I going crazy? I promptly changed the subject, and in an interrogating yet somewhat doubting voice, I demanded, "Then, why didn't you buy me flowers?"

"Honey," he answered, "I'm sorry, I really was going to, but I was so late leaving the dock that I was too late to stop by the store and get you flowers. I wanted to be home for you when you and the ladies came home. I'm so sorry, do you forgive me?"

I began to feel uncomfortable. Yet I had to know one more thing. In an almost quiet, whispering tone I ask, "Why, didn't you pray for our marriage?" He hung his head, "I'm sorry for that too, I thought you were mad at me for trying to rush you out of the house when I yelled, 'You've got five minutes.' "

The Victorious Solution

I was feeling so much shame and guilt by now, the tears rushed out of my eyes and down my face. Larry came around the breakfast table and put his arms around me. I cried, I sobbed. I had been wrong about everything. I begged his forgiveness. I asked him to forgive me for creating a "wedge" of isolation between us. I asked his forgiveness for my night and morning of silence. I asked his forgiveness for thinking bad thoughts of him.

Larry interrupted my confession of sins in a reassuring tone, "Babe, those thoughts were of the evil one, Satan. You were in spiritual warfare. Satan wanted to attack our marriage; he knows how important our marriage is to God. Every time I hear words of slander against you in my mind, I tell Satan to get out. And I renew my mind by thinking of some of my favorite Bible verses."

I felt renewed and spiritually refreshed. We both hugged and Larry led us in prayer. He prayed for repentance for both of us: for my spirit of pride, and for his lack of priority in meeting his wife's needs. We repented, both to God and each other, we forgave each other, and we were reconciled once again in our triune marriage.

Satan doesn't leave us alone just because we strive to live in a *one-flesh, covenant, triune marriage.* He prowls around, looking for the slightest crack in our spiritual armor, always out to destroy us, and he is always throwing his fiery darts at the "heart" of God's children.

In areas of forgiveness, we forget the bond of salvation and its foundation: repentance in and for our sinfulness and Christ's forgiveness at the Cross! And, in our marriages where we meet strife more than any other place, we are no different. We cannot afford even small moments of unforgiveness in our marriages. Not to forgive is a sin, and yet not to repent is to have no reconciliation. The act of forgiveness is not a "feeling." It is the mental activity of "sending away" the transgressions people do to us. The act of not holding onto the hurts and pains they committed against us. Forgiveness is an act of obedience to God. Never let your spouse "out-forgive" you, or "out-repent" you. Repent and ask forgiveness from your spouse even if you feel you are ninety-nine-percent right. It is better to repent and ask forgiveness than to have strife. Confess it as done and then remember the offense *no more!* Give no hold to Satan in your marriage.

A Covenant Marriage in Strife

We just gave you an example of a real-life situation that happened in our marriage. Do you know that God, also, gives examples on how to treat a covenant marriage that is in strife and needs forgiveness? In God's Old Testament of the Bible, He gives us an illustration of what happened in His own covenant marriage to Israel that is acted out in the real life of one of His prophets; Hosea.

The book of Hosea casts the characters as follows: Hosea represents the role of "God," and Hosea's wife, Gomer, plays the role of God's wife, "Israel." (Turn to the book of Hosea in your Bible and follow along if you can.) God starts the illustration at a pre-nuptial stage before the marriage of Hosea and Gomer and gives the audience a glimpse into the future trials of God's wife in the naming of their children.

Hosea, a youthful prophet of God, was of the same era as Amos, Isaiah, and Micah, in about the period of 755-715 B.C. The kingdom of Israel had gone through tribal division; the Northern Kingdom was earmarked "Israel," and the Southern Kingdom "Judah." Hosea's ministry was to the Northern Kingdom, during which King Jeroboam II was enjoying a period of financial wealth and political tranquility.

While enjoying their "freedom from war" time, The Northern Kingdom of Israel was backsliding into gross idolatry. God's bride, the Israel people, no longer loved or worshiped their God. Not one of the nation's nineteen kings after the tribal division was a godly man. God called Hosea to prophesy to the Northern Kingdom of Israel during its last 30 years of nationhood—a prophecy that gave them the future of their life as a nation. Immediately after King Jeroboam II died, Israel began to deteriorate and ran swiftly to its destruction in 722 B.C. In the last 15 or more years Samaria was reduced to rubble and the Israelite people were deported to Assyria.

Hosea's tragic marriage and prophetic words were God's message to Israel during these final chaotic years of its slide to destruction. God drew a parallel between Hosea's marriage to Gomer and God's marriage to Israel. The infidelity of Hosea's wife is recorded as an illustration of Israel's unfaithfulness to God. Gomer runs after other men, while Israel runs after other gods. Gomer commits physical adultery, while Israel commits spiritual adultery. Now that we have had an overview of Israel's history and Hosea's reason for prophesying, let us look at the book of Hosea:

> The beginning of the word of the LORD by Hosea. And the LORD said to
> Hosea, Go take unto thee a wife of whoredoms and children of
> whoredoms: for the land hath committed great whoredom, departing from

the LORD. *So he went and took Gomer ... which conceived, and bare him a son. And the* LORD *said unto him, Call his name Jezreel ... I will avenge the blood of Jezreel ... and will cause to cease the kingdom of Israel ... [Gomer] conceived again and bare a daughter. And God said unto him, Call her name Lo-ruhamah ... Now when she had weaned Lo-ruhamah, she conceived, and bare a son ... Then said God, Call his name Loammi: for ye are not my people and I will not be your God."* (Hosea 1:2-9 KJV)

In these verses, God uses *word images*. For example: (1) Hosea's name in Hebrew means "salvation." God portrays Himself as salvation, not only to Israel, but in the New Testament "to all of the world'; (2) the command to take "an adulterous wife" was a statement of prophesy describing the pre-marital actions of God's covenant bride, the people and nation of Israel; (3) the names of Hosea's children were meant as future predictive signs to Israel on the way God viewed their behavior and what action He would take. The first baby boy was to be named Jezreel, which in Hebrew means "God scatters," and Lo-ruhamah, the female second child, means "not loved." The last baby, who probably did not belong to Hosea, was given the name Lo-Ammi, meaning "not my people" The name itself symbolized the breaking of the covenant marital relationship.

Say ye unto your brethren, Ammi; and to your sisters, Ruhamah. Plead with your mother, plead: for she is not my wife neither am I her husband: let her therefore put away her whoredoms out of her sight, and her adulteries from between her breasts.... (Hosea 2:1-2 KJV)

Chapter 2 of Hosea reflects Hosea's pain and wailing at the desertion of his wife Gomer, he is portraying God's wailing in pain for Israel in her idolatry. Hosea pleads with his children to go to their mother and beg her to stop her adultery. This translates into God calling Hosea to tell the people of Israel to stop their worshiping of other God: idolatry. Gomer runs off and starts a life of physical adultery and immorality, perhaps as a prostitute in the temple of Baal. Her (Israel's) departure from the Lord led not only to false worship, but also to lower moral standards. As life got more debase for Gomer, she was eventually lead into slavery to exist.

Then said the LORD *unto me, Go yet, love a woman beloved of her friend, yet an adulteress, according to the love of the Lord toward the children of Israel, who look to other gods, and love flagons of wine. So I bought her to me for fifteen pieces of silver, and for a homer of barley, and an half homer of barley: And I said unto her, Thou shalt abide for me many days; thou shalt not play the harlot, and thou shalt not be for another man: so will I also be for thee.* (Hosea 3:1-3 KJV)

Chapter 3 depicts Hosea's reconciliation with His wife. It illustrates how God will act in love to Israel. To paraphrase, God says to Hosea, "Go, show your love to your wife again." Hosea is commanded to "go," "express your love," and "care for her again." Hosea had never given up his love for her, just as God had felt, even though his heart was broken. So, in the final stage, Hosea buys her back out of slavery with six ounces of silver, shekels of silver, the price of a slave, and asks for a faithful reconciliation in their marriage.

Throughout the rest of the book, Hosea clearly gives the message that there is a direct relationship between persistent sin and inescapable judgment. Israel finally loses any thread of acclaim as a nation at this point, and doesn't reclaim it back until 1948. But in the story of Hosea, God does remember his covenant to his wife, Israel, and she does repent. The last few chapters of Hosea tell us what God will do to the nations that harm Israel. God does not forget His covenants to His people.

Quite a story, huh? If you were Hosea, what would you have done? How easy would it have been for you to go back and buy Gomer out of her own created debt? Translate that scenario into the year 2013. Would you, could you take most of your next week's paycheck and use it to pay off all your Gomer credit cards, knowing full well the clothes she bought were to lure other men into her bedroom. As your memory reviews the many acts of adultery, and the painful scars they have left on your heart. How would you have acted? Can any of us, consider the real love we had for our spouse at one time, overlook some very real present hurts, and then care enough for that unfaithful one to perform the ultimate act of complete sacrifice at the cost of our own expense?

Sin

What are we to learn from this metaphor? Hosea's marriage was to be an object lesson for the unfaithful Northern Kingdom of Israel. In the book of Hosea, God lays a blueprint for action we must play out if we are to remain in our triune, covenant marriage. The cycle of events that must occur are reflected in the title of this chapter.

Repentance + Forgiveness = Reconciliation

For our purposes we will look at the cycle of events that occur when sin is committed in our marriage:

1. *Offense* is committed
2. *Repentance* is required
3. *Forgiveness* is requested and given
4. *Reconciliation* is achieved

If you will allow me, I'd like to substitute the word *offense* for *sin*. Sin is something we all do daily, whether at work or in our marriages. We are sinful from birth, being born the children of "wrath."

> *Behold, I was shaped in iniquity, and in sin did my mother conceive me.*
> (Psalm 51:5 KJV)

Among whom also we all had our conversation in times past in the lusts of our flesh, fulfilling the desires of the flesh and of the mind; and were by nature the children of wrath, even as others. (Ephesians 2:3 KJV)

From Adam's first sin that poisoned the seed of all future generations; all the rest of mankind was conceived in sin, and that sin is centered in our flesh. In Psalm 51:4, King David confesses that his sin is "ever before" him and in the killing of Bathsheba's husband, his sin was against God, and "God only." However, David is not saying that his sin was not against others, but that it was preeminently against God and His word. To go against God's word through action is to treat the word contemptuously, to scorn it, declaring God to be of little value and unworthy of love and devotion.

Old Testament Sin Management

We know that David was forgiven for his sin. And if this story had been in the New Testament, we all could easily recite his forgiveness "through the blood of Jesus." But David is Old Testament. So how did God deal with David and all of men's sin in the days before the Cross? In all cases of *deliberate sin*, death was the punishment. For sins other than intentional and pre-meditated acts, the offering of sacrifices was regarded as a divine pathway to reconciliation between God and mankind. It was God, Himself, who appointed the giving of sacrifices as an acceptable form of worship to be offered by guilty man. These sacrifices, considered a holy institution in the Old Testament, taught Israel that humans are basically sinful beings whose sins merit death, and in order to achieve atonement for their sins, there must be a substitution.

In the book of Leviticus, there were five *specific sacrificial offerings*, for unintentional sin that required restitution, confession of sin, and cleansing from defilement.

Offerings	Sacrifice was...	Spiritual Significance
Sin offering	Mandatory	To indicate repentance
Guilt offering	Mandatory	To indicate repentance
Burnt offering	Voluntary	To receive forgiveness
Grain offering	Voluntary	To receive forgiveness
Fellowship offering	Voluntary	To be reconciled to God

The sequence of the offerings is what is most important because it illustrates and indicates the *spiritual significance* of the sacrificial system. Let's go through the process.

When an Israelite broke the law, his sin had to be dealt with first; hence, the first offering he was to give was a *sin offering* or *guilt offering*. These were mandatory offerings for *unintentional* sin that required restitution, confession

150

of sin, or cleansing from defilement. The inner man (his spiritual nature) had to recognize that his sin caused a separation between him and God.

> *But your iniquities have separated between you and your God, and your sins have hid His face from you, that He will not hear.* (Isaiah 59:2 KJV)

All of unsaved mankind needs a change of attitude toward its sin. This inner knowledge of wrongdoing is called *repentance*. The act of repentance must come first.

> *Repent ye therefore, and be converted, that your sins may be blotted out When the times of refreshing shall come from the presence of the Lord.* (Acts 3:19 KJV)

First Phase: Repentance

True repentance is a change of mind and attitude, an action that when taken results in a change of one's actions. It is not merely feeling sorry for your sins. There are two Greek words used in the NT to denote repentance (Strong's, *repentance*):

1. *Metamellomai* (met-am-el'-lom-ahee) means "a change of mind," so as to produce regret or remorse on account of sin, but not a change of heart! *Example:* Judas's remorse was so great that he committed suicide.

2. <u>*Metanoeo*</u> (met-an-o-eh'o) meaning "to change one's mind and purpose," as the result of after-knowledge. To reconsider. A change of mind, purpose, and life, to which remission of sin is promised.

Example: Peter's denial of Jesus in Matthew 26:69-75. Jesus' reinstatement of Peter is found in John 21:15-17. Peter was later crucified in Rome under Nero at about the same time Paul was martyred.

While a person may experience emotional grief as they see their sinful actions, this is not true repentance. Repentance will be demonstrated in a conscious choice to change our mind about sin and turn away from it, wanting never to do it again.

True repentance consists of:
1. A godly sense of one's own guilt and sinfulness
2. To hate sin as God hates it, and a turning away from it
3. A comprehension of God's mercy in Christ
4. A determined effort to walk in all of God's ways

Therefore, just as the "sin offering" or "guilt offering" was mandatory, so shall it be mandatory that the first step toward asking for forgiveness from our spouse should be a true spiritual repentance of the heart.

Second Phase: Forgiveness

The act of forgiveness brings into being a *state of atonement*. After the worshiper has dealt with his sin, he now moves onto the second phase in his act of worship by committing himself completely back to God, and voluntarily gives a *burnt offering* or *grain offering*. The physical burnt offering or grain offering was accompanied with the spiritual feeling of being reconciled with God. They recognized God's goodness and His provisions. They felt "cleansed from their sins," in essence, they were forgiven—they were in atonement with God. Their sins had been "covered up" in the blood of the animals that had been sacrificed. *Atonement* means the state of being "one" with God or being reconciled to God. To make atonement is to do that which ceases alienation, allowing reconciliation to be brought about.

Third Phase: Reconciliation

In the third phase, the sinner offers up a voluntary *fellowship offering* which establishes fellowship and communion between the Lord, the priest and the worshiper. Man is now in reconciliation and *fellowship* with God. It is an act of worship.

Fellowship with God consists of our knowing His will and blueprint for our life, being in total agreement with his salvation plan, working toward our own conformity to the image of Jesus Christ, practicing prayer both as a commandment and a way of fellowshipping with God, as well as having mutual affection and joy in his presence.

The sacrificial offerings of the Old Testament were the methods by which God chose until the final sacrifice of Jesus Christ, the new and final covenant! Today, under the new covenant, we see the same elements of the sacrifices in the "Sinner's Prayer": (1) *Confession* (formerly by sin or guilt offering): "I know that I am a sinner" (I understand my sin has separated us); (2) *Repentance* (formerly by burnt or grain offering), "I am sorry"; (3) *Faith* (formerly by fellowship offering), "I believe that Jesus died"; and (4) an *Invitation* (the reconciliation), "I invite you into my heart, and into my life. Please take over my life!" It is through the act of being born that we receive forgiveness and are reconciled with God.

God's Forgiveness

Forgiveness is rooted in the character of God. What, then, happens to our sin against God?

1. They go *out of sight*: "… for thou hast cast all my sins behind thy back." (Isaiah 38:17c KJV)

2. They go *out of reach*: "As far as the east is from the west, so far hath He removed our transgressions from us." (Psalms 103:12 KJV)

    Do you know how far the east is from the west? How do you tell the east from the west? Look at the sun: It rises in the east and set in the west. So, for us in California, the distance from the east where the sun rises to the west where the sun sets is about eight to twelve hours, depending on the

152

season of the year. Wait a minute, God isn't talking about time; He is discussing distance. With curious minds, we would have to figure out a way to start measuring the distance from the east to the west. We would have to start in the east. Hey, where does the east begin? And where does the west stop—at what point on the earth? The North and South Poles have a meeting place at the equator, but it's not the same for the East and the West. And that is God's point exactly! The East *never* meets the West, so God *never* remembers our sin after our repentance.

3. They go *out of mind*: *I, even I, am He that blotteth out thy transgressions for mine own sake, and will not remember thy sins.* (Isaiah 43:25 KJV)

4. They go *out of existence*: *I have blotted out like thick cloud thy transgression, and like a cloud your sins. Return to me, for I have redeemed you.* (Isaiah 44:22 Amp)

God is so good to us. In our repentance and Jesus' forgiveness, we are reconciling to Our Heavenly Father. It is only through realization of our sinful nature and its inability to restore our relationship with God that we understand how badly we need Jesus. We see Him so much more clearly when we see our sins for what they really are: an abomination in the sight of God's glory. Thank God for His sacrifice of Christ, for *He* is our Cross, *He* is our life, *He* is our all!

Natural Man and Forgiveness

Then why, I ask, is it so hard to forgive other people when they offend us? Is it our sinful flesh that refuses to forgive others? Yep, sure it is—that same sinful nature that put Christ on the Cross! I have heard myself say, "I just can't forgive them for what they did to me" when what I really meant was "I *won't* forgive them for what they did to me." From time to time we, in our prideful earthly flesh, get the attitude that the shocking incident they did "to us" is "far worse" than our inability to follow God's commandment concerning forgiveness.

Now, consider this:

> Even if they sin against you seven times in a day and seven times come back to you saying "I repent," you must forgive him. (Luke 17:4 NIV)

Unforgiveness comes from pain, hurt or embarrassment we undergo: set in motion by the words, feelings, or actions of others. We judge some by their actions, while we judge ourselves by our intentions. We judge, or more often misjudge, the significance of the amount of hurt we feel at the moment of the incident. If we stay in this mode too long, the hurt turns to revenge—or worse, a hardened and bitter heart. When the offending person apologizes, it's easier to grant forgiveness. But when the other person is not sensitive to our feelings, and offers no repentance, we tend to keep the hurt to ourselves, rather than confront it. When we get into an uncomfortable place with one another, we want God's judgment for others but mercy for ourselves. And when we

153

continue in our unforgiveness, it brings its own consequences between the offender and the one offended. Eventually, many others will be affected: family, friends, and fellowships. We, often, can avoid people other than our core family when strife arises. However, when we get into a feeling of unforgiveness with our spouse, we need to examine our own hearts and not our spouse's actions when it comes to forgiveness.

Judgment

Very few Christians are aware that there are two kinds of use and interpretation of "judgment": *man's* judgment, and *God's* judgment. Let's look first at man's judgment. *Webster's College Dictionary* (Webster's, *judgment*) cites some *nine definitions* of the word *judgment*. Here are a few: an opinion, estimate, a criticism, or the ability to come to opinions about things and power to compare and decide.

I want to point out two specific examples of how the word *judgment* is expressed in Webster's definition.

Scenario 1

A couple came home late last night from a birthday party that was held down the street at a neighbor's house. They had left their car parked in the driveway. As they approached the home, she heard her husband holler out, "Oh, no!" She watched as he examined the slashed tire.

"Who would do a thing like that? She asked angrily. "I'll bet it was the Smith boy who lives down the street. He's been quite wild lately."

Scenario 2

When the lady saw her husband come home, she was shaken, due to the news she was about to tell him.

"Honey, I went to Betty's house to put flowers on her kitchen table. I wanted them to be a "welcome home" when she comes home from her trip tomorrow. I wanted to leave a note telling her "all was okay" while she was gone; that I had watered all the flowers and had picked up all the papers. As I entered the back door, I heard some noise in her bedroom. I thought she was home, so I ran up stairs and there they were, in bed together. Betty's husband in bed with Silvia!"

They were so embarrassed, and so was I. I felt so awful, I started to cry and ran out of the room. "Honey," I said talking to my husband, "you have to talk with them. That's adultery!"

Scenario 1 and 2 seem, on the surface, to fit Webster's definition of judgment. Each came to an opinion by the power of comparison and the ability to decide. In scenario 1, the tire was slashed—a fact. The Smith boy was going through a mischievous period in life. The woman's conclusion was based on her opinion alone. The Smith boy was not seen doing the "cutting of the tires." She tried to connect the somewhat rebellious behavior of a fifteen-year-old boy with a malicious act, and, hence, made an accusation against his person. In her judgment of this incident, she made a censure of the neighbor and a criticism of the boy. This could have led to character assassination had she shared her opinion with other neighbors. That is *wrong* judgment, and it leads to *sin* on the part of the maker of this kind of judgment—precisely the kind of judgment God warns us about.

> *Judge not, that ye be not judged. For with what judgment ye judge, ye shall be judged: and with what measure ye mete, it shall be measured to you again.* (Matthew 7:1-2 KJV)

However, in scenario 2, this woman based her opinion on some facts. She knew Silvia, and knew she was single. She knew Betty's husband, Jim, and she clearly saw his face, in the bed, in a compromising position called sex. She saw, in action, the sin of adultery. She knew what adultery was, and made the judgment (opinion) that this was adultery occurring before her very eyes. She showed concern enough to ask her husband to go and talk with each of them. We all make judgments every day. Some judgments are good and some are bad, as in the case of scenario one. God knows that we are very quick to give others our own opinions. It is a matter of *pride*. Put more bluntly, we all make judgments on all of life's issues.

Is God telling us not to make judgments? No! In fact, we are told to seek the ability to judge.

> *Teach me good judgment and knowledge: for I have believed Thy commandments.* (Psalm 119:66 KJV)

> *The spiritual man makes judgments about all <u>things</u> but he himself is not subject to any man's judgment.* (1 Corinthians 2:15 KJV)

This verse addresses our attitude toward our Christian brothers and sisters, and their behavior. Jesus is telling us that if we judge others, *the others* will judge us in the same way. He is telling us that the "how" in which we judge people is the same "how" they will judge us! If we judge people unfairly, that is how they will judge us. God would rather we did not even use judgment toward each other, but if we are going to, this is how it will be. It all comes back in the seeds we sow! If we judge family and neighbors fairly, we will be judged by them, in the same method. We can judge our fellow believer, with respect to sin, yet go to him or her "in love" and help them be reconciled to God and their fellow believers by repentance.

Some Christian believers presuppose this passage to be "God's judgment upon us." Actually, He will judge us, but He will use His own form of judgment and in His own setting and timing. God *will not* use the same judgment on us that we use on others. Still others say, "Now, don't judge others or you'll be judged by God." That is not true. This debate among God's children—whether we can escape judgment or not—is a tool of the devil. It is a strategy used by Satan to stop us from making distinctions, decisions and judgments of *any* kind, such as the use of judgment between hell and heaven, or of Satan's own future, or even of the presence of a God! Satan doesn't want us to know any of that. He does not want us to judge people and their behavior. He wants us to be tolerant of all mankind's moral, social, and religious behavior. Then when we abstain from all judgments of sin; we become less sensitive to God's word. We become less active for good in the world. We allow Satan to taint the world with his temptations, and people after people fall into disbelief. We withdraw from teaching our children the morals issues of the Bible, we withhold criticism on the language of their friends and soon we become mute Christians. The witness of the gospel ceases and the world goes to hell. Thank God, He is sovereign and He does control the world, but do not let one of your children be causality.

Yes, we are to make judgments—wise judgments. Judgment comes in attitudes. Our judgments must not be in the flesh, but must come from spiritual discernment. In spiritual discernment, we are aware of the will of God. We need to see and appraise things the way God would. A fair judgment is *honored*, in fact, *needed* for our salvation.

> *For false Christs and false prophets will appear and perform signs and miracles to deceive the elect, if that were possible. So be on your guard ...* (Mark 13:22-23 NIV)

One added thought on *judgment*: Didn't we just say that the Cross forgives *all* sins. Is "judgment" a sin? In some cases, yes. In other cases, no. So in all matters, Jesus' time spent on the Cross *was* for the forgiveness of all sin. I repeat, Jesus died on the Cross for *all* sin.

God's Judgment

When you research the word "judgment" in any Bible dictionary, you will not find any word definitions. You will find headings such as: "Judgment Hall," or "Judgment Seat," "The Final Judgment," and more of the like. All the descriptions in any Bible dictionary will print only what is in the word of God, hence, you can get a quick idea of judgment. You'll learn that God has anointed Jesus to be the final judge. That He does one final judgment and that is in reference to eternal life *with* Him—or eternal Hell *without* Him. God's judgment is life or death, heaven or hell. It is He alone who pronounces judgment upon all men, from Adam to the last living earthly being of this world. For all believers in the Cross of Jesus Christ, judgment means eternal life, for non-believers judgment means damnation. And that is the difference between our judgment and God's judgment. We are only to judge *things (sin), not people*. We are not given the power to damn people to hell, only God can judge people and their actions.

When we come to Jesus and ask for forgiveness in repentance, He forgives us and this seals our reconciliation with Father God. The act of repentance has an element of receiving or the forthcoming of mercy, grace, love, and compassion from God.

Forgiving others is at the very heart of our Christian walk. It is like all commandments, in that we are to do it "as unto the Lord." If and when we find it hard to forgive our spouse, we can ask God to give us some of His forgiveness until it comes more easily to us. When we walk in obedience to God's will for our lives, it is then that our own feelings of pain and anger are overridden by His great love for them and for us.

In examining our hearts for signs of unforgiveness, we also need to make sure that we have not taken up the offense of others: this can be a friend, fellow-worker or a family member. This is very easy to do as husband and wife. If someone, though unwittingly, offends our spouse or our children, we tend to take up their cause. We need to know the difference between "defending" our family and "prideful payback" that leads to meddling quarrels.

> *Like one who seizes a dog by the ears, is a passer-by who meddles in a quarrel not his own.* (Proverbs 26:17 NIV)

Meddling in a quarrel that is not our own is like picking up a dog by the ears. Think of that for a moment. How do you put down a dog that you have picked up by the ears? Anyway you do it you're going to get hurt. Taking up the offense of another is the same thing. It is very difficult to put down. There is only one way to do it. Repent of having taken up the offense in the first place. Help the one offended to forgive. When your spouse is offended, you need to help him or her to forgive. That means, not just feeling sorry for your spouse, but also understanding that he or she has been wounded, and helping them to forgive will bring them healing.

Application to our Marriage

In the power of God there is no obstacle to forgiveness, nor is there a limit to the number of times we are to forgive.

> *I tell you, not seven times, but seventy-seven times.* (Matthew 18:22 NIV)

If our spouse is committing a repetitive sin, we need to be quick to forgive the previous offenses. Each new offense should be treated as though it were the first time. It is imperative that we never bring up past offenses that *we have forgiven them for*, nor speak to others regarding the offenses. The offenses are to be between you and your spouse only (God is included; remember you have a triune marriage).

> *He who covers over an offense promotes love, but who ever repeats the matter separates close friends.* (Proverbs 17:9 NIV)

157

*Therefore, I tell you, her many sins have been forgiven—as her great love
has shown. But whoever has been forgiven little loves little.*
(Luke 7:47 NIV)

Don't dwell on it. Confess it as *done*, then repeat the offense *no more*. If we are
given the opportunity to forgive our spouse often, we can trust that there will
be a return of great love. This is not always possible in our own human power,
but it is possible through the power of God. When we have the Holy Spirit
dwelling within us, He enables us to forgive and trust again.

The act of forgiveness is a sign of spiritual growth. This enters the arena of
"mature Christian" behavior. No longer are we to behave like babies that drink
milk, but we are to taste the meat of the gospel. We should move on to
"perfection" by having digested the elementary things of faith.

*Therefore let us move beyond the elementary teachings about Christ and
move on to maturity, not laying again the foundation [1] of repentance
from dead works and [2] of faith toward God, [3] of the doctrine of
baptisms, [4] of laying on of hands, [5] of resurrection of the dead, and
[6] of eternal judgment.* (Hebrews 6:1-3 NKJV. Numbering added.)

These six principles of the doctrine of Christ are to be learned while in the infancy
of our faith. But we are not to keep reviewing them as one who has forgotten what
we learned in fourth grade and have to repeat the lesson. They are the basic
building blocks of our spiritual growth. Once learned and now wise in these
principles, we must move on to other wisdom and knowledge. These are not to be
forgotten, or demand a reviewing, but are alive in us. If we have to go back to
elementary learning, we cannot develop leadership skills or even move into the role
of being an ambassador for Jesus Christ.

Let us review the six principles Paul states that we should soundly know, not
returning to or revisiting the true meanings:

1. Repentance for Dead Works

All works are dead without faith in Jesus Christ. It is through believing in Jesus
Christ that we are justified, and declared righteous in our faith. No works of our
own can achieve, justify, or cause us to become righteous enough to deserve eternal
residence with God. We must repent of our sins and stand on the blood of Jesus for
our eternal Salvation.

*For it is by grace you have been saved, through faith, and this not from
yourselves, it is the gift of God, not by works, so that no one can boast.*
(Ephesians 2:8-9 NIV)

2. Faith toward God

The saving faith of believer makes God the central core of their life. The believer
understands that their sin separates them from their God, and that their only faith in
Jesus Christ as "true God-true man," and "the only begotten Son of God" is the

salvation that permits him to go straight to the mercy seat and communicate with God. Faith believes in God's grace, mercy, and love as the most essential parts of life.

> *In Him and through faith in Him we may approach God with freedom and confidence.* (Ephesians 3:12 NIV)

3. Baptism

Baptism is a public confession of faith in Jesus Christ, and considered an act of obedience in the Bible according to Acts 2:38. In Matthew 28:19-20, Jesus gives authority to all believers to continue the Baptism of the Holy Spirit across all nations, and promises that He will be with them always. The act of baptism is valid in the following accepted traditions:

• A sprinkling of water upon the believer's head

• The pouring of water over the believer's head and forehead

• The act of submerging the entire body into water

It is the water that represents the washing away of one's sins. It is the blessing and the promise of receiving the Holy Spirit that represents a trust for regeneration of the soul toward the image of Jesus Christ.

> *And Peter said to them, "Repent, and let each of you be baptized in the name of Jesus Christ for the forgiveness of your sins, and you shall receive the gift of the Holy Spirit."* (Acts 2:38 NASB)

> *"Therefore go and make disciples of all nations, baptizing them in the name of the Father and of the Son and of the Holy Spirit, and teaching them to obey everything I have commanded You. And surely I am with you always, to the end of the age."* (Matthew 28:19-20 NIV)

4. Laying on of Hands

"The laying on of hands" is a physical act where one believer (or a group of believers such as in a church setting) lay their hands on the shoulder, back, arm or head of another believer, and go into prayer (independently or through a spokesperson for the group) sending the believer's requests to God. The act of lying on of hands usually accompanies the act of "anointing with oil" (rubbing an approved oil substance on the forehead of the person being prayed for). Any need of a believer can be the object of laying on of the hands and the anointing with oil, however, main purposes still have a tendency for health or family.

> *Is anyone of you sick? He should call the elders of the church to pray over him and anoint him with oil in the name of the Lord. And the prayer offered in faith will make the sick person well; the Lord will raise him up. If he has sinned, he will be forgiven.* (James 5:14-15 NASB)

5. Resurrection of the Dead

The resurrection of the dead is a promise that we all can believe in because Christ, Himself, rose from the dead. After He rose from the dead, the Cross and the burial in the cave, He walked for 40 days on Earth. This was to confirm His promises through witnesses that saw Him. There would be no Easter joy, there would be no heavenly home, and there would be no savior if Christ was not able to accomplish what no other man had ever done in mankind's measure of time. We cannot disput the amount of space the New Testament gives to the resurrection. Paul in 1 Corinthians 15 (read it as time permits) offers Christianity its fundamental life-giving truths in an essential doctrine of the resurrection: that there is a life beyond death, a life that is a higher edict than that of earthly existence.

> *Jesus said to her, "I am the resurrection and the life. He who believes in me will live, even though He dies; and whoever lives and believes in me will never die..."* (John 11:23 NIV)

6. Eternal Judgment

That there are indeed divine judgments taught, in both the Old and New Testaments, is an undeniable fact. The characteristics of judgment occupy both reward and punishment, and it is administered by Christ through the God-given right of the Cross and resurrection. There is a past judgment (the Cross), a present judgment (daily life of the believer), and a future judgment (the Great White Throne, Satan and his following angels, and Israel).

> *For just as the Father raised the dead and gives them life, even so the Son gives life to whom He is pleased to give it. Moreover, the Father judges no one but has entrusted all judgment to the Son, that all may honor the Son just as they honor the Father. He who does not honor the Son does not honor the Father, who sent Him.* (John 5:21-23 NIV)

The writer of Hebrews encourages us to learn six elementary, fundamental teachings of Christ. They are the "milk of salvation" that saves us in our sinful state. After we have absorbed them, digested them, practiced them in our lives, we can witness to others. However, if we never go any further than these six teachings we continue in "a childlike faith," not always knowing "right from wrong," and failing to mature in other critical matters in the Bible. We are not only to advance to maturity in the "whole word," but in fact mature in "suffering for Christ." We are to work toward "perfection" (spiritual maturity).

Closing Prayer

Dearest Father in Heaven, we praise and glorify you. We are so thankful that you sent your only begotten son, Jesus Christ, to die on the Cross for our sins. Your ac of atonement was a heavy ransom to pay of which we could not have done on our own. And, now, because of our dear Lord's blood sacrifice, we stand holy and righteous in your sight. Fall upon us with your power and cover our sin of unforgiveness. Bless our marriages with a spirit that seeks eagerly to forgive one another quickly. Prevent the enemy from accusing us of all failures of our past. We vow to start now, following your image of forgiveness. Amen and Amen.

Chapter 7. Repentance, Forgiveness, and Reconciliation
Summary and Applications for Marriage

- Forgiveness is the very heart of our Christian walk.

- Forgiveness is the benefit of the Cross, released and applied by our own repentance.

- Unforgiveness blocks the promises of God.

- Forgiveness is an act of the will, not a feeling.

- There is no freedom in a relationship where there is no forgiveness.

- When we have no forgiveness, check out "bitterness."

- Don't take up an others "offense," but help the one offended to forgive.

- We need to learn who we are in Christ…who forgave us without our asking.

Visit our website for this book, at **www.NotYourEnemy.info**, where you will be welcome to ask questions or make comments. Enjoy!

We have studied the roles of repentance and forgiveness, with reconciliation being the target in our marriages whenever strife rears its ugly head. The path by which the process of trust can be rebuilt is forgiveness. One doesn't have to forget the offense, just forgive the person. Seeking and granting each other's forgiveness results in restoring our "one-flesh" reconciliation. Healing merges as the feeling of isolation begins to disappear and the seedling of forgiveness produce a better and more mature harvest.

1. Read 2 Corinthians 5:18-20. Answer these questions together:

   a. And all things are of God, who reconciled us to Himself through

   _____ _____ .

   b. That God was in Christ, reconciling the world to Him, and has committed unto us the ministry of _____ , making an appeal through us.

   c. Write in your own words what it is that God is asking us to do in section *a* and *b* above?

   _____

   _____

2. No sin is uncommon to man. Christians, it is our goal to be lead by The Spirit, and not operate in the flesh. When we call upon the Holy Spirit to lead us in forgiveness, He eagerly does so. Below is list a few reasons or feelings that hold you back from forgiving.

   Examples: Stubbornness, anger, fear they would do it again, etc.

   Husband   **Wife**

   _____   _____

   _____   _____

   _____   _____

3. Unforgiveness is often carried around without our knowing, or recognizing that it is so repressed deep down in our soul, (mind, will, emotions) that we get wounded. Do you ever get a queasy feeling in your stomach when a name is mentioned? Do you find yourself getting very busy in the kitchen when certain company comes over?

Why not take time, now, to examine your hearts to see if there is anyone toward whom you are holding unforgiveness. This is hard to do. If there is some hurt connected with an offense, whether by you or someone else, ask Jesus to heal the hurt. Allow Him to give you the courage and strength to get over the feelings of shame or humiliation.

Start a list now, just a few. Write in red to remind yourself that Jesus died for that offense. It is a choice of your will. Don't just think of friends and family members in this section; also think of churches, church friends, ministries, teachers, etc.

Person...   **...needs to forgive or ask forgiveness for...**

_____   _____

_____   _____

_____   _____

Finally, the time has come for you to forgive *each other* for any and all offenses. This is the time to confront any unresolved conflicts between the two of you. Treat each other with the mercy and tenderness that you would want from Jesus if you were talking to Him about your own sin.

Husband		Wife	
Offense	*Need to...*	*Offense*	*Need to...*
	☐ Forgive ☐ Ask forgiveness		☐ Forgive ☐ Ask forgiveness
	☐ Forgive ☐ Ask forgiveness		☐ Forgive ☐ Ask forgiveness
	☐ Forgive ☐ Ask forgiveness		☐ Forgive ☐ Ask forgiveness

As you forgive each other, also repent for any times that you have brought up the past sins that had already been forgiven. When you are finished with all that the Lord has shown you, pray.

Chapter 8
Learn to Pray

Godly Principle 8:
Prayer is essential in every believer's life.

> *The level of intimacy you share*
> *With God is the fullness of intimacy*
> *You practice in your prayer life.*

> *And the level of intimacy you have*
> *In your prayer life is the depth of*
> *Intimacy you will have with your spouse.*

God owes us no repayment for the years we waste in sin, or the suffering we experience while under judgment.

> *I will restore to you the years that the swarming locusts have eaten.*
> (Joel 2:25 ESV)

But God does repay, so richly that we feel nothing has been lost. What a great and glorious God!

The emphasis is on "togetherness." When we pray in the power of agreement, there are no weapons that can cancel out the power.

Before we get into the benefits and activity of prayer, let me ask this question of you. Would you feel a sudden sensation of discomfort if, right now, I was able to call out your name and ask you to pray for both of us "out loud?

Give this some thought. Would you be hesitant to close your eyes, assume a prayerful position, and pray loud enough to be heard in a group? Would you become embarrassed, stumble for words to say, only to finish with a sign of relief and a heart of thankfulness that you got through it?

What is it about talking to God "out loud" in front of others that make us feel so uncomfortable? Is it the act of praying, or is it the act of saying something out loud in front of others? Have you ever been in a Sunday School class or any church meeting where they ask for "prayer requests" and then the teacher asks for volunteers from the class to pray for the different requests? This is called "corporate" prayer. It is the act of one part of the body of Christ taking a petition to God with the hearts of the rest of the body. It is a "unity" prayer, many requests represented in one voice.

Just as in most Christian gatherings, we, too, practice corporate prayer at the lesson's conclusion during our Sunday School class every Sunday. The group is eager in sharing the need for their loved ones, so giving prayer requests isn't so difficult. All of us can think of people we know who need God's love and

His Holy intervention. Corporate prayer brings out the fruit of love and caring in any group of believers. It brings testimony and reassurance of God's love in witnessing His protection, mercy and grace for the body of Christ. It is good for the soul!

In our Sunday school class, our teach writes the requests on the board until everyone is satisfied that all needs have been included in the petition prayer. This is exciting! So many times I have felt the anticipation of the group in their hope in Jesus Christ for the will of God to be done. After the teacher has written down the requests on the blackboard, he asks for volunteers to pray for the requests. At the start of the call for volunteers, hands eagerly rise up, but halfway through the prayer assignments, the ambiance of the room changes. During the transition from putting in prayer requests to the act of volunteering to pray out loud for someone else's request in the group, a silence occurs. Prayer time seems to lose some of its excitement. However, the excitement is recovered as our teacher, who routinely, accepts the challenge to pray for the remainder prayer requests.

The observation of this prayer time in Sunday School has brought me to some real down-to-earth realities about how people feel about praying out-loud. I knew that there were a few people in that classroom that did not submit a prayer request because they felt they might have to "take their turn at praying." There were others who didn't want to volunteer to pray because they felt there were better prayers in the class and they wanted the best for their prayer request. At this point, our wise instructor knowing the benefits of personal involvement in the act of prayer, changed the rules for prayer time. The new approach extended the prayer-requesting person to also be the person to pray for that request; the rationale being that they are more familiar with the circumstances. With this new change, the numbers of prayer requests were less than the other approach. However, it didn't take long for the eager prayer warriors to fill the board with name requests and the class was back to normal. Yet, again, appeared those times of deadly silence. It soon became evident that some persons requesting prayers would finds it too difficult to pray "out-loud" and would ask that someone else pray for their request. Then, there were others who had weekly prayer request, but when they were asked to pray it, they simply refuse. There was, yet, another group of people that feel if they don't know how to pray, that's reason enough not to involve one's self in corporate prayer. It's like mowing the lawn or barbecuing—if you don't know how to do it, you don't have to. However, the backlash of this kind of attitude is that, after a while, they find themselves actually trying to avoid corporate prayer.

Now, we don't mean to give a false impression of our Sunday School Class. Although, there are those whom we just described in the class, there are, also, mighty "prayer warriors" in that class. People who in a moment's notice are eager to indulge in conversation with God. They seem to just open their mouth and warm words of knowledge and wisdom pour out like manna to a hungry soul. Prayer warriors are the salt of the earth, and you always want some of those in any class. However, Instead of accepting the challenge of their example, we lean on them to fill the human position of communication to God for the rest of us. Isn't that what the children of Israel did to Moses at the foot of Mt. Sinai?

> *They stayed at a distance and said to Moses, "Speak to us yourself and we will listen. But do not have God speak to us or we will die."*
> (Exodus 20:18b NIV)

Some questions we might ask of those prayer warriors are: "How did they learn to pray that way?" or "Are they specially gifted by the Holy Spirit?" or "How does Faith play a part in prayer?" Maybe the answers will come readily while studying this lesson.

There are some real legitimate causes for people shying away from praying out loud. Many ask, "I'm not really sure what I'm supposed to pray about, or to whom I should pray to: is it Jesus? Or is God? Or is it the Father? Many people have the sense that they should not "bother" God with small matters. Have you ever heard a person say, "Oh, I would never pray for a parking spot? God is a busy God, a person just can't ask for little things!" A lot of people worry about the place and position of prayer. Should I always be on my knees? What about if I'm in the shower? Attitude has a lot to do with it: "Will God hear my prayer if I'm angry, or mad, or depressed?" Many people feel "speaking in tongues" is sufficient prayer. Then there are those who doubt or who are embarrassed because they prayed for a healing for a relative or friend, and it just didn't happen.

As if the questions of who, when, where, and why weren't enough to cloud our minds, the ultimate confusion comes in the interpretation of God's answers to our prayers.

Yet, the biggest question of all concerns the nature of prayer itself: is praying a *command* from God? Regardless of any intent on our part, we all do pray—in one form or another, in one situation or another—with a gut-level honesty that doesn't question what prayer is. Prayer is a subject we could spend a three-day seminar discussing, so we need to limit our discussion here in order to concentrate on just a few points. Our main themes in this chapter will be how to pray, rules for praying out-loud together as one flesh, and encouragement to practice, practice, practice. Prayer is like forgiveness, you practice it over and over again until it becomes a part of your nature. And, as in forgiveness, we are not alone; the Holy Spirit is in us to give us the power! Prayer helps create deep bonds and helps develop our "spiritual oneness" in our marriage. God sees us as *one*. We are to be inseparable in His eyes. The joy and closeness it will bring to your marriage will bless you with peace and happiness beyond any expectations.

Let us look at four scriptures.

> *Then Jesus told his disciples a parable to show them that they should always pray and not give up.* (Luke 18:1 NIV)
>
> *I want men everywhere to lift holy hands in prayer ...* (1Timothy 2:8 NIV)
>
> *Pray continually ...* (1Thessalonians 5:17 NIV)
>
> *Let us then approach the throne of grace with confidence, so that we may receive mercy and find grace to help us in our time of need."* (Hebrews 4:16 NIV)

These four passages tell us that we are to pray always, that we should pray everywhere and that we are to pray continuously, and that our prayers are welcomed and desired. In Hebrews, we are encouraged to approach the throne of grace where our prayers are welcomed and desired by God. The "throne of grace" is the place from where God's love, help, forgiveness, mercy, spiritual power, outpouring of the Holy Spirit, and all that we need under any circumstances flows!

> *Devote yourselves to prayer, being watchful and thankful.* (Colossians 4:2 NIV)

The Greek word for "devote" means to *continue steadfastly* or to *persevere*. This implies a strong persistence, a holding fast to prayer. In order to devote ourselves intensely to prayer, we must be alert to the many things that would detour us from this purpose.

Prayer gives life, but Satan and the weakness of our human nature will try to cause us to neglect prayer itself or to become distracted while praying. Prayer is a powerful tool for spiritual warfare. We must discipline ourselves to achieve the prayer required for Christian victory. That discipline extends to our own marriage. Prayer is the only scriptural reason given for limiting the sexual love between you and your spouse.

Prayer is the most important lesson in this series, for when we *pray together* the power of prayer is doubled. There is great authority in corporate prayer.

> *Again, I tell you that if two of you on earth agree about anything you ask for, it will be done for you by my Father in heaven."* (Matthew 18:19 NIV)

The reason is that where two or three are gathered together in faith and commitment to Christ, He is in their midst, and *His presence* imparts faith, strength and direction. Praying together is the only way that two can truly become one as God intended. As both spouses submit themselves to the guidance and direction of the Holy Spirit, they reach a level of intimacy not found anywhere else in marriage. It is more intimate than sexual union.

The intimacy of praying together is so profound that it's *the intimacy itself* that often keeps couples from enjoying a one-flesh prayer life. A few lessons ago, we explored the subject of intimacy and the fears of lowering our natural defenses in order to share our deepest desires and feelings. Although we feel very vulnerable when we expose our real feelings, the reaction from our mate is one of "drawing closer" than the rejection we fear. Intimacy tells a lot about a person. Intimacy is the willingness to reach out and bring that beloved one closer.

What is your individual prayer life like? Are you intimate with God? Do you let down your pride and let Him know what you really desire? Do you think that if you ask for something, you really want, that He will think you are selfish? Moreover, if you pray that same "selfish prayer" to God in front of your spouse, will they think you are selfish? Remember this: *The level of intimacy you share with God is the direct intimacy you practice in your prayer. And the level of intimacy you have in your prayer is the direct intimacy you will have with your spouse.*

Although it is essential for each spouse to have daily prayer time with God, alone, a marriage _needs_ the intimacy of spoken one-flesh prayer. This time spent together is more valuable than any other single act you can do for your marriage. The intimacy and nurturing of praying together is essential for the good health and success of our marriage.

To help us get started we will take a look at prayer and some of the elements of prayer. We can be assured that we are praying in "the will of God" when we include two or three of the subjects we are about to discuss. When we understand these five parts of prayer, we can go confidently to the "throne of grace" we talked about, and know in our hearts these are things God loves to hear.

The Elements of Prayer

Praise	Psalms 150
Thanksgiving	Philippians 4:6
Confession	Matthew 6:12
Intercession • Human • Divine	 Romans 15:31 Hebrews 7:24, 25
Petition	Matthew 7:7-8

Most simply put, prayer is "talking with God." It is also "beseeching the Lord," or "making requests of the Holy Spirit," or "drawing near to God." It is the expression of the fullness of our souls with God. Prayer must be offered in faith that God is who He says He is, and that He hears and answerers all prayers; that He will fulfill His word when He said, "ask, and ye shall receive" (John 16:24). There are no *rules* laid down anywhere in Scripture for the exact way to pray. The Lord's Prayer is a model or pattern for prayer rather than a "set prayer" to be offered up to God. When we get into the habit of saying the same prayer over and over again, like "Now, I lay me down to sleep," it becomes a meaningless habit, something that just rolls off our tongue easily from memory. Soon that prayer becomes mumbled, "rote" words, instead of the sincere communication of our hearts and souls.

And when you pray, do not keep on babbling like pagans, for they think they will be heard because of their many words. (Matthew 6:7 NIV)

There are certain guidelines we must follow as we set out to blend together in prayer. Let's go over some *dos* and *don'ts* of prayer together. We'll review the *don'ts* first. Praying together should be a beautiful time of communication between you, your loved one, and God.

1. **A Critical Spirit**

    It is *not a time to criticize or critique* your spouse's prayers. It is not a time to discuss the scriptural validity of prayers. A spouse who is constantly corrected or reprimanded during prayer time will be reluctant to pray out-loud. Remember, if you both are praying with your hearts, you are privileged to sit in on that special conversation. Treat it with the respect it is due.

2. **Timing**

    Be aware of the *length and breadth* of your prayer time together. Sometimes one spouse may desire to pray, on and on for a given need while the other spouse feels that a shorter prayer would cover the topic. If one of you feels a strong burden for someone or a certain situation, that person should take it to their prayer closet, and petition the Lord during their own special time with God. Praying as a couple should not be the only prayer time each of us has with God. All things, ultimately, are just between you and God.

3. **The Words We Say**

    Do not manipulate your words during your prayer time together. What we mean by this is; in your prayer time together, don't bring up issues that are personal to you that concern your spouse's behavior, especially after a quarrel or some strife. Prayer in our native language can and often does carry with it, messages we really want our partner to hear but we disguised them as requests to God. Here are two examples of intimidating prayer "content" to stay away from.

    ### Example 1

    "Oh, Lord, please help my husband to stop smoking. You know how irritating that is to me. It congests me and gives me a headache. You know,

Lord, how often I've asked him to stop but does he care? If he really loved me, he would stop smoking."

Example 2

"Oh Lord, please help my wife to be a better lover. You know how cold she is to me and how frustrating that has been. You know I've done everything I know to do and it hasn't helped. She says she's trying, but I don't see any real effort on her part. Lord, change her heart!"

The 90-Second Daily Prayer

Now that we know "what not to do," let's practice. To encourage each of you in praying out-loud together, we will start off with practicing a "90 second prayer" to do *daily*. Here are the two rules.

• The husband will pray for his wife first, then his wife will pray.
• Pray to God for two things about your spouse. First, thank God for something *good* about your spouse. Second, ask God for something your spouse wants, such as a better job, patience, a physical healing, a gift of the Spirit, peace during commute hours, healing a relationship, a babysitter, a housekeeper, etc.

For All Our Prayers

1. *Open your prayer with praise.*

May the people praise you ... (Psalms 67:3-5 NIV)

With joy and out of a conscious awareness of His presence, we remember that we are His people and He is our shepherd. We should strive to center our thoughts on Him day and night. Remembering God must not be an occasional occurrence, but a repeated experience of looking to heaven in praise, communing with him. Nothing would be better than our first thought of God in the morning and our last thought of God at night so we can be confident of His grace, character, love and plans for us. Prayer always comes out of Praise!

2. *There is a time for us to pray in the spirit, and a time for us to pray with the understanding of our everyday language.*

So what shall I do? I will pray with my spirit, but I will also pray with my understanding [mind]; *I will sing with my spirit, but I will also sing with my understanding* [mind] (1 Corinthians 14:15-17 NIV; brackets added).

When Paul says, "I will pray with my spirit," it means to pray in tongues with one's own spirit under the impulse of the Holy Spirit. The believer's spirit prays as the Holy Spirit gives utterance. Tongues are not just for praying, but also for singing, praising and giving thanks. And, unless you have the gift of "interpretation," you don't know what the prayer is, only the Holy Spirit and God know. Now, Paul also says, "but I will also pray with my understanding" (that is, with my mind) and that refers to prayer in our own language, which is also under the impulse of the Holy Spirit. "Praying in the Spirit" in your together time should be reserved for those couples that are *very comfortable* with speaking in tongues and/or in special occasions.

3. **Pray in the will of God.**

"My Father, if it is possible, may this cup be taken from me. Yet not as I will, but as you will ... My Father, if it is not possible for this cup to be taken away unless I drink it, may your will be done."... so he left them and went away once more and prayed the third time, saying the same thing. (Matthew 26:39-44 NIV)

Jesus is our greatest example. Jesus prayed the same prayer 3 times. He mentions "the cup" and "thy will" 3 times. It is doubtful that Christ was praying to be saved from the physical death as some Bible interpreters would call "the cup." He had resolved to die for the sins of humanity; He was there when the decision was made. It is more probable that he was praying to be delivered from the *punishment of* separation from God. You see, to be "out of God's will" is sin, and to sin is to be separated from God. Christ knew what it meant to take upon Himself all the sins of the world. The Father heard his prayer and He was given the strength to drink "the cup."

Let me just finish the story that means so much to us all. Yes, Jesus drank the cup. He never complained about physical pain, but we know He had reached the height of His suffering in His last two utterances. Scripture tells of ten stages of Christ's death. In Psalm 22:1, Matthew 27:46, and Mark 15:34, Christ cries out in a loud voice, "My God, My God, why have you forsaken me?" These words testify that He experienced separation from God as the sinner's substitute. Here, the sorrow, grief and pain are at their worst. In John 19:30, Christ said, "It is finished," a cry that signifies the end of His suffering and the completion of our redemption. Only then does He offer a final prayer, "Father, into thy hands I commit my spirit" (Psalm 31:5 and Luke 23:46). With this He took His last breath. And, who do we have now to bring us close to Christ? We have His Spirit. His Holy Spirit is eager to teach and lead us in the will and mind of God.

4. **Praying together will bring you into agreement.**

When we submit ourselves to the will of God, we enable Him to mold us and blend us as He desires. We know that when we are both in agreement with God, we are in agreement with each other. Flowing together in consistent agreement in our prayer time will overflow into the other areas of our relationship. We can be assured that when we are speaking the will of God as one, we will see it come to pass.

172

5. **Present your petition.**

Do not be anxious about anything, but in everything, by prayer and petition, with thanksgiving, present your requests to God ... (Philippians 4:6 NIV)

The one essential cure for worry is prayer. Through prayer we renew our trust in the Lord's faithfulness by casting all our anxieties and problems on Him who cares for us. Is there any illness in your family? Give it to God through prayer. Need a new job? Give it to God in prayer. God's peace then comes to guard our hearts and minds as a result of our communion with Christ Jesus. Pray for each other and your marriage.

Therefore confess your sins to each other and pray for each other so that you may be healed. (James 5:16 NIV)

If there is any trouble or strife in your marriage, confess it to one another in love. It is important to remember that much of our one-flesh growth flows out of our prayer time together as a couple. Then move on to other issues. How do you feel about being a parent? Children always give us prayer opportunities. If you want to have intercessory prayer at this time, it should be a mutual decision on those people and situations you *both* want to intercede for.

6. **Allow your joint prayer time to enable you to better understand your spouse's heart.**

As your spouse shares his or her concerns, you will have greater insight into their relationship with the Lord. Prayers edify! It builds us up and gives us strength and courage to be honest and seek the truth.

7. **Prayer is for cleansing.**

Search me, O God, and know my heart; test me and know my anxious thoughts. See if there is any offensive way in me, and lead me in the way everlasting. (Psalm 139:23-24 NIV)

Pray it aloud. God will hear you. He promises to hear, and He will answer. His utmost desire for us is to be completely His. He wants us to be in intimate fellowship with Him. He is our shepherd, we are His sheep and He desires for us to be able to hear His voice, and to be ready to be used for the kingdom of God.

There are some things that happen *only* by prayer. In Mark 9:14-28 is a story about how Jesus gave authority to His disciples to heal people and drive out spirits of sickness. He sent them out only to see them return in failure. One of their failures was a boy who had spirits that threw him to the ground and caused him to foam at the mouth. The father, after arguing with the disciples, told Jesus that the disciples had failed to cure the boy. Jesus seeing the crowd getting bigger, and that they needed to be on their way, quickly healed the boy by rebuking the evil spirit. "You deaf and mute spirit," he said, "I command you, come out of him and never enter him again." Later on the disciples ask Jesus why they couldn't do what Jesus had done. He replied, "This kind can come out only by prayer" (Mark 9:29 NIV).

Jesus didn't mean that a time of prayer was necessary before this kind of evil spirit could be driven out. Rather, a principle is implied here: Where there is little faith, there is little prayer. Where there is much prayer founded on true commitment to God and His word, there is much faith. Had the disciples been maintaining a life of prayer as Jesus did, they could have dealt successfully with this case.

Jesus is our example in everything. He is our example in prayer. Scripture reveals pages of Jesus' prayer life. He came to show us how. *His* Holy Spirit is *our* Holy Spirit. *His* source of power is *our* source of power. When in doubt, do a "WWJD"—which means "What would Jesus do?" And then *do* it, or *pray* it.

Closing Prayer

Dearest Father in heaven, may all glory, honor, and praise be added to your name. We thank You for the intimacy of prayer you have allowed us to have with you. We know that this is made possible only through the sacrifice of your dear Son: Jesus Christ. It is because of His holy blood shed on the Cross, that you welcome our presence in prayer before your Holy Throne. Let joy reign in our hearts as we take our petitions and requests to you. We ask you to send your Holy Spirit to teach us how to pray as one flesh. Jesus, remove our fears and feeling of pride so that we may be able to pray, anywhere and anytime, for others as well as our spouses. We realize that you delight in our prayers, and that you are present in the midst of them. Amen.

- Find a time and a quiet place to start your daily prayer time. Plan "the logistics" in advance to make sure it is not interrupted.

- Praying together gives each other some time to figure out the words they want to say.

- Praying together produces intimacy. Don't let that keep you from enjoying a one-flesh prayer life. Let the intimacy grow.

- In your individual prayer life, we can pray anywhere, any time, and continually; and God is forever there to comfort us.

- There may be legitimate reasons for shying away from corporate prayer, but never from praying with your spouse.

- Keep practicing the "90-second daily prayer." It only takes 1½ minutes!

- Pray with your Spirit—such as "in tongues'—but more than that, pray out loud with your mouth when you are praying with your spouse.

- When you have become comfortable at praying, start your prayer with praise to God and end with "thanks."

Visit our website for this book, at **www.NotYourEnemy.info**, where you will be welcome to ask questions or make comments. Enjoy!

It is going to take consistency and discipline to develop a prayer life together. This doesn't mean you should desert your individual prayer life. Praying together *knits* you as one and *edifies* your "one-flesh" life. In fact, if you will take the time to share with each other what God is saying to you individually, your intimate closeness will bring much joy.

1. Do you *pray* individually everyday?

    Husband: ☐ Yes ☐ No   Wife: ☐ Yes ☐ No

    If you put *no*, please describe your reason(s):

    Husband: _____

    Wife: _____

2. If "Yes," do you find that there is a special time and/or a specific location where you would like to *pray*? Where and when?

    Husband: _____

    Wife: _____

The place in which you are alone is your "prayer closet." Evaluate your prayer closet. Is it free from distractions? Does it have room for an "altar" if you wanted one? An altar is a place where you *mentally* place things like hopes, desires, dreams, health of your mate, job issues, the sins of your kids, anger, envy, and so forth, giving them as an offering to God. You trust God for them and don't take them back in the form of worry or fear. You trust God to work them out for "the good of those who love Him."

3. Do you jointly *pray out-loud* together every day?

    ☐ Yes   ☐ No

    If you put *no*, please describe your reason(s):

    Husband: _____

    Wife: _____

4. Be honest, would you *like* to start praying everyday with your spouse?

    Husband: ☐ Yes ☐ No
    Wife: ☐ Yes ☐ No

5. Would you be *willing* to commit to prayer at least once a day with your mate?

Husband: ☐ Yes ☐ No   Wife: ☐ Yes ☐ No

Start with "the 90-second prayer." Later on, add other praises and thanksgivings. Don't worry about the amount of time you pray. It is most important that every day when you awaken, you attempt to find a prayer time with your spouse. When you have something on your mind, ask your spouse to pray with and for you. Soon it will be a habit with each of you going to the other for prayer! In your own individual prayer time, ask the Lord to bless your time together.

If one of you is just not ready to start prayer time together, and the other is willing, don't be disappointed. The "willing one" should *pray* for courage and strength for the other partner. *Pray* for the Lord to make a convenient time for both of you.

6. For those of you who *do* pray together daily, do you bring up "the deep desires of your heart'?

Husband: ☐ Yes ☐ No ☐ Sometimes
Wife: ☐ Yes ☐ No ☐ Sometimes

7. Do you desire more intimacy during prayer time? (Warning: Wives almost always will answer "yes." Husbands, be prepared to work this out!)

Husband: ☐ Yes ☐ No   Wife: ☐ Yes ☐ No

Discuss this issue of intimacy during prayer time. Listen to each other, in love, and determination to minister to each other. Take this matter to the Lord in prayer right now. He welcomes your every request.

Chapter 9
Marital Agreement

Godly Principle 9:
Agreement is necessary in marriage (Amos 3:3 ESV)

There are two ways to be successful when it comes to marital bliss, but only God's way prevails: the world's approach by way of manipulation through "whatever works" or God's way that lays a loving foundation for your marriage. Learn how to walk in agreement in your godly marriage.

There are always two ways to win an argument: the world's way and God's way. Learn how to walk in agreement in marriage.

Unity is the most important character of a godly marriage. We must be in total agreement in order for our marriage to conform to God's plans for our lives together. To achieve this, we must see things as God see them. Very often when we first glimpse God's plan, we are far from its fulfillment in our lives. When we agree with God and His word, we line up with the will of God, enabling Him to shape purpose and direction to our marriage.

> *Again I say to you, that if two of you agree on earth about anything that they may ask, it shall be done for them by my Father who is in heaven. For where two or three have gathered in My name, there I am in their midst.* (Matthew 18:19-20 NASB)

Yes, even though you have heard it before, it bears repeating. In the last chapter when we studied "prayer" we learned about the immense authority and power that is present in prayer, because Jesus promises to be in our midst whenever two or are gathered *in his name*. "In my name" is the important part of that verse. When we are gathered *in His name*, we are committed to what Jesus is committed to, and Jesus is committed to *the word and will of God, His Father*. His presence in that prayer imparts to the believers faith: strength, direction and grace. The other word in that scripture we don't want to glaze over too fast is "agree." It says "If two of you on earth agree about anything you ask for; it will be done for you." Are you ready and willing to believe this? Agreement is pretty important, or God wouldn't have put this issue in His Word, the Bible. What part does mutual agreement play in your marriage? When the Scripture says, "If two of you," could that mean your and your spouse? God has a principle about "agreement":

> *Do two walk together unless they agree to do so?* (Amos 3:3 NIV)

A marriage cannot exist in a state of love and joy between two people unless they *agree* on fundamental truths. With God, there is no genuine relationship unless we accept his word and *agree with it*. It is impossible to call yourself a believer and at the same time not believe in God's word. When we face circumstances, we can either agree with the devil through doubt and disbelief and allow his plans to come to pass, or we can agree with God's word *and allow His plan* to come to pass. We choose in whom we will place our faith. Faith in God's word and our agreeing with His word is what carries us through as God completes the changes in us that are necessary for His plans in our life. God has expressed His desire in His word that we walk together as one. He has also told us explicitly that He hates to have separated that which He has made into one. Since God has been so clear about His will and desire for us, it is very evident that we need to learn how to come into agreement in our marriage.

> *So they are on longer two, but one. Therefore what God has joined together, let man not separate.* (Matthew 19:6 NIV)

Marriage is "walking together." Marriage is "one flesh." God does not want the separation of His children that walk together in one flesh. Besides the death of a spouse, divorce is the only other method of separation. Since God has been so clear about His will and desire for our marriages, it is very evident that we need to learn how to come into agreement in our marriage. Again, it is only in prayer.

The World's Way

Coming into agreement with our spouse is not always easy. We all have "learned behavior." The world has taught us methods on how to resolve disagreements. See if you discover that your marriage is involved in any of the following styles:

- *Lack of Strife:* A couple calmly considers all the alternatives and reaches agreement without any argument.

- *Expert Opinion:* One spouse has more experience, knowledge, or ego regarding the topic under discussion so the other spouse goes along with them.

- *Compromise:* This method is used by couples who have extremely differing views on a topic. They meet halfway between their differing opinions and enter into a mutually satisfying compromise.

- *Survival of the Fittest:* Here, no attempts at negotiations are made, they fight out their differing opinions until one of them gives in. The one left standing gets their way.

- *Manipulation:* In manipulation, one spouse uses rewards (negative or positive) to get their spouse to agree with them?

- *Emotions versus Logic:* One spouse presents a logical presentation of their view, while the other presents an emotional argument of their view. The couple agrees on the most convincing presentation.

- *Open Door/Closed Door:* If the door is open, the answer is yes, if the door is closed, the answer is no.

Discussion of the Various Approaches

The previous methods are inadequate, even though it is assumed that the point of agreement is important to both spouses. Many agreements are won by lack of interest on the part of one of the spouses. The *Open Door/Closed Door* method used by many Christians can cause bigger problems when the door suddenly slams shut. The couple doesn't really know whether the door has been shut by God, or if the enemy closed it. The problem arises: do they consider the shut door to be a "no" by the Lord, or do they battle Satan to reopen the door. Then what if the door suddenly opens again? Is God saying, "Now's the time," or is it a trap set by the devil? It is really hard to know the will of God by using this seemingly simple strategy of doors.

The fact is, God did not intend us to use any of the above methods for coming into agreement with each other. Most of these methods rely on the ability of one's self to conquer, while the other has to conform to achieve agreement and peace. Each party is willing to compromise, battle or manipulate to gain that which is felt to be the correct decision, thus promoting their own interests. The process of agreement usually involves bringing our spouse over to our way of thinking or going over to theirs, and often not without arguments. The root of the arguments is "selfishness seeking its own way."

> *For where jealousy and selfish ambition exist, there is disorder and every evil thing.* (James 3:16 NASB)

Notice that not one of the methods we reviewed included *first seeking the will of God.* If we are walking in mutual agreement with God, there will be never be a lack of peace in our homes. Hence, our first goal in coming into agreement should always be to fulfill the will of our Father.

> *But the wisdom that comes from heaven is first of all pure, then peace-loving, considerate, submissive, full of mercy and good fruit, impartial and sincere.* (James 3:17 NIV)

How *do* we go about fulfilling the will of God? Jesus showed us many examples while He was here on earth. He always sought to fulfill *the will of His Father.*

> *By myself I can do nothing; I judge only as I hear, and my judgment is just, for I seek not to please myself but him who sent me.* (John 5:30 NIV)

> *"My food," said Jesus, "is to do the will of him who sent me and to finish his work."* (John 4:34 NIV)

Our Father in heaven has a will and a purpose for every stage of our lives. In the will of God is wisdom and "spiritual" understanding. He wants us to know what His intensions are for our marriages, our children, our neighbors, our jobs, and most of all, the future of all living things. It is all written in His book to us, the Bible. We need to seek His will in *all things,* instead of "doing our own thing." When we come into agreement with our spouses, we can be sure that the will of God will be done as He desires. The big question is, how do we know the "will of God"? Defining the will of God requires us to look at three different meanings.

First Meaning of "God's Will"

"The will of God" can often be another way of saying "the law of God." In many passages in the Bible, such as David in the Psalms, for example, the phrase "God's *will*" is comparable in meaning to "God's *law.*"

> *I desire to do your will, O my God; your law is with in my heart.*
> (Psalms 40:8 NASB)

In other words, since God in His law instructs us in the way that He wants us to conduct our lives, the law, therefore, may properly be called "The will of God." David is right; God has put His law in the hearts of all men. All culture known to man, worship some form of god with rituals and traditions. Within these cultures are many taboos, stealing being just one among many.

The Ten Commandments, the most prominent law of the Old Testament, were given in the spirit of behavior. Four are designed for our behavior toward God while six of them are designed for relationships with our family and friends. If we follow their instructions, we will be happy indeed. Although we, in the New Covenant (the New Testament), are no longer under the affliction of breaking these laws, they are still a good standard by which to manage our lives.

In our agreement with God that the Ten Commandments are still a good road map to follow on this earthly journey, we can know that we are in the will of God when we live by them because it is His spoken word.

Second Meaning of "God's Will"

The will of God can also be used to designate anything that God expressly desires. This may properly be called "His perfect will." For example, it is God's revealed will that everyone be saved.

> *For this is good and acceptable in the sight of God our Savior; who will have all men to be saved, and to come unto the knowledge of the truth.*
> (I Timothy 2:3-4 KJV)

God loves all of mankind and wants salvation for each and every person that is alive or who has ever lived on this earth. The Father has appointed the Holy Spirit to resurrect all His believers, just as Jesus, through the Holy Spirit, was resurrected. The Father delegated Jesus to prepare an ever-lasting place of residence for each and every one of us so that he may live among His beloved creation. He desires that no saved believer should fall from grace. This truth

182

does not mean that everyone will be saved, but only that God desires the salvation of everyone.

> *And this is the will of Him who sent Me, that of all that He has given Me, I lose nothing; but raise it up on the last day.* (John 6:39 NASB)

Let us carry this "secondary will" of God a little further, for God does not withhold from us His will for our behavior. We can find many examples of His *perfect will* in the Bible. There are many expressions of His desire that we can actually do. For example, we don't have to question His will when it comes to going to church.

> *Let us not give up meeting together as some are in the habit of doing, but let us encourage one another* (Hebrews 10:25 NIV)

So when He tells us not to forsake the gathering of the brethren, we are in His *perfect will*. When we celebrate every Sunday by going to church and praising His Name, we are *in His perfect will*. When we pray to God requesting someone's salvation, we know it is God's heart that none shall perish, and we are *in His perfect will*. His word is very clear about witnessing in His name, wherever He sends us into the entire world to proclaim His name. Most of the things the Holy Spirit teaches us and reminds us are in the realm of God's *perfect will* for our lives.

Third Meaning of "God's Will"

The will of God can refer to what God *permits* or *allows* to happen, even though He does not specifically desire it. This may properly be called God's "permissive will." Much of what happens in the world is contrary to God's *perfect will,* such as sin, lust, violence, hatred, etc., yet God permits evil to continue, *but only for a limited time.* For example, the decision many people make to remain unsaved—and thus lose eternity—is *permitted* by God, for He does not force saving faith on those who refuse to accept His Son's salvation. Similarly, many troubles and evils that befall a person in life are *permitted* by God.

> *For it is better, if the will of God be so, that ye suffer for well doing, than for evil doing.* (1 Peter 3:17 KJV)

> *Dear friends, do not be surprised at the painful trial you are suffering, as though something strange were happening to you. But rejoice that you participate in the suffering of Christ, so that you may be overjoyed when his glory is revealed. If you are insulted because of the name of Christ, you are blessed, for the Spirit of glory and of God rest on you.*
> (1 Peter 4:12-14 NIV)

Suffering is something we all have a hard time with, yet suffering is not necessarily God's desire or ultimate will for us. The Bible tells us that suffering comes for many reasons. Yet, we will never truly understand the chief source of suffering until we accept the fact the world is ruled by the "evil one," Satan. When Christians outwardly direct their behavior according to the will of Jehovah God, wrongful suffering may occur in their lives. When believers rebuff the accepted evil behaviors of this world, which are at enmity with the will of God, it does not go unnoticed.

In the "suffering" of the righteous, we need to remember that God promised to be with us. He is involved with us in the suffering. And He states that He will not allow us to be tempted beyond what we can bear (1 Corinthians 10:13).

So there they are—three meanings of "the will of God." First, *the law of God*; second, *His perfect will*; and finally, *God's permissive will*. The will of God is in the spoken "word of God." You will find that in the Bible, *the Word* is the Bible! Before God gave us the Bible, God spoke to man. Adam and Eve walked and talked with God in the Garden of Eden. As sin progressed in the world, He chose prophets, then apostles, and finally Jesus. Jesus is "the Word incarnate." Everything that Jesus spoke is the *word of God* for, after all, *He is God*. The Bible, or the word of God, is the written record of what the prophets, apostles and Jesus have spoken. That's where we get the word "Scriptures." Scripture means a collection of sacred writings. The complete Scripture includes both the Old Testament and the New Testament.

We must first all agree that the Bible is the *written word of God*. We know that the inspiration and authority of scripture is by God alone.

> *All Scripture is God-breathed and is useful for teaching, rebuking, correcting and training in righteousness, so that the man of God may be thoroughly equipped for every good word.* (2 Timothy 3: 16-17 NIV)

Scripture is the very life and word of God. Down to the very words of the original manuscripts, the Bible is without error, absolutely true, trustworthy and infallible. The word of God extends into *all that is written*, this includes the words of Moses and David or any other figure such as Paul or Peter in the New Testament. And as we study "the word," we see that it has great authority and power.

> *In the beginning was the Word, and the Word was with God, and the Word was God. He was with God in the beginning. Through him all things were made; without him nothing was made that has been made.*
> (John 1:1-3 NIV)

John says that God used "the Word" to create all things. The Word that God used to create all things was Jesus Christ! The Word of God, which is Jesus Christ, has not only the power to create the world, but the apostle Paul insists that, "in Him, all things hold together" (Colossians 1:17), and that we are born again "through the living and enduring word of God" (1 Peter 1:23). It is for this reason Jesus himself is called "the Word of life" (1John 1:1).

The "Gray Areas"

However, there are times in our life when the Bible doesn't have an exact word on a specific subject. We call these situations the "gray areas" in our life. We know it is the will of God for us to attend church, but which church? What school should our children attend? Which job offer should we take? We need to know *how to seek* God's will for these types of situations in our lives. It is not enough to think this choice looks better or that choice seems wiser. God does have His specific will for each and every situation we find ourselves in. We just need to know how to discern it. No gray areas for God. When we work on our relationship with Jesus Christ, all the other areas of our life flow so much better with less effort than when we try to do it ourselves!

When we, as a couple, seek the will of God regarding a situation, we need to ask Him *together*, as a one-flesh couple. And that's what this lesson is all about; *mutual agreement in a marriage comes only in praying together, where both partners are seeking the will of God*. It is not enough for one spouse to seek God and hear, and the other to go along with the decision. In order for a couple to agree on God's will for them, both must *hear from God*. God tells us that His word is possible for each one of us to hear from Him.

> *Whether you turn to the right or turn to the left, your ears will hear a voice behind you, saying, "This is the way; walk in it."* (Isaiah 30:21 NIV)

Do not be deceived. God desires that everyone hears Him and knows Him. And when God is speaking, both of you will have the *same answer*.

In summary, here are some suggestions when praying together for agreement:

1. Prayer is the recommended approach for couples seeking agreement

We personally believe praying brings you closer to the joy of intimacy that involves the three persons who made the marriage covenant. Above all, these things you must do: Pray *together*! Pray *out-loud* together. Pray out-loud together *holding hands*! We sometimes even hug each other during a prayer time. Your eyes can be open or shut, as you prefer. Again, we often laugh together as we talk to our Lord!

2. Place your trust in God instead of each other

This is not to say that you should not trust your spouse. But as you go to prayer to God as one flesh, your individual focus is on the Lord. It is He whom you put all your trust in, knowing that His guidance is for the both of you. This approach takes away the pressure of possible failure, and assures us that *He is working on the situation*. Our trust is based on the fact that Jesus is bigger than we are, bigger than the problem, and it is He who leads us in victory. When we place our trust in God, we free each other to grow and change in the situation.

We are growing and changing every day. As we said in Lesson 1, we are created in the image of God. When the "fall" came, sin diminished our image. It made us "carnal," spiritually dead. Therefore, God began a "work" in us: work that is a "molding" us toward the image of God. He does this by revealing to us His "truths." We call it moving "from glory to glory." This is God revealing new things to us. We grow more and more, learning more things about the Lord. We are growing and changing (moving from glory to glory) as the Lord molds us toward the image of Christ.

You will never rise higher in your spiritual life than what you think of God.

3. **God is not going to give two differences answers**

If the answers you both received are not the same, it is possible that God has an entirely different plan. This process of agreement may take several prayer sessions and a prolonged period of time, but it takes less time to come into genuine agreement than it takes to unravel the consequences of a wrong decision.

4. **There are no right or wrong answers**

Remember, the only requirement is that you both must agree on an answer. It takes time to pray to God's answers. Often times we are still hearing our opinions. When the answers differ, return to prayer, seeking God's will. God know the timetable of His will for your life; don't be in a hurry to do something without God's conformation.

5. **God's plan will be revealed to both of you**

When God is speaking, both of you will have the same answer. Pray for God's will to be revealed to both of you. You may be the one that is not hearing correctly.

From Glory to Glory

It is the hidden work in our hearts by the Holy Spirit that enables us to move "from glory to glory."

Part of our inheritance is being transformed into new levels of His glory as we become more like Christ. To move from one state of glory to the next, we must receive fresh revelation from God. Often this comes from a visitation of the Holy Spirit.

Time of a Visitation

*   "Chronos," the Greek word for chronological time, such as minutes, hours.
*   "Kairos," the Greek word for "appointed time" or "an opportune time."

Examples: ...*the time of your visitation.* (Luke 19:43-44 NKJV)
  ...*the time of God's coming to you.* (Luke 19:43-44 NIV)

Distinction between the two words:
- "Chronos" is 9 months for pregnancy
- "Kairos" is the time of labor

Reasons for a Visitation

- Miraculous blessings
  - Greatest visitation: Jesus lived on earth for 33 years. People were healed, demoniacs were freed, sin was forgiven, etc.

- Visitation produces glory
  - When God comes, He always releases some kind of strategic information that thrusts us forward in His purpose for our lives

- He preserves our inheritance
  - Every time God's glory comes to us, our spirit is guarded, protected, watched-over by the Spirit of God, as we possess a greater portion of our inheritance

Character of the Visitation

- Not always visible

- Displays of His presence can be seen ...
  - As a fire; dazzling light, cloud, or mist
  - As an act of His mighty power

The visitation leaves us with an impression of His glory burned into our hearts—the act of the Holy Spirit searing the knowledge into our hearts.

Manifestation of the Visitation

- God can speak directly

- God can speak indirectly
  - A strong *impression*
  - A *prophetic word* during ministry or church service
  - In a *conversation* with someone (reveals something new to you)
  - A vivid *dream* (you know it is somehow different)
  - Reading a verse of *scripture* (it jumps out at you; it stirs your spirit, or it's a reminder that rejuvenates your faith

You experience a new realm of God's glory—a new revelation where His glory and presence has caused the atmosphere around you to change.

Why Visitations

We were created in God's image. Before the fall, we could reflect God's love, glory and holiness. After the fall, we lost all that. The Lord wants to bring us back into the image of God, step by step, from glory to glory. Visitations bring glory to us, moving us closer to the image of Christ. When glory comes down, it is a bit of heaven's atmosphere coming down to us.

You Experienced a Visitation

You experienced a visitation at the moment you knew Jesus as your Lord and Savior, or when someone or something suddenly changed the direction of your life!

Objective of a Visitation

Visitations are evidences of God's accomplishment in our lives. God desires active participation and interaction with us.

Do you desire a visitation?

- Take time to pray
- Ask for a clear word
- Be quiet and still
- Be persistent until you know you've heard from the Lord!

To be sensitive to the Holy Spirit moving in your life is the key to moving from glory to glory.

---

6. **Final confirming check**

   The answers you both receive and both agree upon should always line up with the word of God. Any consequence of a decision that does not line up with the word should be a clue to you that you've heard incorrectly. Of course, the more we are in the word, the more our minds will be transformed and the quicker we will recognize His will.

   Do not conform any longer to the pattern of this world, but be transformed by the renewing of your mind. (Romans 12:2 NIV)

7. **The necessity of agreement before action**

   The husband, in his role of headship, must declare that he and his wife will not take any action on a matter without genuine, heartfelt agreement. By achieving agreement in this manner of prayer with his wife, the husband has the added protection of God confirming his prayer! The husband is still responsible to God for the direction his family takes. *You must first agree to agree.* With your first discussions, you may come up with the consensus that you can't agree, so at least agree to wait. It's very interesting that many of those problems will resolve themselves, or at least their importance will diminish with the days. Each of you committing agree will bring more harmony and deeper communion to your marriage than anything else you practice.

8. The danger of setting deadlines as criteria

Do not allow deadlines set by man to be your criteria for decisions. There are times when the husband who has the authority over the family, goes ahead with a decision that is later confirmed as being the wrong choice. Often times the wife will regret her submission. Ladies, your submission is unto the lord. Yes, It is God's will that the husband counsel with the wife and God on family matters. But when a husband brainstorms the family decisions and he's wrong: the husband knows it and God knows it. Let God reveal to your husband his error. We wives don't need to remind them of what went wrong, it's usually very evident, and painful. We are, in fact, commanded to support our husbands in all things, and that goes for wrong choices on his part. However, God did not leave us without hope. Wives go to your prayer closet for your husbands, and "pray up a storm." God will convict the husband in the matter.

As you learn to pray together and move in agreement together with the will of God, one thing is for sure: the Holy Spirit will move powerfully in your lives. When we have prayed and waited on the Lord and can confirm the answer we have received with that which our spouse has received, we can proceed with confidence knowing we have the will of God.

Before we close, we'd like to give you some recent information on how people *communicate*. When we attempt to communication with one another, talking is the most popular way of sending a message. All talking communications have *three factors*: (1) the *content* of the message (the words you use); (2) your *tone of voice*; and (3) your *body language*.

Studies have been done on the effects of these three factors on the receiver side; that is, on the "hearer of the message." The results showed that if the person you are talking to gives you 100% of their attention, 55% of that attention is given to what your *body language* is saying while you talk—your facial expressions, the position of your arms and feet, etc. The *tone of voice* has a 38% impact on the message you are sending, and the words you actually say—the *content* of the message—is only 7% effective, or really "heard" by the receiver! You can believe it when your spouse says, "You haven't heard half of what I'm saying!"

The content of the conversation is the message we really want to send, but often we send confusing messages by the tone of our voice or our body language. These are called "mixed messages" to the listener. Often arms crossed on our chest, clenched fists, trembling hands, tears, sniffles, and eye movements give overwhelming input, taking over 55% of the listener's attention.

Most of us are far more efficient in thinking and speaking than in listening. Learning to listen can be very difficult. Research has indicated that the average individual listens for only seventeen seconds before interrupting and interjecting his own ideas. *Our conversational goal should be to discover our mate's thoughts and feelings, not to defend ourselves.* We can achieve that if we give our spouse our undivided attention while they are talking. We should refrain from defending ourselves or hurling accusations at them, stating our positions. Quality conversation is self-revealing to both the message giver and the listener. Remember, *unresolved conflict* does two things: (1) intensifies future conflicts and (2) leads to isolation.

Closing Prayer

Dear God, the Father, The Son and the Holy Spirit of our souls. How we adore you and praise you! We thank You for filling our hearts, and renewing our minds about Your will in our lives! Your word is sweet to our ears. We ask of Your mercy and grace that you work the changes in our lives so that we may give more time and attention to seeking out agreements in our marriages. Thank you that you hear our prayers. Bind Satan from our prayer time that we may grow in the image of Your Son, Jesus Christ! Forget not thy visitations to each and every one of us. We request a growing from glory to glory for your name's sake. In the name of Jesus Christ we pray. Amen.

- Unity of purpose and direction are complete in God's will. We must be in total agreement with each other to achieve God's will.

- A marriage cannot exist in a state of love and joy between two people unless they agree on fundamental truths.

- Practicing to "agree" is a powerful tool for discerning God's will in our marriages.

- Pray always "in the will of God."

- Inviting "God's will" into our prayers provides us with the faith, strength, direction and grace we need to walk in His plan for our marriage. Praying together in agreement helps us to cover our mate's thoughts and feelings.

- Prayer and patience in seeing our answered prayers brings agreement into our marriages where God is the center of all decisions.

- Prayer produces spiritual in our marriage.

Visit our website for this book, at **www.NotYourEnemy.info**, where you will be welcome to ask questions or make comments. Enjoy!

Chapter 9: Marital Agreement
Thinking It over...

A simple agreement can eliminate heated arguments between you and your spouse. We *suggest* that you both agree to try the following experiment for two months. If it works, use it, if not search for another solution. Here it is: each of you pledge that you will not make one decision concerning the home, your social life, or work lives that affect the other and the rest of the family without being in complete agreement with your spouse.

1. We have reviewed the above suggestion and have agreed to agree:
   Husband: ☐ Yes ☐ No   Date: _____
   Wife: ☐ Yes ☐ No   Date: _____

2. Will you use Prayer as the primary vehicle to seek God's will in your life?
   Husband: ☐ Yes ☐ No   Wife: ☐ Yes ☐ No

3. Will you pray out-loud in your everyday language?
   Husband: ☐ Yes ☐ No   Wife: ☐ Yes ☐ No

4. Are you willing to allow time for God to answer your prayers?
   Husband: ☐ Yes ☐ No   Wife: ☐ Yes ☐ No

Don't expect immediate answers. It may take God longer to expose to one, than the other, the direction you both are to take. God may have to change one's attitude before you can proceed ahead. Remember, God is "weaving a carpet" that include others. All family membership can't be ready at the same time.

5. Are you both ready and willing to submit to God's will for your life?
   Husband: ☐ Yes ☐ No   Wife: ☐ Yes ☐ No

   If you put *no*, please describe your reason(s):

   Husband: _____

   Wife: _____

   ... and be subject to one another in the fear of Christ. (Ephesians 5:21 NASB)

What exactly does that mean? He is speaking to you—*you*! He is saying "one to another," meaning other brothers and sister in Christ. It also means to your wife, "in the *fear* of God," because God wants unity and peace among His people.

6. Can you think of any other place that says "in the fear of God"?

   Husband: _____

   Wife: _____

7. In Matthew 20:26-28 Christ came as a "servant." What does that mean to you? We grow in Christ to *be like Christ*. Explain that:

Husband: _____

_____

Wife: _____

_____

Chapter 10
The Importance of Lifestyle

Godly Principle 10:
We are in spiritual warfare every day!

The conflict of spiritual warfare is God's plans for your life versus Satan's plans for your life!

We must examine our learned lifestyles to see if they are biblical. We have the same abilities that God gave Adam and Eve for spiritual warfare, and together with Christ we will win the victory. The establishing of godly patterns between us and Christ brings healing to our marriage.

Principle 10 declares, "We walk in spiritual warfare every day of our lives." A big statement, huh! How many of us live our lives as if we know that to be true? How many of us think "spiritual warfare" when some things go wrong in our daily life? I heard Joyce Meyer say at a retreat, "We need to recognize that the process of living our lives is taking place on a spiritual battlefield. If we want to keep our marriages on a romantic balcony, we have to tear down "demonic strongholds" on that battlefield." Many Christians are not familiar with "spiritual warfare," and often ask the question, "What is spiritual warfare?" To put it simply, it is a daily struggle against sin and the will of God. It is conflict that is centered in the body as well as the mind and engages fundamental basic of our spiritual faith. As long as we are in the flesh we will have this struggle.

Spiritual warfare involves our own soul as well as the souls of our family members against painful consequences of disobedience to God's will. Sin rears its ugly head in everything we encounter in life: personal habits, school and work, children and friends, doctrine and practices of our church, politics and community customs. God gives us some insights about spiritual warfare.

> *Dear friends, I urge you, as aliens and strangers in the world, to abstain from sinful desires, which war against your soul.* (1 Peter 2:11 NIV)

> Paul writes, *"For I delight in the Law of my God but I see another law in my members, warring against the Law of my mind, and bringing me into captivity to the law of sin which is in my members ... "* (Romans 7:22-25 KJV)

This book has been a guide for you in the study of God's ten principles for marriage. These principles, when put into action are the ways and means by which you will achieve a godly marriage. These ten principles are tools we need to protect our marriages in the fight against spiritual warfare. The word of God is the only standard for a successful marriage. It is important that we have a thorough understanding of each principle. The stability of each principle depends on the solid foundation of its previous principle. It is like building a wall or planting a solid hedge. Each principle gives life to the next one, which when completed, gives us victory in our every day living. If there is any one area in which you still have some confusion or difficulty in applying, go back over that lesson and continue to work on it. The process of changing our lives to totally line up with the word of God is a lifetime project. The "principles" presented in this book are centered in three biblical concepts.

1. **The triune marriage covenant.** In this covenant, Jesus Christ the God of all power and all wisdom and all truth has a plan for our lives. He brings His plan to completion with our co-operation. Without Him as the core of our "being," we are nothing.

2. **The order of family authority.** The key word here is submission! Wives should get their earthly glory from their husband (as Eve got her glory from Adam from whom she was taken). Submission is a hard won victory especially when our spouse hasn't arrived where God wants him to be, but submission has its reward from obedience to God. God has established an earthly order of responsibilities and accountability.

3. **The one-flesh covenant marriage.** Our marriage is an ongoing production. New construction and remolding occurs every time we have another revelation from God. Husbands, if it seems that we have leaned rather heavily upon the male counterpart of the marriage, then you have picked up on one of the major purposes for this book: husbands are the prime center of the marriage and are have responsibilities for the family; that is the word of God.

God continuously addresses the responsibility of the husband so much more than his wife. He loves you men and knows how and why He created you. He wanted you to be directly under Christ in authority. His reward includes growing closer and closer to the image of Christ. Now, 1 Peter 2:9 says, "But you are a chosen people, a royal priesthood." Building on these thoughts, we want to share an important position for the husband as head of the household.

First, we would like to give you a challenge: search the scriptures on a "word-for-word" basis. You can use the concordance in your Bible, or whatever. Except for the passages on love, which are for everyone, there are only a couple of writings that detail a wife's obedience in a marriage: (1) to *be submissive*, and (2) to *respect* her husband. But first we want you to review a few things about your husband. These are the things God will do to your husband if he is willing to do God's will.

Husband as Priest and Prophet in the Home*

Priest	Prophet
Speaking to God on behalf of your family • Praying • Attitudes • Being • Inward work • Preparation • Private life	Speaking to the family of God • Proclaiming • Actions • Doing • Outward work • Proclamation • Public life
Seeking the source of God's power • Impartation	Working with the force of God's power • Revelation
Personal confession and repentance	Calling others to confession and repentance
Isolation in the closet of intimacy with God	Manifestation of spiritual fruit gained in prayer
Consecration and sanctification as an inward work	Consecrated and sanctified lifestyle evident to all
Sacrificing secretly for the sake of your family	Speaking openly to keep your family in touch with God
Closets of prayer alone	Concerts of prayer with others
Anointing yourself with oil	Anointing people with oil for Church office and their roles in public affairs (as the Prophets did for the kings in the Bible)
Development of holiness in your inner man	Exposure of the state of your holiness through your words and deeds

*Author unknown

These godly principles we have been studying, are the words of God, and unless we put them to work, they are just words and thoughts. It is our hope that all of us will continue to search the word for purpose and direction in our lives. Because no matter how much we have grown in our spiritual walk in any given area, there are always new things to learn, and a need for "refreshing" in some previously studied areas.

> *Do not conform any longer to the pattern of this world, but be transformed by the renewing of your mind. Then you will be able to test and approve what God's will is – his good, pleasing, and perfect will.*
> (Romans 12:2 NIV)

197

Let's take a look at our topic, spiritual warfare. Spiritual warfare is an integral part of the entire Christian experience. It is a fact of life. To think that a Christian could avoid spiritual warfare is like imagining that a gardener could grow beautiful flowers without dealing with any weeds. A variety of images come to mind when we think of spiritual warfare—things like spiritual contacts, roaming demons, satanic rituals, darkness, killings, superstitions that come alive, bodies, possessions, and violence of all sorts. What is really meant by "spiritual warfare" and "demonic strongholds"? Many of us can remember various newspaper articles where someone killed a family member thinking they were driving out demons. When we are dealing with spiritual warfare, it will help us to understand the nature and activities of the evil spiritual realm by distinguishing between *destructive superstitions* and what is *true* about the *unseen world.*

From the beginning of time, God equipped Adam and Eve for spiritual warfare. He placed abilities within them, that when combined, were an unbeatable team. In every woman, there lies an "inner feeling" or sense that a problem may be brewing. Some call it "intuition." You know, it's that feeling that prompts you to check the baby at night, or to postpone a trip, or just to pray for your husband, not really knowing that he was having a bad day. This inner feeling or "radar" was originally used as a detector of the enemy's presence. It would scan the horizon and pick up enemy activity at a distance. God calls it "discernment." But for the purpose of discussion, let's call it "radar." The corresponding ability God placed in Adam was the position of warrior in the family. In the heart of Adam, God put the "desire to win," to be the very best. After all, Adam was created in the image of God, and he *was the very best!* God's desire *was* for Adam to triumph over the enemy.

If we recall, Satan and his band of angels were thrown out of heaven, down to the earth, before the creation of man. God knew the enemy was already there. It was God's desire that when the enemy approached, Adam would rise to fight with his warrior quality, knowing he had the victory.

It was Satan's plan to "knock out the radar," so he went to Eve first. He didn't come as the enemy. He simply engaged her in conversation about a tree. Eve answered back, "*God said, "You must not eat fruit from the tree that is in the middle of the garden, and you must not touch it, or you will surely die."* She was quoting God, at least, she thought so. However, God did not say, "You must not touch it." Satan engaged her in further conversation until she became confused about what God had really said, and succumbed to his temptation! She looked at the fruit of the tree, it looked good enough to eat, it pleased her eye, and she really wanted wisdom. Well, don't we all! Wisdom is a desirable trait. She ate the fruit! Satan's diversionary tactic worked, the radar failed and Eve was deceived.

Following the failure of the radar, the warrior also failed. He heard the conversation. Why didn't he rise up and smite the enemy like he was supposed to do. The truth of the matter is that *Adam decided to disobey God*, and ate of the tree of Knowledge of Good and Evil. Many critics of the Bible say it was Eve who ate the "apple" and caused us to sin. (It is common knowledge that we really don't know which fruit it was that Eve was tempted to eat). However, other critics say that since Adam was put in authority over Eve, he should have stopped her from eating the apple. After all, there he was, right beside her!

Here's a cute joke for you to share about Adam and Eve:

> One day Adam was walking in the woods with his two young boys, Cain and Abel. Abel spotted an area in the woods where it was adorned with lush green foliage, but a fence was around it and it look as though it was un-kept despise the beauty. Abel asked his father, "Dad, what is that place over there." Adam replied, "Oh, that's the place where your mother ate us out of house and home. —Anonymous

Immediately, as with everything else, these two abilities in man and woman became perverted. Instead of picking up spiritual signals of the enemy's attack, the radar now picks up things of the flesh like fear, suspicion, criticism, worry, and anxiety. Even though they still register *with the same intensity as spiritual discernment!* And when those fleshly feelings are in overload, it often is expressed as nagging or aggression toward their husbands. The warrior, who was created to excel over his spiritual enemy, now fights to excel over other men. Competition and greed have replaced spiritual superiority. Men fight against men to excel in the sport arena and in the work place. All too often, men tune out their wives and refuse to listen to their counsel. Husband, your wife's counsel is still valuable due to the spiritual discernment she still possesses. You need to pray with her to discern what she is feeling. Is it fleshly anxiety, or a spiritual alert? Wives, help your husbands rise up as a warrior for his family. Call on him when there is some kind of an attack. Support him in the "battle."

Lifestyle Patterns

Before we enter the realm of Satan's activity in the unseen world, let us look at our own lifestyles. Lifestyles are ways of *thinking and acts of responding* that have been *shaped* within *us* throughout our lives. Some of our attitudes and actions we formed our own, but others have been handed down to us, generation after generation, forming "acceptable" family patterns. Generational patterns can be good or bad, yet still acceptable by the family. They can include such things as family traditions, sewing skills, woodworking and even career patterns. However, they also include criticism, procrastination, poverty, little white lies, etc. The Bible refers to them as "generational blessings" or "generational curses."

Thou shall not bow down thyself to them, nor serve them: fore I the Lord
thy God am a jealous God, visiting the iniquity of the fathers upon the
children unto the third and fourth generation of them that hate me; and
showing mercy unto thousands of them that love me, and keep my
commandments. (Exodus 20:5-6 KJV)

The word reveals there are two types of life patterns: godly and ungodly. Any
pattern that does not measure up to the word of God is ungodly. You probably
have both operating in your lives today. Make sure you recognize the godly one
and don't just concentrate on the negative ones. However, as the word begins to
reveal ungodly patterns in your lives, check to see if they are generational
patterns or if they are ones you have developed yourselves.

Is the pattern present in relatives? If so ask the Holy Spirit to help you identify
any generational influences that may be in operation. Here are some examples:

Question	Possible generational issue to be resolved
Do you have a temper?	Did either of your parents have a temper?
Do you get drunk?	Were there "hard drinkers" in your family?
Do you gossip?	Does your family openly "tell on each other'?
Do you think of divorce?	Is divorce an acceptable action in your family?
Find housework difficult?	Any "couch potatoes" in the family?
Feel you have to be perfect?	Were there "negative criticisms" in the home?

Take authority over them, in Jesus' name, and break their hold on your family.

> *For you know that it was not with perishable things such as silver or gold*
> *that you were redeemed from the empty way of life handed down to you*
> *from your forefathers, but the precious Blood of Christ ...*
> (1 Peter 1:18 NIV)

Strongholds

A stronghold is an area in which we are held in bondage (emotional prison)
due to a certain way of thinking. Strongholds are in the mind. These
strongholds are false teachings and misunderstandings about our Christianity
and the person of Christ.

> *For if someone comes to you and preaches a Jesus other than the Jesus we*
> *preached, or if you received a different spirit from the one you received.*
> (2 Corinthians 11:4 NIV)

Paul warns them about listening to "wrong ideas" being taught about Christ.
Here is a lesson for us also. Paul is telling us that our minds can be lead astray
from Jesus when we listen to anyone who preaches a Jesus other than that of

the Bible. Wrong ideas can be put in the minds of believers who have been influenced by demonically inspired teachings! In Matt. 24: 25 Jesus warns us of false prophets and false christs when he reminds us, "Behold, I have told you in advance."

I know your deeds. See, I have placed before you an open door that no one can shut. I know that you have little strength, yet you have kept my word and have not denied my name. (Revelation 3:8 NIV)

As we discussed this in chapter 9, we study about praying for the activities of the "kingdom of God" into our marriages. Here are some of the kingdom of God manifestations we can experience:

- The empowering presence of the Holy Spirit in our lives.
- Union and close relationship with the Lord Jesus Christ.
- Reception and manifestation of the gifts of the Holy Spirit.
- Ability to break free from the bondage of sin.
- Authority over evil spirits.

But getting back to Satan and his plans of destruction, we can know our adversary.

Be self-controlled and alert. Your enemy the devil prowls around like a roaring lion looking for someone to devour. Resist him, standing firm in the faith ... (1 Peter 5:8-9 NIV)

We know that we are the children of God, and that the whole world is under the control of the evil one. (1 John 5:19 NIV)

On another day the angels came to present themselves before the Lord and Satan also came with them to present himself before him. And the Lord said to Satan, "Where have you come from?" Satan answered the Lord, "From roaming through the earth and going back and forth in it." (Job 2:1-2 NIV)

John says, "the whole world is under the control of the evil one" (1 John 5:19). And we know that Satan's roaming is not only territorial but he travels between the earth and the heavens. The apostle Paul described Satan as "the god of this age" (2 Corinthians 4:4). What did he mean by this? He is referring the power he holds over much of the activity of the "here and now." His rule is, however, temporary and conditional. He continues only by God's permissive will until the end of all mankind on earth. Satan is the prince of this present evil age, but that will all end when the kingdom of God is ruled by the Lord Jesus Christ.

As thou hast given Him power over all flesh that He should give eternal life to as many as thou hast given Him and this is life eternal that they might know thee the only true God, and Jesus Christ whom thou hast sent. (John 17:3 KJV)

Believers have little or no idea how wrong and dangerous their thinking is. Satan works very hard to cause us to believe a lie. He wants to hide the truth or distort it in such a way that we fall off the path of discipleship. Spiritual warfare is a way of characterizing our common struggle as Christians. We all face supernatural opposition as we set out to live the Christian life. Spiritual warfare touches every area of our lives; our families, our relationships, our church, our neighborhoods, our cities, our place of employment. It's a power struggle. However, it is not to say that the devil is the only form of evil influence against which we struggle, and is therefore the only one to blame whenever we fall or lapse into sin. Not true. "The devil made me do it" doesn't hold much water these days. The Bible teaches that there are three forms of evil influence that exert their power over us. They are (1) following the ways of this world, Satan's power place; (2) not controlling our sinful nature (our flesh); and (3) following the ruler of the kingdom of the air, Satan. Apart from Christ, the odds of our winning in any spiritual conflict are clearly against us. Again, the evil sources are clearly this world, our own sinful nature (our flesh, or unspiritual heart), and Satan.

Three Matters to Recognize in Understanding Spiritual Warfare

1. **Redemption of our marriage**

   Remember that Jesus has redeemed the marriages of believers back to what Adam and Eve had in their marriage. Jesus is life-giving. John tells us that our covenant with Jesus brings life. What Adam and Eve lost has been regained for us through Jesus. It's time to resurrect those godly abilities in our Christian home. These abilities are going to require fine-tuning and sharpening if we are to recognize the enemy and engage in spiritual warfare. We are to use the kingdom of God manifestations we talked about earlier. Satan's weapons include temptation through worldly ways, which appeal to our flesh. Even though his weapons are limited, they are a continuous bombardment.

2. **The scope of transformation in our spirit**

   Although a person may think that he or she is simply making a decision to follow Christ here on earth, when they confess the "Sinner's Prayer," we must believe that there is a bigger event happening in the spiritual realm: a supernatural transformation occurs in the core of the confessing person. The Christian is identified by his or her connection to Christ. At the center of this person's being now lies a desire for God and a passion to please him in every respect. This is the place of the Holy Spirit's dwelling. No evil spirit can enter here or cause the Holy Spirit to leave. If we look at our bodies as the "temple of God," we could call this core of our being, "the Holy of Holies." It is our spirit. We are spiritually alive!

3. **Satan works in harmony with the flesh**

   The flesh is the inner propensity or inclination to do evil. It is the tainted part of us, from the fall, that remains with us until the day we die. It is our connection to this present evil age. For instance, if a person struggles with lustful thoughts, Satan will take advantage of this and exploit this tendency. He will stimulate the natural inclination and introduce new thoughts and ideas. To be tempted is not to be dominated or controlled by Satan. Temptation is the experience of every Christian. To succumb to the temptation and fail to appropriate the power of the indwelling Spirit of God, is to surrender space in one's heart for the devil to occupy and exercise control. *We must stay in the spirit, for we are stronger in the spirit than in the flesh.*

How do we know if we are being attacked by the devil? How do we know if we are resisting the devil successfully? Satan has two methods with which to attack us: (1) *temptation*; and (2) the creation of *doubt*. His *temptation* is to try to entice someone to do wrong according to Scripture. Many examples are given—lust, adultery, stealing, etc. We are instructed by the Bible to "flee" temptation! But discernment is much harder in the area called "doubt." Satan will always try to bring doubts *about what God says*. We are told that when Satan comes to us creating doubt, we are to *stand and quote Scripture!*

Doubt comes from two sources: Either *yourself* (as in Adam and Eve) or from *someone or something else,* a family member, husband, wife, friend, a book, or from a movie. Satan can work through a lot of forms. The doubt that comes from you may be during an illness, or job security. Here are some examples: (1) you can begin to question if God really loves you, or why would He let this happen; (2) you can doubt His mercy and grace in times of suffering and financial stress. You may feel that God doesn't answer prayer, and in terminal illness; or (3) you may doubt you have eternal life. When we stand and quote scripture, all heaven rejoices in our victory over Satan.

To rebuke doubt the two of you must pray daily and learn to separate the spiritual from the carnal (flesh). Prayer is not to be seen just as another weapon, but as part of the actual conflict itself, where the victory is ours by working together with God. To fail to pray diligently, with all kinds of prayer in all situations, is to surrender to the enemy.

The world is Satan's domain, it is where he focus his energies and power on people of stature, to influence and maintain unhealthy social environments in which we live. He can thereby exert an impact on the course of any culture.

> *For our struggle is not against flesh and blood, but against the rulers, against the authorities, against the powers of this dark world and against the spiritual forces of evil in the heavenly realms.*
> (Ephesians 6:12 NIV)

Satan is organized into a highly systematized empire of evil, with rank and order! This is a very powerful lesson. Satan's main purpose is to keep us from serving Jesus Christ. He doesn't care if we go to Church, or what we believe—as long as what we do is *nothing*! Let's look at the meanings of some important words. The "principalities," comes from a Greek word meaning *chief ranking*, and these consist of the demons in highest authority in Satan's forces. Our word "power" comes from a Greek word meaning *jurisdiction*. These demonic forces are given power over certain portion of the earth. Lastly, our word "rulers" comes from a Greek word meaning *ruler in this world*. These are demons that are assigned to influence world rulers. Our words "spiritual forces" comes from *depravity* in the original Greek. These are the lowest ranking and most numerous of Satan's demonic forces, and are the ones that plague us the most in our every day life. This is why God wants us to flow in unity in our marriage, to be a one-flesh team on the spiritual battlefield. Our unity is the key to successful warfare. Dig into prayer and ask the Holy Spirit to teach you what powers you are fighting.

> *Finally, be strong in the Lord and in His mighty power. Put on the full armor of God so that you can take your stand against the devil's schemes.* (Ephesians 6:10-11 NIV)

The Armor of God

> *Finally, be strong in the Lord and in His mighty power. Put on the full armor of God so that you can take your stand ...* (Ephesians 6:10-11 NIV)

The Helmet of Salvation: Christ's works on the Cross covers your mind and protects our thought. Our security is Christ in whom we are united with, are made alive again, and have co-resurrection, sharing eternal fellowship with God.

Breastplate of Righteousness: in our hearts we strive for obedience, which is righteousness in the sight of God. "Watch over your heart, for from it flows the issues of life." (Proverbs 4:23 NIV). Realize that as you walk right with God in your heart, you stand as one who has been acquitted of all guilt.

The Belt of Truth: get dressed and wear truth! Know the truth of who you are in Christ! Truth shall set you free, even though "darkness of evil" may try to deceive you. Pray for discernment and practice honesty as you live with moral integrity.

The Gospel of Peace: Put your shoes on! *"Watch the path of your feet, and all your ways will be established."* Shod your feet with peace sharing the gospel wherever you go.

204

The Shield of Faith: quench all the fiery of fear and doubt from the enemy. Believe that with God nothing is impossible and that He will enable you to overcome all things. Do not trust circumstances, but abide in your faith, seeking the gifts of the Holy Spirit.

The Sword of The Spirit: This is the word of God. Be in the word daily for victory does not depend upon our own ability. Know Scripture and apply it to every difficult situation. Spread the gospel.

The bottom line is, *pray in faith*. Prayer is so vital because it is the means of intimacy and communication with the Almighty Lord.

God is not sending us into the battlefield unprotected. He has provided armor for us to wear. If you will follow along with us, we will see what Paul meant when he tells us to wear the "full armor of God" (Ephesians 6:11 NIV). Its clothing consists of God's constant Presence, in each and every form of battle.

Be in the word daily, for our spiritual victory in the battlefield does not depend upon our own ability. Know the scriptures and apply it to every difficult situation. Spread the gospel. If we are going to move forward, to win the battle, we must be able to attack. *The word is our sword.*

> *...the word is very near to you; it is in your mouth and in your heart so you can obey it.* (Deuteronomy 30:14 NIV)

The bottom line is *prayer*. Prayer is the heart of spiritual warfare. Prayer is so vital because it is the means of intimacy and communication with the Almighty God. Prayer is an expression of faith. Ask God to strengthen you and other believers to resist temptation and share the gospel effectively.

Other assets have been given to us in the battle with the enemy. As we learn to blend as one in the power of the Spirit, we increase our warfare ability. We have been given authority in Jesus to tear down strongholds and to break satanic holds.

In order to maximize this power, we must learn as husband and wife to patrol our hedges together. The unforeseen hedges that God built around you and your family:

> *Satan said to God, "Have you not put a hedge around him and his household and everything he has? You have blessed the work of his hands ..."* (Job 1:10 NIV)

Because God knows Satan comes to steal, kill and destroy, He places a hedge of protection around His people to shield them from Satan's attacks. The "hedge" is like a spiritual "wall of fire" surrounding God's faithful so that Satan cannot harm them.

205

"And I, myself, will be a wall of fire around it," declares the Lord, "and I will be its glory within." (Zechariah 2:5 NIV)

So all believers who are faithfully striving to love God and follow the leading of the Holy Spirit, have a right to ask, and expect God to place this wall of protection around them and their families. Even when He was preparing a prayer for us, in the scriptures, Jesus asked the Father for protection, not only for our total well being but for our one-flesh marriage.

> *I will remain in the world no longer, but they are still in the world, and I am coming to you. Holy Father, protect them by the power of your name— the name you gave me—so that they may be one as we are one.*
> (John 17:11 NIV)

Jesus asked the Father for protection for all of us. And now, we have the "power of the Holy Spirit praise." *God inhabits the praises of His people.* Praise God frequently in your prayer time and throughout the day. It is a powerful weapon and He is worthy of our praise. Pray to God the Father, in the name of Jesus Christ, to have the Teacher, Holy Spirit tell you everything you need to know. And, lastly, *remember* who you are in Christ!

> *For the grace of God that brings salvation has appeared to all men. It teaches us to say "No" to ungodliness and worldly passions, and to life self-controlled, upright and godly lives in this present age, while we wait for the blessed hope—the glorious appearing of our great God and Savior, Jesus Christ, who gave himself for us to redeem us from all wickedness and to purify for himself a people that are his very own, eager to do what is good. (Titus 2:11-14 NIV)*

Titus (a friend of Paul's whom he named the NT book after) describes how our lives and homes must be. It is not of ourselves that we boast, but in Jesus Christ. The power that God intends for our homes, resides in unity, not division. We must be united in Christ. Jesus has already paid the price to set us free. It is up to us to walk in that freedom. And when trials, suffering and hurt comes your way, remember your Lord has not given you more than you can bare and He is always with you.

A great man, name Joshua once said, "But as for me and my household, we will serve the Lord" (Joshua 24:15). And that's the key—serve, just as Jesus came to serve all of mankind, so we have been called to serve one another. For in Him, and through Him, we share the suffering of the wonderful Cross. Yet, there is no better life than serving the Lord Jesus Christ the Messiah and as we journey through this life we can have the glorious Hope of eternity with our triune God. God Bless you and yours, always.

Closing Prayer

Dear heavenly Father, our God. We praise you and thank you for the honor of coming into your presence. We thank you for your son Jesus Christ and His love for us that He should die for all our sins! Father, we want to praise you and thank you for bringing us your plan for our married lives. You have taught each one of us what we needed to know to bring our lifestyle into you perfect will, and that is only the beginning. Father, don't leave us, but continue to send us your Holy Spirit to teach us and remind us of the Words of your Bible. Holy Father, be with us as we stumble and forget not the wonders of your love and mercy. Send your Holy Spirit's power when we are in spiritual warfare. Help us to up-hold your name in our daily actions, for we were created in your image. Teach us to accept our spouse as part of our own heart, soul, and body. Let the activities of our "one flesh" please you as we strive to live the triune marriage you've covenanted with us. Enrich our prayer life! Honor our praises! We pray this in the name of Jesus Christ, our Lord and Savior. Amen.

Insight: *Who I Am in Christ*

I Am Accepted in Christ	
I am God's child.	John 1:12
I am Christ's friend.	John 15:15
I have been justified.	Romans 5:1
I am united with the Lord and one with Him in Spirit.	1 Corinthians 6:17
I have been bought with a price; I belong to God.	1 Corinthians 6:20
I am a member of Christ's body	1 Corinthians 12:27
I am a saint.	Ephesians 1:1
I have been adopted as God's child.	Ephesians 1:5
I have direct access to God through the indwelling Holy Spirit.	Ephesians 2:15
I have been redeemed and forgiven of all my sins.	Colossians 1:14
I am complete in Christ.	Colossians 2:10

I Am Secure in Christ	
I am free forever from condemnation.	Romans 8:1-2
I am assured that all things work together for good.	Romans 8:28
I am free from any condemning charges against me.	Romans 8:33-34
I cannot be separated from the love of God.	Romans 8:35
I have been established, anointed, and sealed by God.	2 Corinthians 1:21
I am hidden with Christ in God.	Colossians 3:3
I am confident that the good work God has begun in me will be completed.	Philippians 1:6
I am a citizen of Heaven.	Philippians 3:20
I have not been given a spirit of fear but of power and a sound mind.	2 Timothy 1:7
I can find grace and mercy in time of need.	Hebrews 4:16
I am born of God and the evil one cannot touch me.	1 John 5:18

I Am Significant in Christ	
I am the salt and light of the earth.	Matthew 5:13-14
I am a branch of the true vine, a channel of His life.	John 15:1-5
I have been chosen and appointed to bear fruit.	John 15:16
I am a personal witness of Christ.	Acts 1:8
I am God's temple.	1 Corinthians 3:16
I am a minister of reconciliation.	2 Corinthians 6:17-20
I am God's co-worker.	2 Corinthians 6:1
I am seated with Christ in the heavenly realms.	Ephesians 2:6
I am God's workmanship.	Ephesians 2:10
I may approach God with freedom and confidence.	Ephesians 3:12
I can do all things through Christ who strengthens me.	Philippians 4:13

Chapter 10: The Importance of Lifestyle
Summary and Applications for Marriage

- The process of living our lives occurs on a spiritual battlefield.

- Spiritual warfare is continuous and dedicated to our destruction.

- The battlefield is your mind.

- Although God gave abilities to Adam and Eve to deal with spiritual warfare, they became perverted after the fall from sin.

- Identify the enemy: principalities, powers, rulers and spiritual wickedness.

- Use the protection of God: Helmet, breastplate, belt, shoes on your feet, the shield, the sword of the spirit—and prayer.

- Patrol your hedges daily as a one-flesh team.

- Use language like "in the authority of Jesus" and "by the power of the Holy Spirit" and "the Blood of the Cross" to silence the enemy.

- One of the main chief marriage roles for husband and wife are: prayer and intercession.

Visit our website for this book, at **www.NotYourEnemy.info**, where you will be welcome to ask questions or make comments. Enjoy!

Spiritual warfare is *all-encompassing*, in that it touches every area of our lives—our families, our relationships, our church, and our neighborhoods, our communities and our places of employment. There is virtually no part of our existence over which the evil one does not want maintain or assert his unhealthy and perverse influence. Conversely, Jesus longs to reign as Lord over every area of our lives. This is the intense struggle for all believers, and it is a power struggle. To which kingdom and source of power do we yield?

1. Based on what you read in Chapter 10, what are the 3 forms of evil influence against which we struggle?

   a. _____

   b. . _____

   c. . _____

2. Which form of influence has the greatest impact on your lifestyle?

   Husband: _____

   Give an example: _____

   _____

   Wife: _____

   Give an example: _____

   _____

3. Which piece of armor would you use to help you in this spiritual battle?

   Husband: _____

   Wife: _____

   What "generational influences" have you brought into your marriage? Try hard to evaluate your own behavior. Ask your spouse to help you. Examine the behavior of your other sibling. If you just can't come up with anything, you are probably not examining yourself critically enough. But keep trying; the exercise will bring truths about your own flesh that can result in spiritual growth.

Husband, Positive: _____

_____

Wife, Positive: _____

_____

Husband, Negative: _____

_____

Wife, Negative: _____

_____

4. Satan works his temptations on everyone. Read James 1:13-15. At the point
    we "agree" with the temptation in our mind, it has birthed sin. So do you
    believe that Satan's forces can use you, your spouse, your children, a
    family member, a relative, a neighbor, or a person at work as a source to
    bring sin into your life?

    Husband: ☐ Yes ☐ No   Wife: ☐ Yes ☐ No

    If you put *yes*, please give an example:

    Husband: _____

    Wife: _____

    Read Job 1:10, then explain what "patrolling your hedges" means in your
    one-flesh covenant marriage. Discuss this together and come up with a
    definition.

    _____

    _____

    _____

    _____

211

Marriage Overview in One Sentence

Dear loved ones, I have a surprise for you. I have taken several words from each of the ten chapters and put them together in a marriage overview in one sentence, to summarize what it has taught us. Enjoy!

Thank you for reading this book. I *mean* it—a deep thanks to you from the bottom of my heart! Though it has been several years since I started the book, the Lord has once again awakened in me a longing for married couples to be holy in the words of God. Not made holy by the world's standards, but through God's Son, Jesus Christ, the Messiah, who saved you and me, and who loves you and me very much. Step into a real relationship with God!

—Beverly Jean Bentley

Our Godly Marriage	Our Book Study
Our marriage is a *covenant*	1. Covenant
of *one flesh*	2. One flesh
where the *Holy Spirit* dwells	3. Holy Spirit
to work in us the *kingdom of God*	4. Kingdom of God
here on earth and bonds	
us into an *intimate* sexual	5. No Intimacy, No Romance
relationship called a "act of worship"	
so that we *prepare our hearts* for	6. Sowing and Reaping
repentance and good deeds,	
teaching us that *forgiveness*	7. Forgiveness
is an act of the will of God, who	
lends us His power through *prayer*	8. Praying Together
for unity, purpose, direction, and	
agreement in the will of God	9. Praying in Agreement
that will bring about *victory*	10. Spiritual Warfare
until we can experience eternity	
with our triune God.	

Epilogue

Laurence Robert Bentley

I am so proud to have been his wife. He was a privilege to love, and a joy in helping him serve people for the Lord. As we taught these seminars, it soon became a life we lived, every day. And every day our love grew stronger. We served and witnessed, not just to each other but to our friends and neighbors.

During his illness, I was blessed to serve him. He would read the Bible every day, and serve people in whatever he could, this was, and is *love*. Yet in his illness, he taught me: *It's all about Jesus!*

This book was Larry's one-time last-time adventure and opportunity to reach out to people and share God's marriage plans for all people who love and understand the importance of the family. For without a godly marriage that is created, sustained, protected and valued by God, our families would crumble and our society reduced to an immoral nation.

Larry died ten weeks after the appearance of symptoms of a disease that had been diagnosed five years prior to his death, idiopathic pulmonary fibrosis, a disease that would end in his fighting for air—air he would not be able to get. But God was merciful, and he only suffered the ten weeks.

During the last week of his life, Larry was confined to a hospital bed in his home conservatory, a room full of windows overlooking the flowered garden and view of the Delta River. Hospices and I tended to his needs.

Larry served the Lord until twelve hours before he was called home.

On that blessed day, in the afternoon of Larry's departure, a friend called stating that he had to see Larry, and could he come over right now. John also suffered from a lung disease and was also on oxygen therapy like Larry. After trading symptoms, their conversation came around to the topic of death.

Larry, a practicing deacon in the church, asked John if he wanted to go to heaven when death came and was he sure he was going there? John gave a "yes" and a "no" to Larry's two-part question. Larry asked him if he wanted to be sure, and John answered, "What should I do?"

Due to Larry's weakness, John was asked to kneel before Larry's chair so he could place his hand on John's head. I too placed my hand on John's head while Larry anointed John with oil. John's wife, Jackie, began to pray in her holy language, as Larry and I spoke in out-loud prayers for God to save this man, and welcome him into eternity.

Praise be to God who created all things, sacrificed Himself for all, and will provide for all who glorify his Name, for all eternity. God is good—always!

References

Amp: *The Amplified Bible.* The Lockman Foundation.

Chapman: *The Five Love Languages*, by Gary Chapman. Northfield Publishing.

ESV: *The Holy Bible, English Standard Version.* Crossway Bibles, a division of Good News Publishers.

KJV: *The King James Version of the Bible.* Public domain.

LaHaye: *The Act of Marriage*, by Tim & Beverly LaHaye. Zondervan Publishing House.

NASB: *The New American Standard Bible.* The Lockman Foundation.

NIV: *The Holy Bible, New International Version®.* Biblica, Inc.

NKJV: *The Holy Bible, New King James Version.* Thomas Nelson, Inc.

NT: New Testament

OT: Old Testament

Strong's: *The New Strong's Complete Dictionary of Bible Words*. Thomas Nelson, Inc.

Webster's: *Webster's New World College Dictionary, 4th Edition*. Macmillan, USA.

About the Authors

Larry and Beverly had been married for ten years. Beverly had been divorced twice when she realized that the hurt and pain that had touched everyone in her family was because of the divorces, and that was a direct result of her own selfishness. In her repentance at the age of fifty years old, she wanted to start life anew. She knew her first mistake was not requesting God's support for the selection of a husband in either marriage. Regretting this she entered into a covenant with God, a covenant that dedicated the next seven years of her life to Jesus in return for a God-selected husband that would meet her "Five Point Program for Marriage." Larry, who had been "happily single" for the past twelve years raising his daughter, did not realize that his 46-year hiatus from God was about to end.

The first two years of their marriage were a struggle. In the midst of a "blended family" setting, God took the Bentleys through intensive training on how to conduct themselves as a one-flesh team, a godly husband and wife team. Larry was growing by leaps and bounds into a mature Christian through attending every class the Church opened its doors for. As for Beverly, she was searching Scripture and any written material concerning God's will and purpose for their marriage. In their trials and testing, God not only answered Beverly's plea for a "soul-mate" in the "golden years" of her life, but gave them both a desire to minister to each other as they walk the narrow spiritual road of life together.

From their own spiritual growth and marital healings came a heart for other troubled marriages. God had brought them full circle—from an ignorance of God's word on the issue of marriage, to knowledge of God's marital plans for all mankind. The Holy Spirit stirred the Bentleys to write program for troubled couples in their marriages. The sole purpose was to share with others "as God had taught them." The groundwork for their goal of a godly marriage pivoted around two Bible verses: (1) Amos 3:3, which asks the question, "Do two walk together unless they have agreed to do so?" and (2) Hosea 4:6, "My people are destroyed for lack of knowledge."

Their scope of teaching includes six years of conducting marriage workshops in various locations in the East Bay of Northern California. They also have been featured as guest speakers for seminar appearances involving marriage and recovery. Their ten-week workshops were entitled "And the Two Shall Become One." Their book *Your Spouse Is Not Your Enemy!* is a Bible-based presentation structured around God's "Ten Principles for Marriage" from the Bible.

Visit our website for this book, at **www.NotYourEnemy.info**, where you will be welcome to ask questions or make comments. Enjoy!